A Church Without Borders

The Eucharist and the Church in Ecumenical Perspective

Jeffrey VanderWilt

A Michael Glazier Book
THE LITURGICAL PRESS
Collegeville, Minnesota

Cover design by David Manahan, O.S.B. Illustration by Salvador Dali, *The Sacrament of the Last Supper.* © 1963, National Gallery of Art, Washington. Chester Dale Collection. 1963.10.115.

A Michael Glazier Book published by The Liturgical Press

1   2   3   4   5   6   7   8

Library of Congress Cataloging-in-Publication Data

VanderWilt, Jeffrey T. (Jeffrey Thomas), 1962–
    A church without borders : the Eucharist and the church in
  ecumenical perspective / Jeffrey VanderWilt.
      p. cm.
    "A Michael Glazier book."
    Revision of the author's thesis—University of Notre Dame, 1996.
    Includes bibliographical references (p.   ) and index.
    ISBN 0-8146-5878-4 (alk. paper)
    1. Lord's Supper—Catholic Church. 2. Lord's Supper and Christian
  union. I. Title.
  BX2215.2.V36 1998
  262'.001'1—dc21   98-13327
                                                 CIP

To Regis, admiration and thanks

Acknowledgements

This book is a substantial revision of the doctoral dissertation I wrote for the department of theology of the University of Notre Dame from 1993 to 1996. I am grateful for the assistance of Regis Duffy, John Melloh, and Richard McBrien, who, by turns, directed the research and dissertation. Their suggestions and critique continue to assist me.

I am especially thankful for the work of Jean-Marie Tillard. I am grateful for his writings and contribution to ecumenism. Humbly, I draw strength from his wisdom.

I thank my supervisor, co-worker, and friend, Kenneth Smits for reading several rough drafts of this manuscript, for his many helpful comments and reflections. I thank the sisters and staff of Saint Benedict Center, Madison, Wisconsin, for their encouragement and help.

Not least, I acknowledge my parents for their patience and love. The division of the Church and my decision to walk across it caused them not a little anguish. I offer this book to them as some small, entirely inadequate, compensation for the grief this decision once caused us.

Contents

Abbreviations

ARCIC	Anglican-Roman Catholic International Commission.
AAS	*Acta Apostolicae Sedis.*
ASS	*Acta Sancti Sedis.*
BEM	World Council of Churches, *Baptism, Eucharist and Ministry.* Faith and Order Paper 111. Geneva: WCC, 1982.
CDF	Congregation for the Doctrine of the Faith.
CdlE	Jean-Marie Roger Tillard, *Chair de l'Église, Chair du Christ.*
CofC	Jean-Marie Roger Tillard, *Church of Churches.*
EdE	Jean-Marie Roger Tillard, *Église d'Églises.*
GLD	Group of Les Dombes, *Towards a Common Eucharistic Faith.* Theses on the Eucharist. In *Modern Eucharistic Agreement.* London: SPCK, 1973, 51–78.
GS	Vatican II, Pastoral Constitution on the Church in the Modern World, *Gaudium et spes.* December 7, 1965. In Tanner, vol. 2, 1069–1135.
JBL	*Journal of Biblical Literature.*
JES	*Journal of Ecumenical Studies.*
JTS	*Journal of Theological Studies.*
LG	Vatican II, Dogmatic Constitution on the Church, *Lumen gentium.* November 21, 1964. In Tanner, vol. 2, 849–98.
LL	Jean-Marie Roger Tillard, *L'Église locale.*
MC	Pius XII, Encyclical on the mystical body of Christ, *Mystici corporis.* June 29, 1943. *AAS* 35 (1943): 193–248.
MD	Pius XII, Encyclical on the sacred liturgy, *Mediator Dei.* November 20, 1947. *AAS* 39 (1947): 521–95.
NJBC	Raymond E. Brown and others, eds. *The New Jerome Biblical Commentary.* Englewood Cliffs, N.J.: Prentice Hall, 1990.
OIC	*One in Christ.*
Pasch	Jean-Marie Roger Tillard, *The Eucharist: Pasch of God's People.*
PCPCU	Pontifical Council for Promoting Christian Unity.
SC	Vatican II, Constitution on the sacred liturgy, *Sacrosanctum concilium.* December 4, 1963. In Tanner, vol. 2, 820–43.

Tanner   Norman P. Tanner, ed., *Decrees of the Ecumenical Councils*,
              2 vols. (London and Washington, D.C.: Sheed & Ward and
              Georgetown University Press, 1990).

TDNT   Gerhard Kittel, ed. *Theological Dictionary of the New Testa-
              ment*. Geoffrey Bromily, tr. Grand Rapids: Eerdmans, 1964,
              10 vols.

UR   Vatican II, Decree on ecumenism, *Unitatis redintegratio*.
              November 21, 1964. In Tanner, vol. 2, 908–20.

UUS   John Paul II, Encyclical on ecumenism, *Ut unum sint*. May
              25, 1995. *Origins* 25 (June 8, 1995) 49–72.

WCC   World Council of Churches.

Windsor   ARCIC, Agreed statement on the Eucharist. September
              1981.

Introduction

During the 1980s the ecumenical movement appeared to falter. The successes of the World Council of Churches and of bilateral, ecumenical dialogues enthused Christians in the period shortly after World War II and, again, in the first few years after the close of the Vatican Council. Now, however, disagreements among Christians seem more acute. The ecumenical climate has always been concerned to address issues such as ministry and authority, the role and exercise of the papacy, or the meaning of ordination. These concerns, however, have now been joined by others: the authority of the Church to ordain women, the status of gay and lesbian Christians, and Christian culture among non-European peoples. Such apparent growth in disagreement suggests a future of more division among the Churches, not less.[1]

For example, at the Canberra Assembly of the WCC in 1992, a Korean theologian, Chung Hyun Kyung, gave a fascinating, if provocative, presentation on the Korean concept of *han*.[2] Korean friends tell me that *han* is roughly equivalent to the English word "anger." It connotes the energy required for positive, personal change. In this light, *han* seems much like the Western idea of "struggle." Nonetheless, Kyung's presentation generated controversy and widely ranging debate. Orthodox participants wondered aloud whether Kyung had confused the "spirits" of the world, of individuals both living and dead, or of the *zeitgeist*, with the Holy Spirit who "proceeds from the Father and rests in the Son." "We find it impossible," they replied, "to invoke the spirits of 'earth, air, water, and sea creatures,'" as Kyung had done at the beginning of her

---

1. See Konrad Raiser, *Ecumenism in Transition: A Paradigm Shift in the Ecumenical Movement?* tr. Tony Coates (Geneva: WCC Publications, 1991).

2. Chung Hyun Kyung, "Come, Holy Spirit—Renew the Whole Creation," Seventh Assembly of the WCC, Canberra, 1991, in *The Ecumenical Movement: An Anthology of Key Texts and Voices,* ed. Michael Kinnamon and Brian E. Cope (Geneva, Switzerland and Grand Rapids, Mich.: WCC Publications and Eerdmans Publishing Co., 1997) 231–38. Also see her article, "Han-pu-ri: Doing Theology from Korean Women's Perspective," *The Ecumenical Review* 40/1 (1987). Reprinted in Virginia Fabella and Lee Sun Ai, ed., *We Dare to Dream* (Maryknoll, N.Y.: Orbis Books, 1990).

presentation.[3] Evangelicals reflected that they would rather engage in dialogue with other religions from the perspective of a higher christology. They advocated a more careful discernment between the "spirit of particular movements" and the "Spirit of Jesus Christ." There is need, they said, to develop "criteria for and limits to theological diversity."[4]

These proceedings at Canberra demonstrate the difficulty facing the next millennium of Christianity: Can the Christian churches grow beyond their Mediterranean and European cultural and intellectual heritage? When they engage in dialogue with the nations and people of the world, do Christians risk embracing the paradox of a "Christianity without Christ," a bland universalism? Once the proverbial question facing Christians was whether to follow "Athens or Jerusalem, Rome or Geneva." Now it is as likely to be "Asia or Africa, Australia or the indigenous Americas."

Jean-Marie Tillard, a Roman Catholic ecumenist and a participant in the Canberra Assembly, made the following observation about this episode:

> There is the danger of a new division. It will not be the division between East and West. It will no longer be the division between Rome and the Churches stemming from the Reformation. It will be the division between the Churches which brought the gospel to the African, Asian, Polynesian continents and the Churches which were born as a result of this evangelisation.[5]

After reading such remarks it is helpful to remember that the problem of ecumenism became especially acute only *after* the success of Western missionary efforts to African and Asian countries. The centuries-long division of European churches—Oriental, Catholic, and Protestant—was imposed upon the new Christians of these "mission countries." New Christians were made partisans to divisions in the Church that they did not ask for and did not fully understand.

As these "younger Christians" grow into their own perspectives, they will reasonably be expected to challenge the theological hegemony of the European and American churches. The extent to which the "old churches" will be able to receive the "new" augurs the success or failure of Christian ecumenism in the next century.

The present cultural and denominational division opens the question of salvation for human beings as Christians conceive of it. How does

3. Response to Chung's address in *Signs of the Spirit: Official Report,* Seventh Assembly, World Council of Churches, ed. Michael Kinnamon (Geneva, Switzerland and Grand Rapids, Mich.: WCC Publications and Eerdmans Publishing Co., 1991) 280f. Also in Kinnamon, *Ecumenical Movement,* 237.

4. *Ibid.*

5. Jean-Marie Tillard, "Faith and Order after Canberra," *OIC* 27 (1991) 381.

God desire to save us? Does God relate to us primarily as individuals or as a single, collective person? Is God calling everybody to become a Christian or is Christianity one religion among several, equally valid human experiences of the transcendant? Christians claim to be chosen by God. Can they reconcile their status as the "adopted heirs of God" with a universal message of divine goodwill toward all humankind?[6] Must every Christian believe identically in order to be saved? Is identical belief even possible? What is the role of the Church in salvation?

These questions are not new. Early Christians faced a similar difficulty. Gentile Christians of the first century were asking their Jewish Christian companions: "Must we be Jewish in order to be Christian?" After much indecision, Christian leaders abandoned Jewish precepts like circumcision and kosher dietary rules in the interests of the mission to the gentiles.[7] Today, African, Asian, and other Christians ask an equally powerful question: "Must we be Protestant, Catholic or Orthodox according to European or American models in order to be Christian?" Must the Christian be partisan to the division of the churches to be baptized or to be saved?

1. Christian communion is the problem

This problem of inculturation, as I have described it, is very similar to the problem of ecumenism. How are Christians united? How far and how much must they tolerate one another? How far and how much must they speak the same doctrinal language? Must they worship alike? Roman Catholics once looked to the Latin language as a powerful symbol of their unity. Theoretically, one could attend worship in St. Louis, Tokyo, or Buenos Aires with few appreciable differences between the liturgies. Since the reform of the liturgy following Vatican II, the Latin language is no longer the powerful symbol of unity that it once was. The Roman Rite still retains its Latin typical editions, and every vernacular liturgy is a translation from these Latin originals. The next step in liturgical reform facing Roman Catholic churches, however, is to fully immerse the Latin rite in the variety of local cultures and languages. The liturgies in St. Louis, Tokyo, or Buenos Aires, while they will retain substantial similarities, will change to reflect the cultural genius of each local church. Roman Catholic churches are slowly discovering that their unity must exist on a level transcending language and culture. They must learn again how to live in communion with one another.

---

6. Rom. 8:15-17. Raimundo Panikkar, "The Crux of Christian Ecumenism: Can Universality and Chosenness Be Held Simultaneously?" *JES* 26/1 (1989) 82.

7. Cf. Acts 9:36-11:18.

Christian churches are always learning how to live in communion with one another. The reconciliation of diversity in unity has not become easier since the day of Pentecost. This book examines Christian communion because communion is at the heart of the Christian understanding of salvation. It describes our mutual relationship with God. At its simplest, "communion" describes social status—"who is in" and "who is out." Communion, however, is something deeper than mere tolerance or a vague sense of belonging. The problem of Christian communion is not so simple as, say, choosing sides for a friendly game of soccer. For Christians life in communion is difficult. Life in a more perfect communion than exists today is a task to which God is calling all the churches.

Consider a light example. One may imagine few tasks more difficult than that faced by the challengers in an imaginary sporting event. Suppose that the Chicago Bulls, an American basketball team, were slated to play hockey against the New Zealand America's Cup yachting team. Those paving the way toward reconciliation of Christian churches have faced an exponentially more difficult challenge. Like the Bulls and the New Zealanders, Christian churches do not agree on the rules of the game. Most players on both sides would be unfamiliar with (and most likely insecure on) the ice of the hockey arena. Both teams would find the game equipment and the umpire's language strange. "Shooting" and "field goals" are not the same for basketball players as they are for hockey players. Neither hockey players nor basketball players need to know how to exploit the wind for an excellent tack as the yachtsmen do.

Similarly, Christians of different churches have difficulty agreeing on strategies because they are not sure what one needs to do to "score points" and "win." They interpret their most basic sources, the Bible and the early Christian creeds, according to different rules. Large chasms yawn between the faith expressions of "common folk" and the refined theological vocabulary of church leaders and theologians in nearly every denomination. We do not sing the same songs and the words of our prayers come from different glossaries.

Sadly, assessing the matter bluntly, many Christians speak and act as though the practices and doctrine of other churches are either incomprehensible, offensive, or inconsequential. For many churches the Eucharist has been made to symbolize division. Baptized Christians from other churches are explicitly uninvited and unwelcome. The situation is ironic since the Eucharist is celebrated within each Church as the epitome of Christian unity. Communion *within* each Church is very rarely a problem. Communion *between* churches, by contrast, is a difficult problem. By reason of the enforcement of a variety of incompatible church disciplines, the division of the eucharistic table is an ecclesiological fact today.

However, to allow the Eucharist to signify Christian division is untenable. In 1 Corinthians Paul condemns the division of the Church at the Lord's Supper.[8] The Eucharist, Paul teaches, calls the Church to task when people are marginalized by factionalism and party spirit. Similarly, new historical studies indicate how openly Jesus shared meals with marginalized people. Jesus transgressed social boundaries in the interests of drawing all sorts of people into communion: tax collectors, peasants, sinners, and other disreputables. Jesus shared meals with disciples and others around a nearly "borderless board." Jesus' "borderless board" calls the Church to gather in a similarly "borderless" fashion. That is why I titled this book *A Church without Borders*. The meal that Jesus shares with us makes a claim upon the churches. His meal with the churches takes place at a "borderless board." The Church that gathers around a "borderless board" will necessarily also be borderless. The borderless character of the Eucharist represents one of the most substantial arguments for Christian ecumenism. How will the churches respond?

2. The Eucharist and the churches

In the last few decades theologians from several traditions have offered systematic reflections on the nature and origin of the Church. One may conveniently call these reflections "eucharistic ecclesiologies" or "ecclesiologies of communion." (From now on I will simply call them "communion ecclesiologies.") Contributions to communion ecclesiology have been provided by ecumenists or systematic theologians. Authors were interested primarily in the theology of the Church by itself or in particular questions about the ecclesiological status of other churches. In this book, I hope to offer some small contribution to communion ecclesiology.

As a liturgical theologian, I offer a perspective slightly different from that found in ecclesiology. I am far more interested in understanding how the Eucharist creates and sustains the Church in Christian communion. I am less inclined to consider the Church and its structures for their own sake. If others judge that I have not given certain structural or dogmatic issues such as the magisterium, infallibility, or primacy their proper ecclesiological emphasis, I might agree. This book does not pretend to be a comprehensive treatise on the Church. Instead, I simply hope to show how the Eucharist makes demands upon the Church and its structures, given that both share in this special, saving reality we call "communion."

I will make four claims about Christian communion and the relationship between the Eucharist and the Church.

First, communion ecclesiologies understand that the Church is a communion in the body of Christ. Christians receiving Holy Communion in the Eucharist sacramentally participate in the body of Christ. The

8. 1 Cor 11:18-20.

Church is made by the Eucharist. No mere opinion, this claim is found in the earliest layers of Christian tradition. Communion in Christ is both immediate and mediated. We receive communion immediately by way of the Holy Spirit and mediately by way of a lifetime of participation in our particular Churches. Communion is transmitted through divine *and* human activity.

Second, I will argue that there is a communication of idioms between the Eucharist and the Church. The term "communication of idioms" comes from christology. Christology is the theological consideration of the union of God—the second person of the Trinity—and humanity in the person and works of Jesus Christ. In christology, the term "communication of idioms" refers to the general principle that claims about Jesus' humanity may also be made about his divinity and vice-versa. The principle of the communication of idioms allows the Christian to speak about Jesus holistically, as both Son of God and child of Mary, because of the hypostatic union of divine and human natures in his one person. I will argue that Christian theologies of the Eucharist make claims that can be transferred, by a modified application of the communication of idioms, to the Church. These are specific, qualitative demands upon the nature of the Church. They are grounded in the nature of the Eucharist as a participation by the Christian in the paschal mystery of Jesus' life, death, and resurrection through the power of the Holy Spirit. The Church must live and move in synchrony with these qualitative considerations if it is to be truly a eucharistic church, the body of Christ.

Third, the eucharistic quality of the Church makes equally weighty claims upon its ecumenical character. I will argue, for instance, that the eucharistic Church is a participant in Christ's paschal sacrifice. For a Church truly to participate in Christ's sacrifice, its rituals and doctrines may not be used to swell that church's sense of self-distinction. Instead, ritual and doctrine should only protect and enhance that church's communion in the One who "took the form of a slave."[9] Sectarianism is incompatible with communion in Christ.

Ironically, rather than safeguarding communion, sectarian strategies destroy communion because, by avoiding participation in the *kenosis* of Jesus, they prematurely close relationships with others for the sake of maintaining a nearly idolatrous attachment to verbal formulations of divine truth. I do not oppose strongly christocentric formulations of Christian faith, nor would I advocate any kind of "saltless Christianity" stripped of the always scandalous particularity of communion with Jesus of Nazareth and all the (sometimes misguided or mistaken) men and women who have tried to follow him. I do oppose, however, the sectarian

9. Phil 2:7.

"use" of doctrine or practices to distance one's self from or to belittle the hard-won faith of other Christians.

Finally, how Christians imagine salvation is apparent in how they live in communion. I call this a "soteriological norm." What any Christian group determines its members must do and believe in order to be Christian are important indications of their "soteriological norm." Soteriological norms are expressed in actions as often as in words. Soteriological norms consciously and unconsciously undergird the ways people worship, make doctrines, sanction taboos, speak, write laws, and exercise authority. How a church worships, professes belief, or sanctions behavior is always a concrete, collective (occasionally wrong-headed) response to its understanding of God's offer of salvation in Jesus Christ. Nearly every division among Christians begins and ends where disciples have heard different answers to this question: "What must I do to inherit eternal life?"[10]

Given the fragmentation of modern societies, Christians sometimes speak and act in parts of their lives as if they were agnostic about salvation—one of the great risks facing Christianity today.[11] As much as secularity, individualism challenges our understanding of salvation. Some Christians speak and act as though they would be saved alone, "Jesus and me."[12] A more biblical concept of salvation, however, is the collective conception. One of the chief signs of salvation is the restoration of justice. The re-creation of human relationships according to God's grace is a theme with deep biblical roots. The biblical conception of God's peace, *shalom*, Gerhard von Rad reminds us, is a radically social concept.[13] The Holy Spirit offers the peace of salvation, Christ's risen life, to all who would receive it.

The paschal mystery of salvation is at the heart of communion. Members of the Church receive their knowledge of the paschal mystery first-hand in the Eucharist, just as they receive their understanding of the Church at the very same table. Their knowledge of communion is related to their conceptions of the Church, of the Eucharist, and of salvation in Christ.

---

10. Luke 18:18.

11. Robert Wuthnow, *Christianity in the Twenty-first Century: Reflections on the Challenges Ahead* (New York: Oxford University Press, 1993) 140–41, 216–17.

12. Wuthnow, *Christianity*, 7, reminds us that religious identity—which necessarily includes an idea of salvation—must be developed in relation to some community. Our understanding of who we are is fundamentally relational.

13. *TDNT* 2, 406, s. v. εἰρήνη, "Eiréne," by Gerhard von Rad.

FOR FURTHER READING

Kinnamon, Michael and Brian E. Cope, eds. *The Ecumenical Movement: An Anthology of Key Texts and Voices.* Geneva: WCC Publications, 1997.

Panikkar, Raimundo. "The Crux of Christian Ecumenism: Can Universality and Chosenness Be Held Simultaneously?" *JES* 26/1 (1989) 82–99.

Raiser, Konrad. *Ecumenism in Transition: A Paradigm Shift in the Ecumenical Movement?* Tony Coates, tr. Geneva: WCC Publications, 1991.

Wuthnow, Robert. *Christianity in the Twenty-first Century: Reflections on the Challenges Ahead.* New York: Oxford University Press, 1993.

CHAPTER ONE

Communion in Christ

For many Christians, childhood conceptions of the Church persist as an important background to their faith. They never seem to grow out of their "Sunday school" faith. For instance, I recall the first time I heard the word *koinonia* in junior high Sunday school. The teacher explained that the word meant "fellowship." She did not connect "fellowship" and "communion" for us. We knew that "communion" referred primarily to the Lord's Supper. Although my adolescent peers and I confused "fellowship" with "chumminess," we should kindly forgive my Reformed Church Sunday school teacher for accentuating the social character of Christian communion at the expense of the eucharistic. Our church's piety and doctrine had all too often overemphasized religious individualism ("me and Jesus") at the expense of communion.

For centuries, the relationship between "communion" in the body of Christ (sacramental union with Christ) and "communion" with all the other members of the body (fellowship) has been hidden behind doctrines more concerned with church structures and sacramental realism. However much Catholics and Protestants differed, their doctrines of the Eucharist centered around the presence of Christ in the consecrated elements of bread and wine (however differently they conceived of it). More or less in all the Churches, eucharistic piety had abandoned social considerations long ago in favor of individualized experiences of union with Christ. Christians minimized the profound, sacramental character of living in Christian communion with others. Among Protestants, "communion" tended to connote voluntary association; among Catholics, relationship to church authorities.

During the past century theologians have sought to reunite both dimensions of communion. Communion in its horizontal dimension (in human social relationships) is profoundly related to communion in its vertical dimension (as human participation in divine grace). Theologians were successful in this effort to the extent that they remained close to biblical and early Christian sources. This chapter is devoted to the discussion of biblical sources for a Christian conception of communion; the next chapter will consider more recent sources and developments.

The English word "communion" comes from the Latin *communio*, which in turn is a translation of the Greek word *koinonia*. Christians did not invent the term "communion" though we have extended its meaning far beyond its origins in Greek political theory. For the Greeks *koinonia* referred to partnerships created by holding goods in common.[1] "Goods in common" might mean land or commodities or it could refer to social ideals, like "beauty," "balance," or "harmony." Sharing goods, the Greeks thought, is the foundation of human sociality. Members of modern consumer societies like Great Britain or the United States, by contrast, might believe the "social contract" or the "marketplace" is the foundation for society. Modern societies tend to emphasize tolerance for differences, valorizing "freedom" and "choice."[2] Ancient Greeks like Plato and Aristotle, however, wrote that what makes human beings essentially "human" are the things that they hold in common with one another, rather than the things that make them different. Because we are similar and share common values and points of views, common needs and desires, we are able to establish mutually beneficial relationships with one another. Commonality is at the heart of the Greek understanding of society. While modern world-views emphasize how societies are organized for the mutual benefit of their members, the ancients emphasized how society is founded on shared needs and values.

Aristotle said we are "political animals."[3] We are human, he thought, only to the extent that we have communion with other human beings. Because we are political animals, our ability to share goods—both material and conceptual—with other people makes us human. Important for our considerations, Aristotle thought that communion was part of the *telos* (roughly, the "end" or the "ultimate goal") of human being. For Aristotle, the *telos* of a thing describes the natural state of a thing, the place where a thing "wants" to end up. Note this crucial distinction. For us the word "natural" connotes the observed, relatively undisturbed state of a thing. For Aristotle, however, "natural" connotes the final state of a thing, the state a thing "intends" to become. "Natural" therefore describes a thing as it ought to exist in an ideal state. It does not necessarily describe a thing as it presently exists. For instance, the "nature" of a cat is to spend one half the day chasing mice and the other half bathing

1. *TDNT* 3, 800-803, s. v. κοινῶνια, *Koinonia*, by Friedrich Hauck.
2. Ulrich Duchrow, "Christianity in the Context of Globalized Capitalistic Markets," tr. John Bowden, in *Outside the Market No Salvation?* ed. Dietmar Mieth and Marciano Vidal, *Concilium* 1997/2 (Maryknoll, N.Y.: Orbis, 1997) 40.
3. Aristotle, *Politics,* I, 2.

in the sun of the African savannah, even though he lives in a Midwestern apartment complex and has never once enjoyed the taste of a fresh mouse. Domestic cats are always being made to behave against their nature. Human nature causes us to join in relationships with one another, even though exigencies may conspire to deprive us of the quality relationships we most desire. We derive great pleasure from social games, sufficient to warrant huge expenditures of time, energy, and material resources in such pursuits. Human beings regularly collaborate for social advantage. As frequently, we conspire to marginalize or diminish the social status of others. Sociality, therefore, is fundamental to human nature and to the human *telos*.

Although human nature possesses a radically social quality, we must concede that our social behaviors are not always inclined toward higher morality.[4] If Christians are going to use the Greek conception of *koinonia*, they will have to allow the word to mean something beyond mere conviviality or "chumminess." Christian conceptions of *koinonia* will have to reach beyond "fellowship" to grasp the possible origins, purposes, and rationales for our having a communion with one another. For example, Christian conceptions of human nature may be called "doxological." Whether they are found in hymns, prayers, or catechisms, Christian descriptions of human being are themselves acts of praise to the God who created our life, sustains and redeems us.[5] While "mere communion" could imply collaboration in vice as much as in virtue; "Christian communion" may not. Christian communion, we will see, must always be linked to a "soteriological norm." Christian communion is not aimed toward the social *telos* of humankind alone but toward the fulfillment or salvation of our social nature as such.

1. Communion for Paul

The first recorded Christian application of the word *koinonia* is found in 1 Corinthians 10 and 11. The apostle Paul used terms like "communion" and the "body of Christ" in other letters, but he discusses them in direct correlation to the Eucharist only in 1 Corinthians.[6] There

---

4. For a fascinating study of human and primate ethology, see Frans B. M. de Waal, *Good Natured: The Origins of Right and Wrong in Humans and Other Animals* (Cambridge, Mass.: Harvard University Press, 1996). De Waal shows that all primates learn and exhibit "ethical behaviors." Many behaviors that were once thought "uniquely human," e. g., care for the disabled, social leveling, pranksterism, and scapegoating, can be observed among most primates, in particular the great apes, chimpanzees, bonobos, baboons and gorillas.

5. For example, *Catechism of the Catholic Church* (Washington, D.C.: U. S. Catholic Conference, 1994) I, 1.

6. For Paul's use of the term in general see George Panikulam, *Koinonia in the New Testament: A Dynamic Expression of Christian Life* (Rome: Biblical Institute Press, 1979).

they appear within the context of a classical argument for group cohesion. To understand such concepts and the argument in which they appear, consider the social situation at Corinth, the context in which Paul's letter was written. Recent studies by Gerd Theissen, Wayne Meeks, Margaret Mitchell, and Paul Bradshaw allow us to make several observations about the social conditions of the Corinthian church, and therefore also, the situation toward which Paul's arguments were addressed.[7]

No less than any other small group, Corinthian Christians had to engage in processes of social organization. From primitive, perhaps charismatic, origins, Pauline churches, like the one in Corinth, would grow into mature, urban communities. From Paul's letters to Corinth, we may infer that the Corinthian church was in such a process of social transformation. This type of change, as one easily concludes from observing modern communities, is never easy. The fractiousness of the Corinthian church, as Paul described in this letter, is sufficient evidence of the difficulties.[8] Through his correspondence, Paul hoped to convince Christians in Corinth to adopt practices and beliefs that were more consistent with the Gospel he had received and handed over to them. Throughout the letter, Paul used standard techniques of Greek rhetoric to persuade the church community to become aware of the ill effects of their divisions and to work together for unity.[9]

Paul's discussion of the Eucharist takes place in the middle of Corinthian divisiveness. Paul knew that the Lord's table was the main stage on which Corinthian Christians acted out social and theological arguments, yet he desired their church to manifest unity and peace at the Lord's table freely and willingly. The unity and peace they enjoyed at the table could then extend into other relationships as well. Paul's discussion of the Eucharist was an essential part of this rhetorical strategy. Paul called the Christian community the "body of Christ." He defined the boundaries of the Church on the basis of participation in the meal in

---

TDNT 4, 798, s. v. κοινῶνια, *"Koinonia,"* by Friedrich Hauck. H. Seeseman, *Der Begriff Koinônia im Neuen Testament* (Giessen: 1933). G. V. Jourdan, "Koinônia in 1 Cor. 10:16," *JBL* 57 (1948) 113.

7. Gerd Theissen, *The Social Setting of Pauline Christianity. Essays on Corinth,* tr. J. H. Schütz (Philadelphia: Fortress Press, 1982). Wayne Meeks, *The First Urban Christians: The Social World of the Apostle Paul* (New Haven, Conn.: Yale University Press, 1983). Margaret M. Mitchell, *Paul and the Rhetoric of Reconciliation: An Exegetical Investigation of the Language and Composition of 1 Corinthians* (Louisville, Ky.: Westminster/John Knox Press, 1991). Paul Bradshaw, *The Search for the Origins of Christian Worship* (New York: Oxford University Press, 1992).

8. 1 Cor 1:10-13.

9. Cf. Aristotle, *Rhetoric,* 1, c. 2-3. Mitchell, *Rhetoric of Reconciliation,* 66. See especially her chapter 2, "1 Corinthians as Deliberative Rhetoric," 20–64.

which Christ's body is shared.[10] The Lord's Supper creates social cohesion and shared identity. Paul believed that exclusion from the meal was a powerful social sanction.

According to Wayne Meeks, Paul believed the Lord's Supper is a "symbolic expression of the group's solidarity and of its boundaries."[11] Paul thought the Eucharist, rightly enacted, could exert social force for group cohesion.[12] More than eucharistic doctrines, the acts of the Christian community, gathering to bless, eat, and drink, enhanced the possibility of social cohesion among the members of the community. Such practices secured the external limits of their community. The "body" consisted of those who gathered around the table and vice versa.

Among Americans the occurrence of daily family meals has decreased during the last decade. A recent commercial for a popular fried-chicken franchise made light of this. As a typical nuclear family of four gathered for supper, mom and dad took time to get reacquainted with their children. They had forgotten the children's names. As mom asked daughter about her piano lessons, daughter reminded mom that she played the clarinet, not the piano. The message of the commercial? Sharing meals (preferably meals centered around certain products) enhances family togetherness. Advertisers easily exploit this truism for commercial advantage by playing upon our desires for more intensely satisfying family relationships. Far more basic than how people "talk about" being members of a family, is how often and with what level of commitment they perform the "rites" of being family members.

Churches, like families, are societies in the ordinary sense of the term. Like any other society, churches are founded on social contracts and require ethically motivated members in order to exist and survive. They require rituals and symbols of belonging, such as baptism, meals, stories, and other recognizable patterns of speech and behavior to sustain themselves as a recognizable group. No church exists without members who have freely chosen to speak and act according to that church's particular (or occasionally peculiar) style. On an ordinary, entirely pragmatic level, churches break bread and drink from the cup in order to be what they are, a society of those who, because they are baptized, may go together to the table.[13]

The spectacle of the Corinthian church at supper symbolized their lack of solidarity in Christ and with one another. Their attempts to enact communion at the Eucharist failed and were, in effect, the opposite of a

10. 1 Cor 10:17.
11. Meeks, *Urban Christians*, 102f.
12. *Ibid.* 85.
13. Werner Elert, *Eucharist and Church Fellowship in the First Four Centuries*, tr. N. E. Nagel (St. Louis, Mo.: Concordia Publishing House, 1966) 16.

sacrament. Their words and actions at the table symbolized division and limitation within the group rather than communion in Christ who transcends their divisions.

Unfortunately, there is every reason to believe that Paul's doctrines and arguments failed to change the manner in which Corinthian Christians observed the Supper. Commentaries on the Pauline Eucharist frequently fail to distinguish between Pauline "prescription" and historical "description." One cannot move from Paul's writing about the Eucharist immediately to a discussion of the way that the Corinthian Christians must have acted out and thought about what they were doing at the table. Even less validly could one deduce every ancient practice and conception of the Eucharist from Paul's arguments.[14] Paul's discussion of the Lord's Supper is better evidence for Corinthian behaviors which annoyed him than it is for Christians ever having eaten the Lord's Supper in the manner he was promoting. While Paul's rhetoric sounds authoritative to us, it is no evidence for the obedience of his Corinthian audience.[15]

Paul's doctrine on the Eucharist was aimed to correct the Corinthians' understanding of the Eucharist. Their meal-time behaviors betrayed a misunderstanding of the rite and its purpose. If they understood the Eucharist properly, they might also perform the Eucharist properly. They should eat and drink, Paul states, "discerning the body."[16] The Corinthians were not "discerning the body," because they were eating and drinking without waiting for one another.[17] Some ate and drank their fill, and so became drunk; while others left the meal hungry. Dissension in the community had infected their source of communion. Paul's arguments are offered as a remedy, to restore ideal communion practices among the members of a local church.

1.1. Communion in Christ

When Paul wrote to the Corinthians, he said their communion should be a communion in Christ. Yet Paul acknowledged their communion was only one kind of communion among several. Temple banquets and pagan meals also had a kind of communion. Paul said eating the meats sacrificed in the Jerusalem Temple is a form of communion "in the altar." The meals of pagan dining societies also included ritualized sharing of bread, wine, and other foods. At this time, we believe, the Christian Eucharist was barely distinguishable from such festal banquets.

---

14. Mitchell, *Rhetoric of Reconciliation*, 303. *New Jerome Biblical Commentary* (Englewood Cliffs, N.J.: Prentice Hall, 1990) s. v. "Paul," by Joseph A. Fitzmyer, 1336.
15. See Bradshaw, 67f.
16. 1 Cor 11:29.
17. 1 Cor 11:29, 33.

The Eucharist was not yet the rarefied, symbol of a meal that it later became. If there were prayers and a Liturgy of the Word, they were observed within the context of a robust, hearty meal. The Christian banquets, eating and drinking bread and wine, and the circumstances in which they were held, may have appeared very much like their pagan and Jewish counterparts. How were first-century Corinthians to distinguish their Eucharist from the sacred meals of the other groups?

Paul understood that Christian communion is one subset of a more general, social phenomenon. Even pagans have their own sorts of "communion." They have communion with their gods through sharing in temple meals.[18] To get an idea of what such meals, or *symposia*, may have been like, one need consult only a few of the numerous examples found in classical literature. Plato's *Republic* and his aptly titled *Symposium* center around the relaxed debate of a company of men who had been dining together. Homer's *Odyssey* concludes with a heavily ironic, comedic banquet where the unexpected Odysseus vindicates his honor and defeats his wife's suitors. For a Roman example, consider the decadent banquet scene in Petronius's *Satyricon*. At the *symposia of* Graeco-Roman temple cults, libations and toasts in honor of the various gods was a central element, as was the period of after-dinner entertainment, which might include discussion, dancing, music, games, or even erotic liaisons among guests.[19]

Similarly, Paul said the Jews share a communion with the altar by eating the meats that had been sacrificed there.[20] In later Christian theologies of the Eucharist, the Eucharist was often compared to the temple sacrifices, especially that of the Passover Lamb. Unlike later theologians, Paul did not expect his Christian audience to refute or dismiss these examples of communion outside of Christianity. Rather, he expected them to understand Christian communion in light of the others.[21] The Church is not a "dining society" because its Eucharist is not a pagan symposium, even though the Eucharist bears similarities to the symposium. The Church is not a "temple" because its Eucharist is not a holocaust.

The chief difference between the pagan meal, Jewish sacrifices, and the Christian Eucharist was not founded upon the ethos, the ethical and behavioral conventions, of the different groups. Even pagans made rules against fractious disputation at the table.[22] Paul chose to distinguish these

18. 1 Cor 10:20.

19. Dennis E. Smith and Hal E. Taussig, *Many Tables: The Eucharist in the New Testament and Liturgy Today* (London and Philadelphia: SCM Press and Trinity Press International, 1990) 25ff.

20. 1 Cor 10:19.

21. Meeks, *Urban Christians*, 158.

22. Smith and Taussig note that the by-laws of the Guild of Zeus Hypsistos, for example, forbid "making factions," 32. See Colin Roberts, T. C. Skeat and A. D. Nock, "The Guild of Zeus Hypsistos," *Harvard Theological Review* 29 (1936) 40–42.

meals not on the basis of "how" they were celebrated, but on the basis of the ones in "whom" one had communion at the meal. Each cultic community, pagan, Jewish, and Christian, was grounded in a single, shared relationship. Pagans had communion in their gods. Jews had communion with the altar. Christians have communion with Christ.[23] Sharing a meal with others was *ipso facto* to be "communicant" (a translation of Paul's word, *koinonous*) with them in a transcendent reality. To generalize, in the Greek literature, *koinonia* describes social inclusion on the basis of a shared economy, a sharing of things or ideas. Christian communion arises from a shared communion in Christ rather than from common cultural conventions.[24] In 1 Corinthians "communion" describes social inclusion on the basis of participation in Christ to the exclusion of all opposing powers.[25]

1.2. Communion implies accessibility

If Christian communion is a communion in Christ, it must depend upon the accessibility of the person of Christ to communicants. Christ must be accessible to communicants in the Lord's Supper or else the Christian meal is no different from other meals. Paul believed that Christ is accessible to communicants in the symbols of the bread "that we have broken" and "cup of blessing that we have blessed."[26] Classical eucharistic doctrines such as transubstantiation may be interpreted as strong affirmations of the accessibility of Christ in the eucharistic elements themselves.

Some more recent attempts to accommodate eucharistic doctrine to a world less inclined to accept medieval metaphysics have emphasized the accessibility of Christ through the acts of breaking the bread and blessing the cup.[27] These are gestures, one could say, which irrevocably change the significance of those items for us. Finally, ecumenical dialogue partners have found the affirmation of Christ's promise to remain present, "This is my body broken for you," an important foundation for Christian affirmation of the accessibility of Christ in and through the Eucharist.[28]

---

23. 1 Cor 10:18-19a.

24. Hans von Soden, "Sakrament und Ethik bei Paulus zür Frage der literarischen und theologischen Einheitlichkeit von 1 Kor. 8-10," in *Urchristentum und Geschichte Gesammelte Aufsätze und Vorträge*, vol. 1 (Tübingen: J. C. B. Mohr, 1951) 239–75.

25. Panikulam, 28f.

26. 1 Cor 10:16.

27. Perhaps the first to recover the performative dimension of the liturgy was Gregory Dix. See his *The Shape of the Liturgy*, with notes by Paul Marshall (New York: Seabury Press, 1983), a reprint of the 1945 ed., especially chapter 2, "The Performance of the Liturgy," 12–35. See also Edward Schillebeeckx, *The Eucharist*, tr. N. D. Smith (New York: Sheed and Ward, 1968) 134ff.

28. BEM, 13. Joseph M. Powers, *Eucharistic Theology* (New York: Herder and Herder, 1967) 86. Powers called the Eucharist a "sign-act." "Sign-acts," like kissing or shaking hands, he says, convey "the total personal reality" of one person to another.

At the very least we must say the Lord's Supper is the locus of accessibility to Christ. Christ is no less accessible whether the Eucharist is conceived in terms of material objects like bread and wine or the actions the Church performs with bread and wine. The Eucharist is both action and thing acted upon. At the Eucharist communicants receive a share and become communicants *(koinountes)* in Christ and in the saving acts which Christ has accomplished for them. At the Eucharist they receive a share and become communicants in the broken bread and the blessed cup. They also become communicants in the breaking of the bread and the blessing of the cup. Their role is not passive.[29]

Christian doctrine claims that Christ is present in the Eucharist. To understand this doctrine we must move beyond the claim for his eucharistic accessibility, to consider also the promises of Christ to be present in a particular way. Christ is present "for" us. For example, the Eucharist is incorrectly understood if it is thought the place for us to cower before an omnipotent tyrant. Rather, we are given access to Christ so as to trust, rejoice, thank, and praise him "in the presence of the fountain of every good thing." "We seek God," Randall Zachman reminds us in an article on the theology of John Calvin, "not because we have no other choice . . . [but] because God kindly invites us and gently allures us by the sweetness of God's goodness."[30]

Where theologians like John Calvin especially emphasized the presence of God's revealing Word in sacred Scripture, we may add balance to his view by equally emphasizing the presence of God's revealing Word in the members of Christ's body, the Christian community throughout the ages. The doctrine of the presence of Christ in the Eucharist primarily refers to the self-communication of Christ by the Holy Spirit in and through those who partake of the Eucharist.[31] Secondarily, it refers to the sacramental means of that self-communication—the symbols of bread and wine and the symbols of the Church's actions with bread and wine. In other words, Christian doctrine should insist upon the communion of the bread and cup in the person of Christ insofar as our participation in Christ (our communion) is possible only through a sharing in that bread and cup.

If Christ is present in the Eucharist, he is not present as a mere object like bread or wine, but also as a person who invites us into a saving

---

29. Cf. Jerome Kodell, *The Eucharist in the New Testament*, (Wilmington, Michael Glazier, 1988) 73. See also Jerome Murphy-O'Connor, "Eucharist and Community in First Corinthians," *Worship* 51 (1977) 59.

30. Randall Zachman, "Theologian in the Service of Piety: A New Portrait of Calvin," *Christian Century* 114/14 (April 23–30, 1997) 417.

31. "The *res sacramenti* is: the *koinonia tou kyriou*, the self-communication of the Lord." von Soden, 264, 266, my translation.

relationship. The eucharistic presence of Christ is not passive or "thing-like." Christ's presence is active, for it has its own proper work to perform on us. It is relational, for it draws Christians into relationship with Christ and with one another. It is effective, for the relationship between Christ and the eucharistic bread and wine does not end with the consecration—as though the Eucharist were fulfilled in mere presence—but the mission of Christ finds its fulfillment in the salvation of those whom Christ touches. By means of sharing in the consecrated bread and wine, communicants are invited to a saving relationship with Christ and one another by the agency of the Holy Spirit.

1.3 Accessibility through communion depends on the Spirit

Our dependence upon the work of the Holy Spirit for establishing communion with Christ must not be underestimated. The Holy Spirit is always at work in the community, cultivating the preconditions for communion, gathering and ordering the assembly of the baptized, and sustaining the effects of communion among us by giving us the ability to perform acts of mercy and mission in the name of Christ. For Paul, the presence of Christ to the Church is always a spiritual presence.[32] The Spirit defines the mode of existence of the risen Lord, who has extended his Spirit over the Christian community in a decisive act of power.[33]

Roman Catholic Dutch theologian Piet Schoonenberg may assist our understanding of the role of the Spirit in the communion of the Church. Schoonenberg's "Spirit christology" develops the biblical understanding of the special relationship between the Spirit and the Word. On his view, the Spirit is the Spirit of "sonship." The Spirit who spoke in the voice of the prophets is the Spirit who speaks in Jesus and in the Church. The Spirit, resting on Jesus at his baptism and in his resurrection, unites him in love to the Father as the Father's Word. The Spirit speaks prophetically in the Word and Jesus walks the lonely path of the prophet in all its vicissitudes. By the light of his resurrection, Jesus' union with God by the Spirit is finally and fully revealed. The mere fact of God's presence in the Son is not enough to simply satisfy an orthodox theology of the incarnation. The Son is given in Jesus, the Messiah, "for" us. Our salvation depends on recognizing "the kind of Word" God has spoken to us in Jesus. This view has important consequences for our understanding of the Church. It is not enough to continue referring to church structures. Church structures are given "for us" (and not we for them). Our salvation depends on recognizing "the kind of Word" God is speaking to the

---

32. 2 Cor 5:16.
33. *TDNT* 6, 419 s. v. πνεῦμα III. Paul, "Pneuma. III. Paul," by Eduard Schweizer.

world in the Church. The Word the Spirit speaks is prophetic and, like Jesus, the Church must walk the lonely path of the prophet in all its vicissitudes.[34]

Paul's letter indicates the Eucharist is a perpetual memorial of Christ's death to be performed "until he comes in glory."[35] The presence of Christ to the Church in the Spirit may therefore be called a "proleptic" presence. *Prolepsis* refers to those signs of the fulfillment which are given to the Church as a token or pledge of the promised completion of the world in Christ. Christ's presence is experienced in the Eucharist as both a present reality by the work of the Spirit and as the pledge of his absolute presence at the end of time.[36] This is congruent with Paul's understanding that the gift of the Spirit is no mere "overture" to the second coming. The existence of the community itself is sign of the Lord's having already arrived among us through the power of his Spirit.[37]

The effectiveness of the Eucharist therefore depends upon both the accessibility of Christ and upon the power of the Holy Spirit in, through, over, and under the actions of the Christian assembly. The Spirit provides the power by which the Eucharist becomes more than just another meal with bread and wine, but a complex sign through which Christ is made known to us. Only in the Spirit are we able to discern the body and blood of the Redeemer in the assembly of individual men and women who form the Church. The Spirit rescues us from judgment.[38]

Nonetheless, the power and presence of the Spirit cannot normally be presumed, but must be discerned. The presence of God's Spirit among human beings may not be listed among one's list of prior assumptions. Rather, biblical and historical examples indicate that the Church has more often recognized the work of the Spirit through hindsight than by plan or request. Instead, our public stance toward God must begin with the open acknowledgment of our dependency upon God's merciful, free, and loving Spirit.[39] Eucharistic theology has adopted the Greek term *epiclesis*, which means, literally, "something cried out for" to describe the pneumatological dimension of the sacrament.[40]

34. Piet Schoonenberg, *De Geest, Het Woord en de Zoon: Theologische Overdenkingen over Geest-Christologie, Logos-Christologie en drieëenheidsleer* (Averbode and Kampen/Altiora and Kok, 1991) 41f.

35. 1 Cor 11:26.

36. Michael Bouttier, *Christianity According to Paul*, tr. Frank Clarke, Studies in Biblical Theology 40 (London: SCM Press, 1966) 47f.

37. Schweizer, 417.

38. 1 Cor 11:29.

39. By "confidence," we mean a radical openness, a *parrhesia*, to the saving power of God. *TDNT* 5, 882–84, s. v. παρρῆσια, "Parrhesia," by Heinrich Schlier.

40. *TDNT* 3, 496–500, s. v. ἐπικαλεω, "Epikaleo," by Karl L. Schmidt. For Paul's pneumatology see also *TDNT* 6, 415–37, s. v. πνεῦμα III. Paul, "Pneuma. III. Paul," by Eduard Schweizer.

Every Christian Eucharist must include this epicletic character. The Church takes a chance on God every time it performs such deeds and speaks such words. The rite alone would be a meaningless agglomeration of words and deeds were it not performed by men and women suffused with the power and Spirit of the risen Christ. None of the symbols of the Eucharist can be said to do their saving work by an intrinsic power. They do their work only as much as the men and women who perform them are receptive to and dependent upon the will of God revealed through Christ, now made effective by the power of the Spirit.

If some theological systems stress the character of sacramental symbols to perform their work *ex opere operatum*, "by the work itself," they do so within pneumatological brackets. Our degree of confidence in what the Eucharist accomplishes for us is proportionate to our degree of confidence in God who creates the communion which the Eucharist symbolizes. As Paul wrote in Romans 5:5, "Hope does not disappoint us, because God's love has been poured into our hearts through the Holy Spirit that has been given to us." Theologies that express a high level of confidence in the saving power of the Eucharist do so because they first have expressed a high level of confidence in the loving mercy of God, who, they say, condescends to touch us in and through the Church's eucharistic words and deeds. Even poor instruments, like human beings, can be effective signs of God's salvation.

1.4. Communion in the spiritual body of the risen Christ

Commentators have sometimes distinguished between "vertical" and "horizontal" communion. By "horizontal" communion they referred to the "mere communion" of voluntary association. By "vertical" communion they meant the communion of individuals by the Spirit with the Lord Jesus. If anything can be shown from the previous section, the "vertical" and the "horizontal" aspects of communion are not so easily separated. Christian communion implies far more than the "mere communion" of voluntary association. The individualized conception of salvation contained in the idea of a merely "vertical" communion does no justice to the biblical conception of communion. Rather, the "horizontal" and "vertical" aspects of Christian communion must be held in tension, for participation in the one symbolizes and creates the possibility of participation in the other. The meal creates the possibility for "both" vertical and horizontal dimensions of communion.[41] The communion created by the Eucharist is both social and personal. It includes both the everyday and ordinary along with the transcendent and eschatological.

---

41. Paul Neuenzeit, *Das Herrenmahl* (Munich: Kösel-Verlag, 1960) 140.

In the Pauline writings the "body of Christ" image is a remarkable example of how Paul has held together both "vertical" and "horizontal" aspects in a dynamic tension. Paul's discussion of the body works "horizontally" for it neutralizes factionalist rhetoric. It works "vertically" for it vividly interprets the relation between the Church and Christ, the "body" and the "head of the body," who is the cornerstone of the Church.[42] The "horizontal" communions of Christians comprise the "vertical" communion of the risen body of Christ and manifest the outward form of his Spirit.[43] The eucharistic bread is a functional symbol of communion in the body. Partaking from the meal, Christians are made part of the entire social organism of which the bread is a symbol, the communion of Christ's body. "The community," Hans Conzelmann remarked, "is interpreted in and through the meal."[44] The meal is a synecdoche, for it summarizes the aspirations of the Christian community to be united with their Savior.

The Lord's Supper is not only about union with Christ. The Lord's Supper is also for our knowledge of Christ, of ourselves as members of Christ's body joined to one another. When one looks at the Church, one does not see one more social or cultural organization in the world. Instead, one sees, first, the risen Christ himself, the members of the body vivified by the power of his Spirit.[45] While the members of the body first recognize Christ at the Supper, those outside of the body recognize Christ in the powerful love and communion of his members. The Church thus represents a corporate personality—Christ, both head and members—unfolding through time and place in an historical communion among the baptized men and women who enact the Eucharist. Christ alone performs the Eucharist to a saving effect, yet he does so in the person of his body, the communion of the Church. As we will see in chapter two, this leads to the conclusion that the Church is a continuation or extension of the incarnation. If the Eucharist is effective, as we believe it is, then we must also believe in a continuity between the Church and the incarnate Christ.[46]

The incarnation of Christ in the physical body of Jesus of Nazareth is an essential and incomplete—though immense—part of the mystery of incarnation. Christ is also incarnate "at the right hand of God" and "as head of the Church," his body.[47] The Eucharist is a place where Christ is

42. 1 Cor 11:29. Mitchell, *Rhetoric of Reconciliation*, 161.

43. John A. T. Robinson, *The Body: A Study in Pauline Theology* (Philadelphia: Westminster Press, 1952) 14, 51.

44. Hans Conzelmann, *1 Corinthians*, tr. James W. Leitch (Philadelphia: Fortress Press, 1975) 172.

45. Neuenzeit, 218.

46. Murphy-O'Connor, "Eucharist and Community," 115.

47. Acts 2:32-33; Col 1:18; Eph 1:22-23.

made intimately accessible to the members of his body. The intimate accessibility of Christ through the Eucharist, declared by doctrines of his eucharistic presence, must never be divorced from the ecclesial modality of that presence—Christ is present in his assembled body—or from the purpose for that presence—Christ is present as the Church for the salvation of all. Historically, doctrinal affirmations of the presence of Christ have been encumbered by ancient polemics or by philosophical and metaphysical speculations. Hopefully, the Church of the next millennium will fruitfully subordinate these polemics and speculations in favor of a renewed emphasis on the place of the Eucharist within God's saving design. By the power of the Spirit, Christ has extended the redemptive work of God beyond first-century Palestine in and through the life and mission of his risen body, the Church.

1.5. Communion in the Cross

In an ecumenical context, where few answers may be taken for granted, it may be useful to consider this seldom-asked question: Why should Christians repeat the Lord's Supper?[48] Paul's argument for repeating the Lord's Supper rests on the command of Jesus to bless the cup and break the bread "in his memory."[49] The Greek word for "memory" is *anamnesis*, which may be roughly translated as "not forgetting."[50] Paul wrote that as often as one eats the bread and drinks the cup, one "proclaims the Lord's death until he comes."[51] Eating and drinking the Eucharist proclaims the gospel of salvation.[52] Paul's words mean that eating and drinking at the Eucharist are truly "evangelical" acts. When we do so we proclaim the Gospel as much as when we read the words of Scripture. The evangelical mission of the Church is fulfilled as much in preaching as in receiving the Eucharist. We should be clear about this for "evangelical" Churches, on the one hand, tend to minimize the practice of the sacraments in favor of an emphasis on preaching. "Sacramental" churches, on the other hand, tend to downplay the evangelical witness of the Eucharist in favor of an emphasis on reception as a personal expression of faith or as a location for mystical encounter.

The memorial of Christ and the proclamation of his death are closely linked to the act of receiving the body and blood of Christ in the Eu-

---

48. This question is not moot. There are several Churches who do not, or very seldom, observe the Lord's Supper. Such "non-sacramental" Churches include the Salvation Army or the Society of Friends (Quakers).

49. 1 Cor 11:24-25. D. Jones, "Anamnesis in the LXX and the Interpretation of 1 Cor XI.25," *JTS* 6 (1955) 183–91.

50. The root word *amnesis* is the basis for the English word "amnesia."

51. 1 Cor 11:26.

52. Murphy-O'Connor, "Eucharist and Community," 112f.

charist. Each Eucharist is a proclamation of the Gospel, of the death of the Lord. Each time we perform the Eucharist we remember the Savior.[53] The memorial of Christ—the *anamnesis* of Christ's death and resurrection—is central to the mission of the Church. Thus, the Lord's Supper is not a "private forum" for members of the Church to observe in solitude. The Eucharist may not be separated from the public gathering of the Church. Neither may the Eucharist be separated from the death of Christ. An examination of the Eucharist as a communion in the death of Christ will help us to understand the sacrificial character of the Eucharist.

In his first letter to the Corinthians Paul used an interesting combination of Greek words to refer to the body and blood of Christ. The Greek word for body, *soma*, and the Greek word for blood, *haima*, do not correlate.[54] They do not form a conceptual pair like the English words "body" and "blood." Paul's Greek audience would have usually heard *sarx* (flesh) and *haima* (blood) together. *Sarx* had negative connotations for Paul. It referred to human being in the world, sinful and living in isolation from God. In contrast to *sarx*, *soma* refers to the entire person, not to the anatomy alone. *Soma* denotes instead the human person made alive by the power of Christ's Spirit.[55]

Just as *soma* does not refer simply to the flesh and sinews of the human body, so also *haima* does not refer simply to the fluid of the veins and arteries. In Paul's letter the word "blood" refers to Christ's death on the cross and to the memorial of his death in the members of his body. Just as the "body of Christ" is a functional symbol for the Church's communion in Christ's body, so the "blood of Christ" is a functional symbol for the Church's communion in the death of Jesus. Modern Christians may "know about" the Cross because they read and hear the Gospels; but they are "participants" in the Cross at the Eucharist.

This connection between the Cross and the Lord's Supper must be carefully traced. Paul understood Christ's death as an atoning sacrifice, the definitive turning point in the relationship between God and humankind.[56] In the passages from 1 Corinthians which we have been considering, he linked the death of Christ to the Eucharist. Moreover, all of the synoptic passion narratives join Paul and set the institution of the Eucharist "on the night when he [Jesus] was betrayed."[57] According to Hans von Soden, communion in the blood of Christ refers to participation

53. Neuenzeit, 127. Murphy-O'Connor, "Eucharist and Community," 20.
54. Conzelmann, 172.
55. Robinson, 17–31.
56. See Ernst Käsemann, *Perspectives on Paul*, tr. Margaret Kohl (Philadelphia: Fortress Press, 1978) 32–59. Henri de Lubac, "*Mysterium crucis*," in *Catholicism: A Study of Dogma in Relation to the Corporate Destiny of Mankind* (New York: Sheed and Ward, 1958) 206f.
57. 1 Cor 11:23; cf. Matt 26:26-29; Mark 14:22-25; and Luke 22:14-20.

in the death of Christ. Likewise, Günther Bornkamm wrote that "'participation in the blood' and 'participation in the body' mean to share in the death of Christ and thus in Christ himself, the Lord present in the sacrament who died for us and offers himself to us in the bread and cup."[58]

The soteriological value of the Eucharist may not be separated from the sacrifice of the Cross. In his eucharistic presence for us, Christ comes as the crucified One, risen and victorious over death and sin. Communion in the Eucharist means little if it is not also a communion in the salvation Christ's conquest has created. Only because "Christians have died in, with and through the crucified body of the Lord," John Robinson reminds us, are they now "in and of His body in the 'life that he liveth unto God', viz., the body of the Church." The participation of the Christian in the death that Jesus died, "once and for all," is so complete and thorough, Robinson concludes, that literally everything that happened in and through Christ's body "in the flesh" can be repeated "in and through [the Christian] now."[59] We do not die in Christ alone and by ourselves. We have a communion in the death of Christ for Christ shares this death and all its glorious consequences with the members of his body through baptism.

How, then, do we share in the death of Christ at the Eucharist? In his landmark study of 1 Corinthians, Hans Conzelmann described the communion as a two-tiered participation in the new covenant of Christ's blood. The first tier: when we partake in the meal, we partake in the blood of Christ. The second tier: partaking the blood of Christ, we partake of the new covenant of salvation which Christ's blood has created. Conzelmann concluded that our communion is in the atoning power of Christ's blood.[60] Conzelmann's observation is consonant with human experience, for we must first receive the meal itself. Second, we receive the connection between the meal and the blood of Christ. Finally, we receive the blood of Christ as ultimate sign of his victory over death and sin, as the definitive act in the restoration of the world to communion with God. Only because it is first known as the blood of Christ may the cup of blessing be called a cup of salvation.

Paul's doctrine of the Eucharist, therefore, does not emphasize the mere presence of Christ as though it were a sheer fact. Rather, Paul's argument suggests that he wanted to draw the attention of his readers first

---

58. von Soden, 263, my translation. Günther Bornkamm, "Lord's Supper and Church in Paul," in *Early Christian Experience*, tr. Paul L. Hammer (London: SCM Press, 1969) 145. Conzelmann disagrees, 199f. For him, the key term is not "blood," but "covenant." The communion is not in the sacrifice *per se*, but in the new covenant established by Jesus when his blood was shed.

59. Rom 6:10, 7:4. Robinson, 47.

60. Conzelmann, 171.

to the eucharistic meal and its components—the elements of bread and wine and the gestures the Church performs with them. Second, he spoke of the meal as an occasion—as "the" occasion *par excellence*—for communion in the atoning presence of Christ. Finally, he reminded his readers of the salvation which Christ created on the Cross. Because Christ is risen and present, in the Spirit, to the members of his body, salvation is also offered and accepted in the context of the eucharistic meal. The acts which comprise the Eucharist, taking, blessing, breaking, pouring, receiving and so forth, rehearse us in confident dependence upon God.[61]

Conzelmann proposes a two-tiered scheme for communion which joins three levels of meaning in Paul's description of the Eucharist. In Paul's description of the Eucharist "body" and "blood" first refer to themselves. Second, they signify the whole Christ. Finally, they signify Christ who saves and forms the Church.[62] The three levels of meaning are joined in two levels of "communion." First, there is the mere communion of a meal of bread and wine in the body and blood of Christ, both head and members. There is, second, a communion in salvation which is given to communicants in Christ's body.[63]

The first level of communion, communion in bread and wine, which could take place in any context—religious or secular, Christian or non-Christian—does not necessarily draw people into the Church or save them. Rather, the second level, offered and received in the context of eucharistic meals, both forms and saves the Church by drawing it in to the love and unity of God by the power of Christ's Spirit. In some Protestant Churches it was once customary to call the sacraments "saving ordinances." The Eucharist is a saving ordinance only if it is a sacrament of Christ who saves.

2. Meals with Jesus—the borderless board

Salvador Dali's painting of the Last Supper was completed in 1955 and now hangs in the National Gallery of Art in Washington, D.C.[64] This

---

61. Cf. Käsemann, 40.

62. Neuenzeit, 60.

63. The three levels of communion may be understood roughly to correspond to the medieval distinction between the *res tantum, res et sacramentum,* and *sacramentum tantum* developed by Peter Lombard and later confirmed by Innocent III. *Sacramentum tantum,* the "sacrament itself," refers to the bread and wine and the actions we perform with them. *Res et sacramentum,* the "reality and the sacrament," refers to the body and blood of Christ, both head and members. *Res tantum,* the "reality itself," refers to the unity and love of God in which we participate for the sake of our salvation.

64. Dozens of images of the painting may be easily found by searching on the World Wide Web. One of the best images was found at <http://www.empower.net/dali/last-supp.html> (July 1997).

painting is a personal favorite for its juxtaposition of mystical and modern elements. Jesus and the disciples—including Judas—are collected around a monumental, perfectly proportioned, stone table. Above the scene is a large, male torso—the mystical body of Christ—whose arms are outstretched to embrace all the figures in the painting. Bread and wine are set at the center of the table where they perfectly coincide with the center of the large torso and the body of Jesus. At the front of the painting two disciples reverently kneel. In the space between these two disciples the viewer is drawn into the painting. The upper room, a dodecahedron, opens onto a panoramic vista of Dali's Catelonian homeland. The structural elements of the room are incomplete in the foreground suggesting that the back of the room is behind the viewer. The room in effect reaches beyond the canvas to draw in the audience.

The painting is an example of what Dali called "nuclear mysticism," in which he combined elements of Christian mysticism with modern science.[65] My point in describing the painting is not to expound on Dali's image of the Last Supper, but to use his painting as illustration of two ecclesiological qualities which find their source in the Eucharist: the mystical body of Christ and the borderless character of the eucharistic table. The large, looming torso above the tableau unifies and embraces those gathered around the table. Dali's use of the figure in his painting implies a "body of Christ" *beyond* the body of Jesus, who is pointing skyward toward the mystical body image. This mystical body image includes all who have gathered around the table. Glimpsed only in part, the body of Christ seems to extend into another realm of existence. The entire tableau—Jesus, the disciples, the bread and wine—are described, visually, as the "mystical body of Christ" because of the unifying embrace of that large, partially visible, male torso. Dali's painting was completed in the mid-1950s, at nearly the same time Pius XII wrote his important encyclical *Mystici corporis*, on the mystical body of Christ. This "mystical body" idea will be a central theme of chapter 2.

The Eucharist may be considered a sacramental extension of the Last Supper through time and place. The space in the foreground of Dali's painting, between the two disciples, might represent that extension, its "boundless" and "borderless" qualities. Wherever the disciples gather, they are "sacramentally" located at the original table in the original Upper Room. The open quality of Dali's upper room and the space between the two disciples in the foreground contributes powerfully to this impression. The twelve do not so closely surround the altar that no one else may join their circle. The walls do not seal the room from the world.

65. N. a., "The Last Supper," <http://www.empower.net/dali/lastsupp.html> (July 1997). See also "The Sacrament of the Last Supper," <http://www.ionet.net/~jellenc/dali.html> (April 1998).

The table is not closed to latter-day men and women. Dali thus emphasized the open-ended quality of the Upper Room.

Recent studies of the Gospels have remarked upon the radical "openness" of the meals of Jesus. Conceptually it is not far to move from the openness of Jesus' historical meals where marginal men and women (e.g., the "tax collectors and sinners") were welcomed to the openness of Jesus' eucharistic table where men and women of all times and places are now welcomed.[66] The main difference is this. The second type of openness depends upon the first, historical kind of openness for its specific content. The meals of the historical Jesus prefigure the limitless reconciliation of the human community toward which he has sent the Church. There is no reason to suppose that the Church should open its tables if the historical Jesus had not "opened" his.

For Jesus' contemporaries, the margins between social categories like Jew and gentile, holy and profane, righteousness and forgiveness were strongly motivating, realistic, and powerful. Jesus' mealtime practices blurred those lines of social division and threatened the status quo for the first-century men and women who encountered Jesus and his movement. Take another conceptual step, as did the earliest generation of Christians, and the death of Jesus follows a similar movement. One who blurred the margins between poor and the strong, the pure and the polluted in his life has also abolished the margins between the living and the dead, between the present and the absolute future in his death. This second type of openness, a post-resurrection, conceptual extrapolation from the disciple's experience of Jesus' earthly life and ministry, was no less earth-shattering. The "openness" of Jesus' table is social, but also cosmic. As the meals of Jesus reached beyond the Upper Room into an uncountable number of later times and other places, they increasingly exhibit the second type of openness. The Eucharist depends not just on the historical ministry of the earthly Jesus, but also upon the resurrection of Christ and the gift of his Spirit for its effectiveness. Because of the paschal mystery, the tables of the historical Jesus have their counterpart in the altars of the cosmic Christ.

The extension of the Eucharist to all times and places and to all types of men and women is a powerful and important balance to Paul's theology of atonement and the Cross. If Paul's description of the Lord's Supper sounds limited, the gospel portraits of Jesus at table with men and women—also written in light of the Church's later eucharistic experiences—offer additional images, both powerful and profound, by which to describe the Eucharist and the Church.

66. Cf. Mark 2:15-17; Matt 9:9-13; and Luke 5:27-32.

For example, the preaching and ministry of Jesus may be interpreted under the category of the approaching reign of God.[67] Jesus' own table-fellowship is sometimes viewed from this perspective. The way in which Jesus shared meals, therefore, is considered a striking model of the reign of God. As described in the Gospels, the meals Jesus shared with others reinforced the parables and other words he was preaching about the approaching kingdom. Just as the parables described a "kingdom" that is open to all and which is given lavishly and abundantly—even upon the "least deserving"—so the meals that Jesus shared enacted the same kingdom message and were, in a sense, the "proof to the pudding" of Jesus' preaching. The radically open character of Jesus' meals was an integral component of his message.

I have little doubt most of Jesus' meals were shared intimately, with his closest companions alone. The Gospels are clear that the Last Supper was one such "intimate" meal. Still, the Gospels also show Jesus sharing meals with nearly indiscriminate openness. The gospel writers could not avoid mentioning the scandal such meals apparently provoked. The Gospels uniformly report Jesus' opponents leveling accusations against him. Prominent among the charges: "He dined with tax collectors and sinners."[68] Confidence in the historicity of such meal practices is high. The situation is part of the triple tradition (they appear in all three synoptic Gospels); and the account was a potential embarrassment to early Christians. On the other hand, the stories point up supposed differences between Jesus and the Pharisees, who were less likely to have been the historical opponents of Jesus than they were the historical opponents of early Christians.[69] Jesus' practice of sharing mealtime hospitality with nearly scandalous disregard for social conventions is sometimes referred to as his "open commensality." Open table practices were not simply a technique Jesus used to attract crowds for his message. They were part of Jesus' goal to reconstruct peasant community on radically different social foundations. Eschewing the usual categories of honor, shame, clients and patronage, Jesus was, according to Bible historian John Dominic Crossan, truly egalitarian.[70]

---

67. John Macquarrie, *Jesus Christ in Modern Thought* (London and Philadelphia: SCM Press and Trinity Press International, 1990) 33ff. John P. Meier, "Jesus (III) Basic Message of Jesus, (A) Kingdom of God," *NJBC* 78:17. *Idem. A Marginal Jew: Rethinking the Historical Jesus*, vol. 1: The Roots of the Problem and the Person, Anchor Bible Reference Library (New York: Doubleday, 1991) 174–77.

68. Matt 9:10-11; Mark 2:15-16; Luke 5:30.

69. See Meier, *Marginal Jew*, chapter 6, 167–95.

70. Dennis E. Smith, *Social Obligation in the Context of Communal Meals: A Study of the Christian Meal in 1 Corinthians in Comparison with Graeco-Roman Communal Meals*, Th. D. dissertation: Harvard University, 1980. Lee Edward Klosinski, *The Meals in Mark*,

The radicality of Jesus' commensality must not be misunderstood or understated. At the original heart of Jesus' ministry, in the words of John Crossan, is a "shared egalitarianism of spiritual and material resources."[71] Unlike the urban and cultural thrust of Paul's preaching and mission, Jesus' original movement was concerned with common meals and a shared hearth. To share a meal with Jesus is to become committed to sharing a meal with those who opened their home to him. These men and women were not the power-elites of first-century Palestine. They were the peasants. They were handicapped. They were collaborators with Roman tyranny. As Crossan observed, as an itinerant preacher Jesus could have easily satisfied the economic needs of his teaching ministry with alms, wages or fees. Alms and wages were standard means of finance for itinerant teachers of Jesus' day.[72] Instead, Jesus chose to share meals and to enter the homes of the women and men he intended to change by his message. "Commensality," Crossan states, "was . . . a strategy for building or rebuilding peasant community on radically different principles. . . ."[73] "Kingdom of God" is the name Jesus gave to those radical social, ethical, and religious principles. The gospel writers favorably compared meals with Jesus to the meals of the kingdom of God.[74] The meals are a wedding feast; the kingdom, a banquet.[75] The community meal derives its power to reconfigure the peasant community because it is a symbol of the messianic kingdom, because it is a sign of abundance, and because it deliberately thwarts the social barriers created and maintained by religious and political elites.

Current scholars of the "historical Jesus" school were not the first to identify the theme of "open commensality" in Jesus' life and ministry. Hans Lietzmann, a German scholar whose work has been too easily dismissed by later scholars, distinguished between Pauline and gospel traditions on the Eucharist. In his classic work *Mass and Lord's Supper*, Lietzmann described not one but two types of primitive Christian Eucharists. He said that the first form of the Eucharist was the primitive, early form, a continuation of the table-fellowship, or *haburah* meals, which Jesus once shared with his disciples. Celebratory, agapic "meals of

---

Ph. D. dissertation: Claremont University, 1988. John Dominic Crossan, *The Historical Jesus: The Life of a Mediterranean Jewish Peasant* (San Francisco: HarperSanFrancisco, 1991) 344.

71. Crossan, 341.

72. Crossan, 344.

73. Ibid.

74. William R. Crockett, *Eucharist: Symbol of Transformation* (New York: Paulist Press, 1989) 6f.

75. Matt 8:11; Luke 13:29.

the kingdom," represented in the stories of the multiplication of loaves, form the heart of this tradition.

The *haburah* meals of the earthly Jesus and early Christian communities contrast, Lietzmann believed, with a second, less primitive form of the Eucharist. The cultic form, apparent in the synoptic and Pauline narratives of the Upper Room, closely linked the meaning of the Eucharist to the sacrificial and atoning death of Jesus. Lietzmann called the first strand of eucharistic tradition "agapic"; the second, he called cultic.

Lietzmann believed that the agapic form of the meal, though it began "in the time of the historic Jesus," in the early 30s C.E., was continued immediately with the risen Lord among the disciples. Consider the Emmaus story or John's accounts of post-resurrection breakfasts at the Sea of Galilee.[76] Lietzmann supposed that the cultic form of the Eucharist, by contrast, originated around 50 C.E., in an old tradition known to the author of Mark's Gospel. The cultic form emphasizes the death of Jesus and, through the consumption of his body and blood, establishes a "spiritual reality," the *corpus mysticum* of the Church.[77] Lietzmann's views were similar to, though less extreme than, those of Adolf von Harnack and others who valorized "primitive" Christianity at the expense of later developments. Lietzmann thought there was a historical development from agapic to cultic forms of the Eucharist. Unlike his contemporaries, he did not deny the possible origins of the cultic form of the Eucharist with Jesus. Lietzmann thought that Paul's discussion of the Lord's Supper in 1 Corinthians was the primary source for the cultic tradition. When Paul therefore spoke of the meal as coming to him "from the Lord," Lietzmann believed Paul was referring to a vision or a special revelation from the "risen" Savior to Paul. Paul, he says, was the "human author" of the cultic form of the Eucharist.[78]

Lietzmann's identification of the agapic and cultic types of Eucharist was creative and ingenious. Certainly, both emphases form a major portion of early Christian preaching and practice. Nonetheless, his views have suffered understandably severe criticism. Günther Bornkamm and Hans Conzelmann, for instance, dismissed Lietzmann's analysis with brief footnotes.[79] If Lietzmann's scheme, from agapic to cultic meal types, is understood to describe only a process of historical development from one set of eucharistic practices to another, one must concur with Bornkamm and Conzelmann. There is no verifiable evidence for such development in existing historical records. On the other hand, should his

---

76. Luke 24:30-31; John 21:12. Hans Lietzmann, *Mass and Lord's Supper: A Study in the History of the Liturgy*, tr. Dorothea H. G. Reeve (Leiden: Brill, 1979) 204.

77. Lietzmann, 205.

78. Lietzmann, 208.

79. Bornkamm, 127. Conzelmann, 201.

scheme be understood as offering eucharistic *typologies* within early Christianity, we must give Lietzmann's idea a second glance.

Even if Paul was not the creator of a cultic form of the Eucharist, as Lietzmann surmised, the description of the Eucharist in 1 Corinthians is consistent with a struggle between the apostle and his Corinthian opponents to synthesize conflicting interpretations. By Lietzmann's own definitions, the conflicts we deduced from Paul's 1 Corinthian rhetoric are easily named "agapic" or "cultic." Paul is emphasizing "cultic" at the expense of "agapic" interpretations and practices. He was attempting to dissuade his readers from excessive mealtime habits and immodest drinking by reference to a more solemn dimension at the core of the meal. Where his Corinthian readers may have understood the meal in a nearly libertine fashion as an agapic, "resurrection feast," Paul wanted also to remind them of the memorial character of the meal, as a communion in the death of the Savior.

It is possible but not likely that the practice of an explicitly agapic, *haburah*-type meal ended after Jesus' death.[80] The Gospels and other early Christian sources, such as the *Didache*, indicate that early Christians maintained a collective memory of *haburah*-type meals with Jesus. The cultic form of the meal, by definition, could not have existed before the Last Supper. At the Last Supper, then, either Jesus had an unusually precise premonition of his death or the gospel writers had projected later eucharistic theologies onto their accounts of the last earthly meal Jesus shared with the disciples. John Meier concludes that the final meal of Jesus did not "fit neatly under any conventional religious rubric of the time."[81] The authors of the synoptic Gospels were, therefore, the first to try to make an extraordinary meal fit under the rubric of the Jewish Passover. This is why, if Meier is correct, the Johannine tradition on the Last Supper may have historical priority over the synoptic. If you remove the Passover themes from the narratives of the Last Supper, you are left with a typical (though final) *haburah* meal. The strong likelihood is that the Last Supper, the meal at the foundation of the eucharistic cult, was an agape, not the Passover haggadah.

Paul's Corinthian opponents, therefore, could have been maintaining legitimate traditions of the Lord's Supper and they could have heard the apostle's complaints as bold, "new" interpretations. Paul's argument, therefore, should not be interpreted as introducing a "ban" on the holding of eucharistic feasts, but an imposition of cultic meaning on every meal. Whenever the Church gathers to eat in Corinth, they should do so in memory of the death of Christ, discerning his body and partaking the

---

80. Meier, *Marginal Jew*, 399.
81. Ibid.

covenant of his blood.[82] In sum, the cultic tradition of the Eucharist should not be understood as a "negation" of the agapic dimensions of the meal, but as a "corrective" offered and exercised entirely within the agapic tradition of the meal.

Just as Lietzmann defined two types of early Christian traditions on the Eucharist, he also identified two, corresponding types of communion. Lietzmann believed that the agapic meals were observed in an atmosphere of eschatological jubilation. The agape, he imagined, was "celebrated 'with gladness'; and in answer to the 'Maranatha,' the 'Come, Lord Jesus,' of their leader, the company at table hailed the longed-for Lord with glad hosannas."[83] The agapic meal, Lietzmann thought, produced a horizontal communion. It was the egalitarian communion of disciples gathered for the messianic feast. The horizontal communion is an earthly community, eating and drinking in continuity with the meals Jesus once shared with his intimates and friends.

Lietzmann also spoke of a "mystical communion." This second type of communion corresponds to the cultic traditions of the Eucharist. It does not describe an earthly fellowship of equals. Rather, it speaks of the "vertical" relationship between God and human beings. If there is any sort of "community" as a result of the "mystical communion," it is the covenant community formed in the blood of Christ. "The new covenant in Christ's blood," Lietzmann wrote, is the divinely ordained "counterpart to the covenant on Mt. Sinai."[84] When one partakes in the elements of the meal, because Christ is "so essentially in the elements," one is incorporated into Christ and so becomes one person with him.[85] This type of communion is the communion of the mystical body and it roughly follows upon Paul's analogy when he compared the Lord's Supper to the temple meals of the Jews and of pagans. Each of the three meals had the effect "of establishing a *koinonia* [communion] with the appropriate god. . . ." The passage in 1 Corinthians 10:16, "communion in the body of Christ," should be interpreted, Lietzmann concluded, "in the sense of a Hellenic-Oriental cult-mysticism."[86] Unlike horizontal communion, mystical communion refers to an injection or donation of divine life into the life of human participants.

Lietzmann's dichotomy between the two types of communion, both horizontal and mystical, is helpful. Communion among human beings is of a strikingly different order than communion between human beings and the divine. One is given to wonder which sort of communion is more

82. 1 Cor 11:29. Cf. Conzelmann, 202f.
83. Lietzmann, 204.
84. Lietzmann, 183.
85. Ibid. John 17:11-12.
86. Lietzmann, 185.

difficult to achieve. The fantasy of a "communion" with an idea of "god" is much easier to achieve than is true communion with flesh-and-blood human beings. Communion, Lietzmann rightly pointed out, does not originate solely at the Cross. Communion also has a place in the earlier, simple meals of Jesus, the Galilean rabbi. Communion with Christ is not only the awesome, fascinating, and mystical establishment of a relationship between an infinite God and several finite creatures. It is also found in the humble, simple meal of sinful men and women ("tax collectors and sinners"). Communion also points beyond the meals Jesus shared with disciples in the past. It points beyond the meals he shares with disciples today, toward the horizon of God's absolute future, where both agapic and cultic, both horizontal and mystical forms of communion blend and merge.

3. Communion as salvation—a soteriological norm

When we consider how the Eucharist is observed in churches today, we sometimes despair whether we shall ever recover the beautiful, pristine character of those simple meals that Jesus shared with his disciples. Paintings depicting the Last Supper like the one by Salvador Dali allow our imaginations of a lovely meal to persist. We prefer to imagine that Jesus and the disciples were acting in full self-possession. We suppose they really knew what their acts were accomplishing and how they would be remembered. The meal, we like to think, was as solemn as the one in Zefirelli's movie. Then we look at our hurried Masses, the accumulation of private Eucharists, or the monthly or bi-monthly Communion services tacked on to the end of services for the private devotion of a few. We consider the huge, festival celebrations, sometimes filling sports stadiums. The mega-church of the Promise Keepers or the papal Mass are very similar, both for their methods of crowd-control as well as for the enormous social energies they generate. We are very, very far from the Last Supper revealed in Scripture through historical study.

The Eucharist today must be a sign for us of the salvation which God has promised through Jesus Christ and is, even now, making real in our world by the power of the Holy Spirit. I say "must" not because God is not free to do other things, or because we are not free to believe other ideas. Rather, the Eucharist "must" be a sign of salvation only if Jesus Christ, by the power of his Spirit, is the true means of human salvation. Even so, our Eucharists—as we actually do them—are necessarily partial signs of the whole salvation, a central idea for the remainder of this book. As Paul reminds us, our ability to discern the body of Christ in the communion of men and women gathered at any given table is a wounded ability. But discern we must, even if our eyes must squint, our imaginations wander, and the volume is turned way up on our hearing aids.

Communion, our brief biblical survey suggests, depends upon a love that is both sacrificial (cultic) and relational (agapic). It has both qualitative and quantitative dimensions, dimensions which seem equally powerful to build or destroy the effectiveness of the Eucharist as a proclamation of Jesus and the kingdom of God. Our eucharistic meals are impaired if they are not, like Jesus', open commensalities celebrated around a borderless table. If we could see the "end of the table," it could not be the Eucharist, because it had not extended far enough to be fully in communion with the table of Christ. Our eucharistic meals are impaired if they are not places where all are welcomed and embraced with a self-sacrificing (cultic) love until the Savior returns. Our ability to see salvation from our place at the altar depends upon the communion between our Eucharist and the paschal sacrifice of Jesus, between our Eucharist and the earthly meals of Jesus, between our Eucharist and the heavenly banquet of the Reign of God.

The Christian idea of salvation holds that our end exists in the radical, boundless inclusion of human persons "hidden together in Christ with God."[87] Salvation and communion, therefore also the Eucharist, are intrinsically linked because they all originate in a single act. They originate in the act of divine love. The Eucharist, as a sacrament of the Last Supper, of the death of Jesus, and of his love for the outcast and marginalized, is a place where divine love is expressed in and signified by an essentially borderless communion of men and women, the Church.

4. Conclusion

Communion in Christ and among human participants is offered in and through the Eucharist. Eucharistic communion has both "horizontal" (social) and "vertical" (transcendent) dimensions. It is both agapic and cultic, though the cultic dimension is understood as a corrective within the agapic tradition of the meal. Paul believed that communion in the death of Christ constituted the saving effect of the Eucharist. He also believed the Church is manifested in eucharistic communion as the body of Christ. No mere metaphor, the body of Christ comprises both the head and members enlivened by the Spirit of God. The Church is also manifested at the Eucharist as a communion of men and women in the sacrificial love of the crucified Savior. The bread is a functional symbol for it is a communion in the body of Christ, signifying both Jesus, by the promise of his own words, and the Church. The cup is also a functional symbol for it is a communion in the death of the Savior and in the new covenant which was created in the death of Christ. To partake of the eucharistic cup is to proclaim and remember the death of Christ.

87. Gal 3:3. Bornkamm, 145.

Finally, eucharistic Communion is a living sign of the salvation which Christ has prepared and is now offering human beings through the power of the Holy Spirit. The eucharistic Communion signifies the saving acts of God both past, present and future. The Communion announces (in part) the whole (borderless) kingdom of God. Since the Eucharist is a meal with Jesus, a dinner with "tax collectors and sinners," in commemoration of his death (and all that his death has accomplished), eucharistic Communion directs our knowledge and understanding toward the love of God which is being assembled, relationship by relationship, with and among all the people who will ever gather in Christian communion.

The Eucharist is therefore rich with ecclesiological implications. The Church is created not only because it celebrates the Eucharist (rituals often have strong sociological effects), but because in some measure, it is synonymous with the communion Christ creates by the Holy Spirit in the Eucharist. The communion effected at the Eucharist is the communion of the body and blood of Christ, the myriad relationships that exist between the head and all his members. In a brief slogan, the Church makes the Eucharist and the Eucharist makes the Church.

Questions for meditation and dialogue on "Communion in Christ"

Each chapter includes a section of "Questions for meditation and dia-logue." These questions are offered as a way for readers to ground the theo-retical concerns of the chapter in their own experience and knowledge. The success of world-wide ecumenism depends on the success of ecumenism locally. Were readers to engage in small, informal dialogue groups, they could begin together to imagine and build a "borderless Church" for their own place and time. How could their own local churches and congregations become more closely and fruitfully joined in communion?

1. *Communion and fellowship.* In or out of church, where have you ex-perienced communion most powerfully? In your experience, what dif-ferentiates the levels of intensity in communion, from "fellowship" to "communion," from "a kind of communion" to "full communion"? Do you experience a difference between "mere sociality" and the com-munion you receive in church?

2. *Eucharist and communion.* Paul compared the Christian communion of the Eucharist to Jewish and pagan meals. Have you ever recognized "communion" in contexts outside of church? Is there a kind of com-munion "in the world"—at football games, the Olympics, during na-tional tragedies, through the media? How do these types of communion differ from Christian communion?

3. *Agapic and cultic.* If you were to describe the Eucharist or the Lord's Supper in your church, would it follow more closely the pattern of the "agapic" meal or of the "cultic" meal? Are the members of your church more likely to emphasize the "sacrificial" elements of the meal or the "celebratory" elements? When you look to churches or con-gregations in your city or town that emphasize the opposite end of the spectrum, do you find elements of the "sacrificial" or "celebratory" uncomfortable or compelling?

4. *Salvation and the "borderless table."* Consider some of your ideas about salvation. Who is included and who is excluded from your idea of salvation and why? Are there ways in which your church acts out a collective "idea of salvation" at the Eucharist? Who is included and who is excluded from receiving Communion at your church and why? Does your church's practice of exclusion or inclusion have any bearing on who your church believes God has called to salvation? Could your dialogue group agree that salvation is "limitless" and that the table of Jesus is also "borderless"?

FOR FURTHER READING

Bradshaw, Paul. *The Search for the Origins of Christian Worship*. New York: Oxford University Press, 1992.

Lietzmann, Hans. *Mass and Lord's Supper: A Study in the History of the Liturgy*. Dorothea H. G. Reeve, tr. Leiden: Brill, 1979.

Meeks, Wayne. *The First Urban Christians: The Social World of the Apostle Paul*. New Haven, Conn.: Yale University Press, 1983.

Mitchell, Margaret. *Paul and the Rhetoric of Reconciliation: An Exegetical Investigation of the Language and Composition of 1 Corinthians*. Louisville, Ky.: Westminster/John Knox Press, 1991.

Panikulam, George. *Koinonia in the New Testament: A Dynamic Expression of Christian Life*. Rome: Biblical Institute Press, 1979.

Robinson, John A. T. *The Body: A Study in Pauline Theology*. Philadelphia: Westminster Press, 1952.

Smith, Dennis E. and Hal E. Taussig. *Many Tables: The Eucharist in the New Testament and Liturgy Today*. London and Philadelphia: SCM Press and Trinity Press International, 1990.

Theissen, Gerd. *The Social Setting of Pauline Christianity. Essays on Corinth*. J. H. Schütz, tr. Philadelphia: Fortress Press, 1982.

CHAPTER TWO

Communion Ecclesiology

Roman Catholics and others commonly use the word "Church" when they are really talking about priests and bishops. They talk of the Church in terms of their real perception of those who have power. By and large, they are right. At the same time, I have heard many people speak of "the Church" as though it were primarily a land-holding owner of religious monuments. We imagine "the Church" to be a religious building distinct from the people who gather there. Especially in the United States, one sometimes hears a third use of the term "Church." It is a good idea, people advise, to "worship at the church of your choice." In this example, using the lingo of television public service announcements, "the Church" is reduced to a voluntary object, a personal decision. It hardly seems strange to us: referring to the selection of church affiliation in terms most often used to describe one's favorite brand of laundry soap, or joining a public service fraternity like the Elks or the Rotary Club. Middle-class Americans have been acclimated to such treatment. They are consumers first; believers, second.

Though it has institutional structures, the Church is not identical to its clerical organization. Similarly, though it holds buildings and properties, it is not a building or a land-holding corporation. The Church is not a voluntary association of like-minded religious consumers. No, to arrive at an understanding of the Church we must scratch deeper, beneath the surface, diving toward the structures where the Church's life and meaning are shaped and framed. Baptized Christians, whether ordained or lay, must not be edited out of the Church's self-understanding. The Church's real estate is certainly not its most valuable possession. Arguably, the Church could divest from many of its holdings with no great loss to its nature or purpose. We should not assume that Christians join the Church or remain with the Church by choice, for Christians—especially those who come to Christianity later in life—rarely speak of the Church as something they choose. More often, Christians understand that the Church "chooses" them.

It is possible to say something positive about the deeper structure and characteristics of the Church. What does the Eucharist impress upon the structure and character of the Church? In this chapter, then, let us search for some rationale, within the Roman Catholic perspective, by which to ask the question. How were we led to suppose the Eucharist has anything to say about the structure or character of the Church?

One of the essential affirmations of Roman Catholic ecclesiology, in contrast to some Protestant ecclesiologies, is its insistence on the "visible" Church. The Church, we say, is not an invisible body of people known only to God. Not content to merely state the negative, since the Reformation Roman Catholic theologians have also asserted that the Church is not divisible from its earthly, visible, institutional manifestation. Counter-Reformation theologian and cardinal, Robert Bellarmine (1542–1621) once wrote, "The church is indeed a community *(coetus)* of men, as visible and palpable as the community of the Roman people, or the kingdom of France, or the republic of Venice."[1] Bellarmine called the Church a *societas perfecta*, a "perfected society." The Church of Jesus Christ, he thought, is coextensive with the Roman Catholic Church. Against the Protestant reformers, Roman Catholic theologians, like Bellarmine, stressed continuity from the visible, external form of the earthly Church to the invisible, internal form of the Church. The "invisible Church"—an idea left over from Augustine's idea of the "heavenly city" that dwells invisibly within the "earthly"—is constituted by grace as the body of God's elect. The body of God's elect has an earthly organization. The "visible Church," they maintained, is the Roman Catholic Church.

Bellarmine concluded that the Church had a three-fold constitution: magisterial, ministerial and juridical. The Church, he said, professes the true faith (magisterially) and maintains the communion of the sacraments (ministerially) under submission to recognized authorities (juridically). These three powers of the Church derive from Christ himself, who bestows them on the apostles and their successors.[2]

The ecclesiology of communion, as developed by Roman Catholic theologians of this century, is an answer, in part, to the emphasis of earlier ecclesiology—like Bellarmine's—upon the hierarchy, the domination of the clergy over the laity, and legalistic understandings of grace and reconciliation. Indeed, some recent authors, like Yves Congar, have dismissed these ecclesiologies as little more than "hierarchologies."[3] By this,

1. Cited in Jerome Hamer, *The Church Is a Communion*, tr. Ronald Matthews (London: Geoffrey Chapman, 1964) 84.

2. Joachim Salaverri, "De Ecclesia Christi," in *Sacrae Theologiae Summa*, 5th ed. (Madrid: Library of Christian Authors, 1962). Richard McBrien, *Catholicism*, (San Francisco: HarperCollins, 1994) 657–59.

3. Yves Congar, *Lay People in the Church*, tr. David Attwater (Westminster, Md.: Newman, 1959) 39. Richard McBrien, *Do We Need the Church?* (New York: Harper and Row, 1969) 103.

they meant to say that earlier theologies were content to define the structure of the Church and proof-text their claims with scriptural references. Less attention was given to the quality of authority in the Church (as service) or to the sacramental character of the "visible" Church as an expression and means of grace. It is fair to say that the institutional charter of the Church was made to weigh in over the charismatic element in the Church. Additionally, the importance of baptism and the ministry of the baptized tended to be overshadowed by an inordinately high estimation of the value of vowed religious life and ordination.

1. Succession of images for the Church

During the twentieth century Roman Catholic ecclesiology took up the task of revising the Church from outside and from within its "hierarchological" frame of mind. Looking back upon the century, one might claim to see a "succession of images" as the authors of each decade recovered biblical and patristic metaphors for the Church. At the beginning of the century, the "kingdom of God" image held sway. By mid-century, all were speaking of the Church as a "mystical body." With Vatican II and the encyclicals of Paul VI, the Church is the "people of God." Now, in recent decades, there is the Church as "communion." One image succeeded another, synchronous with the great social upheavals of the era: World War I, World War II, the Cold War, and in the last few decades, the Cold Peace of corporate multinationalism. If the Church as a "communion" idea is just one more metaphor in a succession of images, then a recent essayist was fair in his assessment that "the life-expectancy of a given biblical image in ecclesiology seems to be two to three decades."[4] Under the author's prognosis, we should soon see another image or model for the Church come to the foreground.

Images for the Church, however, are not simply the products of "fads" or "trends." The truth of the Church's constitution as a communion does not negate the truth of the Church's constitution as body of Christ. The metaphors build upon, correct, and correlate to one another. Each image successfully points to facets of the mystery. These facets come to the foreground and recede, rotating in and out of focus. They are authentic answers to questions facing people who live in historical times and places. It is true that certain terms and metaphors will rise and fall, that certain ideas will be more or less appealing in various historical and cultural circumstances. The succession of images for the Church during this century tells us just as much about ourselves as it does about the Church.

4. John Ford, "*Koinonia* and Roman Catholic Ecclesiology," *Ecumenical Trends* 26/3 (March 1997) 42.

I hope the succession of images for the Church is not ephemeral, but represents a real development. All the images outlined above originate in renewed biblical and patristic scholarship, scholarship that was not available to Bellarmine or other neo-scholastic theologians. Roman Catholic theologians have worked diligently to recover and appropriate biblical and patristic sources. Whereas Counter-Reformation theologies were full of anti-Protestant polemic, theologians of this century have begun to rely upon renewed appraisals of historical sources. Such studies have typically tried to understand the ancient writings from within an appreciation for their contemporary social milieus. An easy example is found in the first letter to the Corinthians. As was shown in chapter 1, Paul's admonition to celebrate the Lord's Supper can be interpreted variously in light of the social context envisioned. If a friendly, appreciative audience is envisioned, one's interpretation would differ than if one assumes Paul's Corinthian audience was hostile to his authority.

A second trend has also marked modern Roman Catholic theologies. There has been a renewed appreciation for the concrete qualities of human life. Earlier theologians may have been content to describe human behaviors and motivations in abstractions. Discussions of ethics, liturgy, sacraments, or grace were made to depend upon general principles drawn from narrowly conceived understandings of medieval philosophies and metaphysics. Contemporary theologians have used more empirical methods and have adapted modern philosophies, especially existentialism, to serve Christian ends. Divine grace touches individuals conditioned by history and culture. Contemporary social and psychological sciences have become vital sources for the theological investigation of human behaviors and motivations.

Both trends—historical study and the renewed appreciation for the human subject—suggest that there is a renewed interest in human particularity among theologians. Theology does not need to describe universal or generalized ideas of human beings. After all, God does not save an abstraction of a human being, a generalized, universal "man/woman." God saves individuals, men and women, one at a time, each inhabiting a unique place, time, and culture. The particularities of culture, intelligence, genetics, differences in talents and abilities can no longer be ignored by theologians and theology, for they all bear on the nature and capacities of the human person whom God is reaching into (and out of) with love, revelation, mercy, and salvation. The new theologians' reliance upon the social sciences has been a great benefit, with one important proviso. Unlike the social scientist, the Christian theologian must insist on at least one *a priori* assertion: humans and human cultures are always understood as potentially open to God, to God's revelation, and to love of God and neighbor. The theologian may not presume that humans and human cultures are existentially closed to the possibility of a real encounter with or knowledge of the transcendent, a necessary prerequisite for the possibility of salvation.[5]

An extended example will make these points clear and offer material for further considerations. In his 1987 work *The Sacrifice We Offer*, David Power claims that the Council of Trent did not attempt to teach the fullness of eucharistic doctrine. Instead, Power concludes that the bishops at Trent sought only to preserve a part of their contemporary, eucharistic practices. They believed these practices were threatened by certain strains of Protestant critique.[6] Power states that the doctrinal issues raised at Trent can be understood only "in conjunction with the argument over right practice." That is, they should not be understood as universal statements of truth covering every possible celebration of the Eucharist. They should be understood as partial statements made within the context of an argument to preserve particular, threatened practices. Power concludes from his examination of the teachings of Trent that the eucharistic theology espoused by the bishops, especially in its treatment of the Eucharist as a sacrifice, "was a theology of the power and act of the ordained priest."[7]

The bishops of Trent, Power reminds his readers, deliberately allowed several questions about the Eucharist to remain unanswered and undefined. The intention of the Council was to act upon and preserve only those few aspects of contemporary eucharistic practice which the bishops felt were threatened. Later theologians read the decrees of Trent without respect for the questions the council was addressing. These theologians read the decrees and canons as though they were "full and adequate statements of Catholic belief and practice," Power concludes.[8]

Occasionally, eucharistic doctrines from Trent were used as a means to augment ecclesial and clerical power at the expense of the baptismal dignity of the laity. The assembly of lay Christians was considered nearly expendable in the celebration of the liturgy. By the time of Trent, popular understanding of the Eucharist had already departed from its patristic fullness. The Eucharist, they thought, was primarily an act of consecration, confected by the validly ordained priest alone, while speaking the words of Christ over the gifts of bread and wine. Long before the Reformation, for numerous historical reasons the "low Mass" had become the

5. Bernard Lonergan, *Method in Theology* (New York: Herder and Herder, 1972) 344–46. Karl Rahner, *Foundations of Christian Faith: An Introduction to the Idea of Christianity*, tr. William V. Dych (New York: Crossroad, 1982) 21–22, 24–25.

6. David N. Power, *The Sacrifice We Offer: The Tridentine Dogma and Its Reinterpretation* (New York: Crossroad, 1987) 51.

7. Power, 65.

8. Power, 122.

ordinary rite for the Eucharist in the Western Church. Liturgical assemblies were treated as an audience for the acts of a solitary priest.[9] Such developments provided the liturgical context of eucharistic theology for both Reformation and Counter-Reformation theologians and pastors. This was the Mass condemned by Luther, Zwingli, and Calvin. This was the practice the Tridentine bishops tried to protect, preserve, and reform.

1.1. Nineteenth-century antecedents

The "ecclesiology of communion," as developed by Roman Catholic theologians of this century, is a partial answer to the emphasis of earlier ecclesiologies on the clerical hierarchy and the sacramental minimalism of those who understood the teachings of Trent to comprise an entire sacramental system.[10] The task of creating a more complete theology of the Church was delayed until quite recently. The Counter-Reformation forgot the biblical-patristic understanding of the Church as related to the kingdom of God. Even the conception of the Church as "body of Christ" had been twisted around to serve the needs of a Church that understood itself as living under siege. The task of twentieth-century ecclesiology has been to reconstruct the biblical-patristic understanding, to revitalize it for modern women and men, and to reassert the centrality of Christ and his message of the imminent reign of God among humankind.[11]

Communion ecclesiology in Roman Catholicism has a complex history. Contemporary proponents point to a variety of nineteenth- and twentieth-century origins. German Protestant theologian and pastor Friedrich Schleiermacher (1768–1834) provides a helpful perspective, for Roman Catholic communion ecclesiology can be interpreted both as a reaction against and a cautious embrace of his perspectives. For Schleiermacher, the communion of the Church is "created through the voluntary actions of men and only through [ethics] does [the Church] continue to exist."[12] Like my Reformed Church Sunday school teacher, he regarded the Church as a special category of "fellowship," or *gemeinschaft*.[13] The Church is a voluntary association of individuals, with a corporate life in Jesus, redeemed in the context of this fellowship.[14] This concept dominated Schleiermacher's idea of the Church.

---

9. Cyrille Vogel, "An Alienated Liturgy," in *Liturgy: Self-expression of the Church*, ed. Herman Schmidt, Concilium 72 (New York: Herder and Herder, 1972) 11–25.

10. Congar, 39. McBrien, *Do We Need the Church?* 103.

11. McBrien, *Do We Need the Church?* 114.

12. Friedrich Schleiermacher, *The Christian Faith*, tr. H. R. Mackintosh and J. S. Stewart (Philadelphia: Fortress Press, 1976) 2.2.1.

13. Elert, 2.

14. Dennis M. Doyle, "Möhler, Schleiermacher, and the Roots of Communion Ecclesiology," *TS* 57 (1996) 472f.

Nineteenth-century German Catholic theologian Johan Adam Möhler may be regarded the founder of modern Roman Catholic communion ecclesiology. Möhler's classic text in ecclesiology *Unity in the Church* develops several of the main themes that continue to shape and inform communion ecclesiologies.[15] His book can be seen, largely, as a response to Schleiermacher's views. Möhler, it must be said at the outset, was in full agreement with Schleiermacher on many points. He agreed that the Church is a communion, the Spirit draws Christians into community with one another and with Christ, only in this community do they find redemption.[16] Both Möhler and Schleiermacher called the Eucharist the highest representation of Christian unity.[17] Both rejected the narrow, juridical approach to unity. The Church, Möhler wrote, contains within itself "all legitimate positions." Contraries and antitheses remaining within the "tension of the Church" are categorically distinct from contradictions carried on "outside the Church."[18] The ministry of unity in the Church is not to maintain uniformity, but to hold legitimate diversity in check. On disputed questions, the Church must allow all voices to speak and be heard. The practical effects of work by visionary theologians like Möhler have taken many years to percolate into the everyday experience of the Catholic Church.

1.2. Liturgical reform leads the way to new understandings of the Church

Pius X (1835–1914) endorsed the principle that Roman Catholics ought not only be passively present at the Eucharist but should also actively participate in the liturgy. Pius X understood the liturgical participation of the laity to consist of three activities: song, prayer, and the reception of Holy Communion. In his *motu proprio* on the restoration of church music *Tra le sollecitudini,* the Pope demonstrated his high esteem for the participation of the laity in liturgical acts.[19] He imagined the Gregorian chants, the "normative music," could be learned and sung by all. While the Pope never said such words, many of the read-along missals named after Pius X credited him with the slogan, "Do not pray at Mass; pray the Mass." In a 1946 presentation, liturgical scholar Godfrey Diekmann concluded that, although the Pope has been misquoted, he was not

---

15. Doyle, 468. Johan Möhler, *Unity in the Church or the Principle of Catholicism Presented in the Spirit of the Church Fathers of the First Three Centuries,* tr. Peter C. Erb (Washington, D.C.: Catholic University of America, 1996).

16. Doyle, 476f. *Unity,* 91, 85, 210, 166, 94.

17. Doyle, 468, 476. *Unity,* 82, 166.

18. Doyle, 477. *Unity,* 197.

19. Pius X, *Tra le sollecitudini,* November 22, 1903; *ASS* 36 (1903) 329–39, 331.

misunderstood.[20] The slogan epitomized one of the primary aims of Pius X's pontificate: to invigorate what had become a marginalized and inactive laity.

The chief hallmark of Pius X's papacy, arguably among the most influential events in the history of twentieth-century Roman Catholicism, is his influence on the early and frequent reception of the Eucharist. In 1905 his Sacred Congregation of the Council issued the decree on the frequent and daily reception of Holy Communion, *Sacra Tridentina*.[21] Frequent reception, this decree stated, is an antidote for moral failings. Urging frequent, even daily reception of the sacrament, the congregation wrote, "Access to the table must be freely opened to those who approach it with a right and devout intention." In 1910 his Congregation of the Sacraments issued the decree on the discipline of first Communion, *Quam singulari*, encouraging early reception of Communion.[22] The congregation wrote that the obligation to receive Communion annually, the so-called "Easter duty," begins at the "age of reason." Full and perfect knowledge is not necessary to receive Holy Communion. The only knowledge necessary is the ability meaningfully to distinguish between natural bread and the consecrated bread of the sacrament. The obligation to teach and to encourage early reception of Communion, they concluded, rests on pastors, parents and catechists.

The Vatican authors of these documents were cautious. They felt they could not teach that Communion by the laity touches in any way upon the validity of the sacrament. They could not rescind the condemnation of certain Jansenist claims that the Communion of the laity was essential to the celebration of the Mass.[23] Such hesitancy aside, *Sacra Tridentina* and *Quam singulari* together affirmed the benefits of frequent reception of Communion by lay people at most Masses and by children who had attained the age of reason. The Pope's encouragement to frequent Communion did not immediately increase the frequency of reception by the laity. Nearly thirty years later, speakers would repeat the Pope's words to advance arguments for the practice of permitting Communion of the laity at every Eucharist.[24] It is fair to say that Catholics of this century would learn again how to receive the Eucharist. Learning

20. Godfrey Diekmann, "Lay Participation in the Liturgy of the Church," in *A Symposium on the Life and Works of Pope Pius X* (Washington, D.C.: Confraternity of Christian Doctrine, 1946) 137–58.

21. Sacred Congregation of the Council, *Sacra Tridentina*, December 20, 1905.

22. Sacred Congregation of the Sacraments, *Quam singulari*, August 8, 1910.

23. Gerald Ellard, "The Eucharistic Banquet: Frequent and Daily Communion," in *A Symposium on the Life and Works of Pope Pius X* (Washington, D.C.: Confraternity of Christian Doctrine, 1946) 177f.

24. Ellard, 117f.

again to "receive" the body and blood of Christ, they would also learn again how to "be" the body and blood of Christ.

Pius X's encouragement of liturgical song, prayer, and frequent Communion was not a new idea. Prosper Guéranger (1805–1875) had written his three-volume work *Institutions liturgiques* fifty years previously. Guéranger's agenda for reform included the restoration of the Benedictine order in France and the revival of communal life and prayer. Guéranger hoped to dispel post-Enlightenment individualism. He promoted public worship as an alternative to popular devotion. Guéranger advocated two principles, which continue to inform the pastoral norms for the liturgy: the liturgy is a true source for spiritual life; the liturgy is the work of the entire Church.[25] As Annibale Bugnini summarized, Guéranger's aim "was to restore as fully as possible the expressive and sanctifying power of the liturgy and to bring the faithful back to full participation."[26]

Another early liturgical reformer, Belgian monk Lambert Beauduin (1873–1960), followed the work of Pius X closely. Beauduin's agenda for liturgical renewal was to redress the spiritual malaise he observed among Christians of his day. He thought that individualism, the abandonment of prayer, and misdirected piety originated in the "failure to maintain the liturgy as the true center" of Christian devotion.[27] Beauduin believed that the active participation of all in the Mass and in the Liturgy of the Hours would support and invigorate an authentic private devotion as opposed to an all-consuming quest for what he thought were "pious novelties."[28] Beauduin was a lonely pioneer among Roman Catholics engaged in early ecumenical discussions.

Guéranger and Beauduin alike helped lay practical foundations for communion ecclesiology. Christians form their primary conceptions of Christ and the Church in response to experience, from participation in liturgical rites. Liturgical and devotional practices that sustained an impoverished ideal of Christian communion had to be challenged, if renewed conceptions of the Church were ever to take root and grow. Until recently, it is fair to say many ecclesiastical authorities were as alienated from the liturgy as the laity. They had little interest in the liturgy as a source for Christian spirituality and theology. Just as the importance of

25. A. M. Roguet, "Pastoral-Liturgical Action," in *The Church at Prayer: Introduction to the Liturgy*, ed. A. G. Martimort (New York, Desclée, 1968), 221. Michael Kwatera, "Prosper Guéranger: Founder of the Modern Liturgical Movement," in *How Firm a Foundation: Leaders of the Liturgical Movement*, ed. Robert L. Tuzik (Chicago: Liturgy Training Publications, 1990) 18f.

26. Annibale Bugnini, *The Reform of the Liturgy: 1948–1975*, tr. Matthew J. O'Connell (Collegeville: The Liturgical Press, 1990) 6.

27. Richard G. Leggett, "Lambert Beauduin: The Vision Awaits Its Time," in *How Firm a Foundation*, 25.

28. Leggett, 25.

the laity tended to be devalued in the liturgical assembly, ironically, so too was the role of the priest and other ministers. If the laity is considered an assembly of mere consumers of grace, then priests and ministers become little more than dispensaries. Clericalism and minimalism, at least in the liturgy, tend to walk hand in hand. Beauduin, Guéranger, and, to some extent, Pius X helped to rescue the liturgy and the Church from such minimalism. It is difficult to imagine the development of an ecclesiology of communion in this century if the minimization of the liturgy and of the liturgical assembly had not been challenged theoretically and pastorally.

2. The mystical body of Christ

Henri de Lubac (1896–1991) decisively linked the Church and the Eucharist for twentieth-century theology. Unable to teach during World War II since the Nazis had closed the schools, De Lubac retired to a monastery library and wrote one of the most important books of Catholic theology this century. *Corpus mysticum*, a study of the idea of the body of Christ in early Christian writings, was the book to come from this period of seclusion. De Lubac offered a serious reappraisal of medieval and early Christian writings on the Eucharist. He looked far beyond post-Vatican I neo-scholasticism to examine original sources. His contemporaries more often esteemed ancient sources for their value as proof-texts, than for the various perspectives they offered. De Lubac was free to examine sources as independent voices; rather than for their ability to bolster the doctrinal status quo. De Lubac therefore discovered that before the twelfth century the word "communion" did not principally refer to the reception of the Eucharist. Instead, it referred to the social reality the Eucharist creates, the "communion of the church."[29]

2.1. The contribution of Henri de Lubac

De Lubac found that the Church of his time had inherited its theology of the body of Christ from late scholasticism. Late scholastic and neo-scholastic theologians regularly distinguished the *corpus Christi verum* (the "true body of Christ") from the *corpus Christi mysticum* (the "mystical body of Christ"). The true body of Christ *(verum corpus)*, they believed, is Christ's eucharistic body, his body sacramentally present as consecrated bread and wine. The mystical body *(corpus mysticum)*, they thought, referred to the body of the Church.[30]

---

29. Henri de Lubac, *Corpus mysticum: L'Eucharistie et l'Église au moyen âge*, 2nd ed. (Paris: Aubrie, 1944) 28.

30. Lubac, *Corpus mysticum*, 95–96, 116–21. Paul McPartlan, *The Eucharist Makes the Church: Henri de Lubac and John Zizioulas in Dialogue* (Edinburgh: T&T Clark, 1993) 76.

De Lubac discovered that theologians writing before the twelfth century defined the terms in exactly reverse fashion. Early Christian writers like Augustine and Gregory the Great, along with authors as late as Hugh and Richard of St. Victor, referred to the Church as the true body of Christ *(corpus verum)*. They referred to the Eucharist as the mystical body of Christ *(corpus mysticum)*.[31] "Mystical" in the historical context did not refer to the ecstatic experiences of mystics. Rather, it designates the sacramental quality of Christ's eucharistic presence. *Mysticum*, we must remember, derives from the Greek word *mysterion*, by which Oriental Christians still refer to the sacraments.[32] Thus de Lubac wrote: "Christ in his Eucharist is truly the heart of the church."[33] The Church is the sacrament of Christ, containing and "vitalising *[sic]* all [the] others."[34]

De Lubac's work demonstrates how the contents of ideas like "mystical body" could change with time. He documented that the definitions of the terms had reversed. Changes in the meaning of doctrinal terms are not always signs of heresy, even when they touch on matters close to the heart of faith. Doctrine, we observe, is similar to other cultural artifacts. It has its own dialectic and a history.

Additionally, de Lubac skirted the neo-scholastic preoccupation with juridical and structural interpretations of the Church. His book focused, instead, on theological images and metaphors for the Church. Since then ecclesiology has approached the doctrine of the Church differently. It could no longer continue to describe the Church in structural categories alone.[35] Qualitative considerations, stemming from a concern to represent the role of the Church in salvation history accurately, must be included as well. The attention of Roman Catholic ecclesiology, therefore, has turned to consider why the Church exists and not only that it exists. The structures of the Church must somehow be related to their function in God's saving design. Rather than assuming the Church has already fulfilled God's intentions, contemporary ecclesiology needed to consider how the Church is *not yet* true to itself.

2.2. Pius XII's *Mystici corporis*

De Lubac's understanding of the Church as "mystical body" was at first misunderstood. Yet, in 1943, Pius XII issued the encyclical *Mystici corporis*. This encyclical is thought by many to have been the Pope's an-

---

31. Lubac, *Corpus mysticum*, 126.

32. I. H. Dalmais, "Liturgy and the Mystery of Salvation," in Martimort, 199f.

33. Lubac, *The Splendour of the Church* (London: Sheed and Ward, 1956) 110. Mc-Partlan, 70.

34. Lubac, *Catholicism* (London: Burns and Oats, 1962) 28. Idem. *Splendour*, 147. McPartlan, 70.

35. Cf. McPartlan, 96f.

swer to de Lubac's scholarship. From this perspective, the encyclical represents the partial vindication of de Lubac's beleaguered point of view. From the end of World War II until Vatican II, Catholics referred to the idea of Christ's presence in the Church primarily by reference to the "mystical body of Christ" concept.

Pius XII's idea of the mystical body, set forth in *Mystici corporis*, did not arise from a theological vacuum. Even de Lubac's contribution depended upon the work of earlier authors. For example, Möhler had written that the Church is a continuation of the incarnation through time and place. The Church in some fashion extends Christ, he said. The Church is "incarnational" because it is Christ's body and because it ensues from the mystery of the hypostatic union.[36] Both Möhler and Carlo Passaglia (1812–1887), another eminent theologian of the nineteenth century, began their treatises on the Church with an examination of the mystical body. For them, the Church as mystical body of Christ was the central ecclesiological category.

The first Vatican Council also called the Church the "mystical body of Christ" in the preface to its dogmatic constitution on the Catholic faith, *Dei Filius*.[37] There is no evidence that the phrase, in its context, meant anything more substantial than a poetic allusion. In its Dogmatic Constitution on the Church, *Pastor aeternus*, the council focused primarily on the role of the papacy.[38] The unity of Christians was said to depend upon their adherence to the successors of Peter, who were, by definition, unswervingly faithful to the dominical foundations of the Church. Although Vatican I was aware of the mystical body of Christ idea, it did not integrate this into the official decrees. The council fathers were afraid, one commentator remarked, that the conception was too vague and imprecise.[39] They did not conceive of Christian communion as flowing out of a common life in Christ. Rather, built from the top down, communion for them was signified chiefly by assent to the jurisdictional authority of the bishop of Rome.[40]

Pius XII's *Mystici corporis* was presented in 1943, at the height of World War II.[41] The war provided a context of urgency for the problem of Christian unity. In particular, what were Christians to do when the political authorities compelled them to engage in war against other Chris-

36. Edward J. Kilmartin, *Christian Liturgy,* vol. 1: Theology and Practice (Kansas City, Mo.: Sheed and Ward, 1988) 218.

37. Vatican I, *Dei Filius*, April 24, 1870; Tanner, vol. 2, 804–11.

38. Vatican I, *Pastor aeternus*, July 18, 1870; Tanner, vol. 2, 811–16.

39. Karl Rahner, ed. *Sacramentum Mundi: An Encyclopedia of Theology*, vol. 1 (New York: Herder and Herder, 1968) s. v. "Church," by Marie-Joseph le Guillou, 320.

40. *Pastor aeternus;* Tanner, 813.

41. Pius XII, *Mystici corporis Christi*, June 29, 1943; *AAS* 35 (1943) 193–248.

tians? Because Christians fought on both sides of the warring powers, was the *mystical body* also divided against itself? Pius hoped that the exposition of the doctrine of the mystical body would draw people to the Church, having seen a divinely given unity in what he termed its "fellowship of charity."

In the encyclical, the Pope wrote that the Church is a body and so it must be visible and tangible like other bodies. He described three types of body: physical, moral, and mystical. The physical body refers to the union of physical members, sinew, and vital organs. Men and women united for a common socio-political goal form a moral body. Moral bodies include the nation-states, unions, corporations, and so forth.[42] Like the moral bodies, the mystical body is also composed of the union of physical bodies toward a common end. The mystical body, unlike the moral body, is supplemented by a "supernatural principle." There is an "uncreated" and "infinite" quality to the mystical body that is not given to moral bodies. For Pius XII the Church was basically a social institution with supernatural powers. The Church was in effect the social body of Jesus Christ, therefore, his mystical body.

The culmination of the union of the mystical body, the Pope said, is found in the Eucharist. However, the union of Christ and the Church, in Pius' view, remained focused in the person and actions of the priest. The encyclical said that the baptized are united "in prayer and desire" with the sacramental minister, "whose words alone" have a sacramental effect. The assembly is accessory to the action of the priest. Christ's eucharistic presence was understood in an entirely local, spatially limited fashion, as the "Immaculate Lamb . . . present on the altar."[43]

Pius described the Eucharist as a "striking and wonderful figure of the unity of the Church." The Pope did not say the Eucharist is an effective cause of Christian unity. It appears that he thought of the Eucharist more as a symbol of unity manifested "after the fact." In the Eucharist, he wrote, "many grains go to form one whole." Christ is "given to us" and gives communicants "a spirit of charity." Members of the Church are "bidden to live . . . no longer [their] own life . . . and to love the Redeemer . . . in all the members of his social Body."[44]

In its day *Mystici corporis* significantly reoriented Roman Catholic ecclesiology. In the words of Jerome Hamer, it "revived the great idea of communion" and it emphasized the idea of the Church as both a mystery and a society.[45] On the negative side, the encyclical reinforced the idea that the Roman Catholic Church and the mystical body of Christ are

42. MC, 62.
43. MC, 82.
44. MC, 83.
45. Jerome Hamer, *The Church is a Communion*, 1.

identical.[46] It too heavily focused on the role of the clergy and did not conceive of a larger, essential role for the baptized members of the assembly. Finally, the encyclical did not adequately describe the difference between moral bodies and the mystical body, for the difference, as contemporary theology now understands it, is pneumatological. The encyclicals of Pius XII express little appreciation of the role of the Spirit in both the incarnation and the constitution of the Church as the body of Christ.[47]

2.3. Pius XII's *Mediator Dei*

Four years after *Mystici corporis*, Pius XII issued another major encyclical, *Mediator Dei*, "On the Sacred Liturgy."[48] The world in 1947, the world of *Mediator Dei*, was entirely different from the world of 1943, the world of *Mystici corporis*. World War II had ended and Europe was engaged in massive rebuilding and repair efforts. The Church, repairing buildings destroyed by years of bombing, was also rebuilding the liturgical rites that would take place in those buildings. Pius XII was not "reforming" the liturgy with this encyclical. He was "rebuilding" it. His legislation proposed a project of liturgical restoration.

Like *Mystici corporis*, *Mediator Dei* called the church a "divine society." The Church "should always increase and extend itself by means of its doctrine and its government, by means of the sacrifice and the sacraments which [Christ] instituted. . . ."[49] The Pope concluded that "in every liturgical action" Christ is present. He is present, the Pope wrote,

> in the august sacrifice of the altar, both in the person of [Christ's] minister and especially under the eucharistic species; He is present in the sacraments by His power which pours into them that they may be efficacious instruments of sanctity; He is present in the praises and in the petitions directed to God . . . .[50]

I quote this statement at length for it, or words similar to it, will appear again in Vatican II's *Sacrosanctum concilium*, in Paul VI's *Mysterium fidei*, in the Anglican-Roman Catholic International Commission's "Windsor Statement" on the Eucharist, and in the World Council of Churches' "Lima document," *Baptism, Eucharist and Ministry*.[51] Compared to this early statement, the later formulations show a marked development and sophistication.

---

46. Hamer, 23.
47. Kilmartin, *Christian Liturgy*, 219.
48. Pius XII, *Mediator Dei*, November 20, 1947; *AAS* 39 (1947) 521–95.
49. MD, 27.
50. MD, 28.
51. SC, 7; Paul VI, *Mysterium fidei*, September 3, 1965; *AAS* 57 (1965) 753–74, section 35; Windsor, 7; BEM, 13–14.

Note how Pius XII described Christ as a powerful presence alongside the Church. He described Christ's presence as "in" or "under" certain objects, persons, or actions. Note how the presence of Christ was not said to exist in the assembly of the Church as such. Christ is said to be present, rather, in the actions of the priest and in the praise and prayer of the assembly. The Church as a whole praises and prays, but the minister alone acts in the place of Christ, taking, blessing, breaking, and giving. Whereas the apostle Paul described the bread and cup in entirely corporate terms ("the bread . . . which *we* break," "the cup . . . which *we* bless"), Pius understood the verbs in the singular, the actions of a single person. [52] When would ecclesiology accord the Christian assembly of the baptized its full stature?

3. *The sacramental presence of the Church for the world—the contribution of Vatican II*

Building on and surpassing the legacy of Pius XII, the decrees of the Second Vatican Council describe the Church in new language. The council moved toward a "people of God" ecclesiology, without also abandoning the "mystical body" theology of the earlier part of the century. The bishops of Vatican II embraced two, uncomfortably synthesized ecclesiological visions.[53] The council used organizational and institutional categories to describe the Church nearly as often as it used relational and soteriological categories. The ecclesiology of Vatican II was two-fold. It incorporated both "universal" and "eucharistic-local" elements. In the liturgical documents especially, conciliar statements emphasized the local and eucharistic character of the Church. The council used "universal" and institutional language, however, to describe the Church as a worldwide organization ordered toward the salvation of all humankind.[54] In the years since the council, Roman Catholics have either worked hard to reconcile the contradictions inherent in these two approaches, or they have worked hard to defeat the proponents of the other type of language.

3.1. The liturgical presence of Christ—*Sacrosanctum concilium*

First of the council documents, Vatican II's Dogmatic Constitution on the Sacred Liturgy, *Sacrosanctum concilium*, focused especially on the

---

52. The verbs in Greek are plural participles: *ton arton hon* klomen, *to poterion tēs eulogias hon* eulogoumen. Cf. 1 Cor 10:16.

53. Herwi Rikhof, *The Concept of Church: A Methodological Inquiry into the Use of Metaphors in Ecclesiology* (London: Sheed and Ward/Patmos Press, 1981) 37.

54. Anton Thaler, *Gemeinde und Eucharistie: Grundlegung einer eucharistischen Ekklesiologie*, Praktische Theologie im Dialog, Band 2 (Freiburg, Switzerland: Universitätsverlag, 1988) 224. Bernard Forte, *La chiesa nella eucaristia: Per un ecclesiologia eucaristica alla luce del Vaticano II*, Biblioteca teologica napolitana 6 (Naples: 1975) 276.

liturgical activity and manifestation of the Church.[55] Paragraph 7, for instance, repeated nearly verbatim the modes of Christ's presence once outlined in *Mediator Dei*, adding only a fifth mode of presence. First, Christ is present through the sacrifice of the Mass, in the person of his minister, "the same one who then offered himself on a cross is now making his offering through the agency of priests." Second, he is present through the sacrifice of the Mass "most fully, under the eucharistic species." Third, he is present through his power in the sacraments, so that "when anyone baptizes, Christ himself is baptizing." Fourth, Christ is present in the proclamation of his word. "[H]e himself is speaking when scripture is read in church." Fifth, Christ is present when the Church prays and sings.[56] The liturgical assembly, the council concluded, is the ordinary visible manifestation of the Church.[57]

While the authors of *Sacrosanctum concilium* maintained the emphasis on the role of the priest, they also defined the sacramentality of several other ecclesial acts, such as baptism and the proclamation of the Word. Except for the presence of Christ in the eucharistic species, the council did not associate the presence of Christ with material things, focusing instead on the actions of the Church. Actions like praying, singing, baptizing, preaching, and reading, are corporate acts of the Church, performed as Christ and in the name of Christ. In a word *Sacrosanctum concilium* enshrines the principle that, in the performance of its sacraments, the Church itself is a sacrament.

3.2. The Church in light of salvation—*Lumen gentium*

The Dogmatic Constitution on the Church, *Lumen gentium*, affirmed the sacramental character of the Church.[58] The Church, the bishops said, exists to "enlighten all people with [Christ's] brightness." It does not exist for its own sake, but as a means to a higher end. The Church is "a sacrament or instrumental sign of intimate union with God and of the unity of all humanity. . . ."[59] The Church is not the whole of God's saving plan, though it has an essential role to play. Every covenant between God and humankind described in the Hebrew Scriptures prefigures the Church. The Church looks forward to the "glorious completion [of God's plan] at the end of time" when all the just, "from Abel . . . to the last of the elect" will be gathered into the universal "Church of God."[60]

---

55. Vatican II, *Sacrosanctum concilium*, December 4, 1963; Tanner, vol. 2, 820–43.
56. SC, 7. I. H. Dalmais, "Liturgy and the Mystery," in Martimort, 195ff.
57. SC, 4. A. G. Martimort, "The Assembly," in Martimort, 83ff.
58. Vatican II, *Lumen gentium*, November 21, 1964; Tanner, vol. 2, 849–98.
59. LG, 1.
60. LG, 2.

Lumen gentium extended Pius XII's idea of the social body. Just as all of humankind forms a social body, so there is a body within humankind who are the faithful in Christ and whose head is Christ.[61] The Church is a chosen, or "elected" people, given a mission of love and mercy toward the world. The Church is established by Christ "as a communion of life, love, and truth, . . . taken up as the instrument of salvation for all and sent as a mission to the whole world. . . ."[62] Within the people of God, the hierarchical structure of the Church as a juridical body is intact. The priestly people are themselves ruled by the ministerial or hierarchical priesthood. These two priesthoods share in the one priesthood of Christ, "though they differ in essence and not simply in degree."[63]

The participation of the entire people of God in the Eucharist is given a credible explanation. The council wrote:

> The faithful, . . . by virtue of their royal priesthood, join in the offering of the eucharist, and they exercise their priesthood in receiving the sacraments, in prayer and thanksgiving, through the witness of a holy life, by self-denial, and by active charity.[64]

The Eucharist, on these grounds, is no longer the performance of one person acting on behalf of the Church. It is, instead, the act of the entire Church, performed as the holy people of God. Although the Church as a whole mediates the relationship between Christ and the world, within the Church there are some by whose ministry the relationship between Christ and the Church is mediated.

The Church is a sign and effective cause of salvation. Even when the Church's proclamations judge and call the Church to repentance, the Church remains a sacramental sign of the fullness of communion in God. If the Church is a "pledge" or token of salvation, then one may extrapolate from the circumstances of the earthly Church to an image or idea, however dim, of salvation as the fullness of communion with God.[65] Vatican II called the Church "the kingdom of Christ—already present in mystery," growing, visible, and not wholly self-possessed, but dependent upon the "power of God in the world."[66] The Church must depend upon

61. LG, 7.
62. LG, 9.
63. LG, 10. The Latin text reads, "licet essentia et non gradu tantum differant." The emphasis in the Latin text is clearly on the participation of both types of priesthood (baptismal and ordained) in the one priesthood of Christ. For discussion, see R. Kevin Seasoltz, "The Liturgical Assembly: Light from Some Recent Scholarship," in *Rule of Prayer, Rule of Faith: Essays in Honor of Aidan Kavanagh, O.S.B.*, eds. Nathan Mitchell and John F. Baldovin (Collegeville: The Liturgical Press, 1996), 315. Michael Richards, "Hierarchy and Priesthood," *Priests and People* (June 1993) 229.
64. LG, 10.
65. Eph 1:14.
66. LG, 3.

the grace of the Holy Spirit to "become" what it already signifies. Just as there is a fundamentally epicletic or pneumatological character to the Eucharist, there is also a fundamentally epicletic or pneumatological character to the Church. The Church prays for and depends on the Spirit to become and remain the communion of the people of God, the body of Christ.

Lumen gentium did not carry the idea of communion to its conclusion. Later chapters of the document, especially chapters 3, 4, and 5, exhibit a narrower, juridical approach. Dutch theologian Herwi Rikhof concludes that "*Lumen gentium* is an attempt to integrate what cannot and should not be integrated, . . . it does not present a coherent and consistent view of the church."[67] In his view, later chapters of *Lumen gentium* "coddle the tendency to treat the Church from a narrow, apologetic, organizational, or juridical approach." Beneath the document as a whole, however, he sees the attempt to bring the entire doctrine of the Church under the term "communion." Thus exists the possibility of synthesizing the dichotomies of *Lumen gentium*. Rikhof advocates subordinating the structural and juridical means of the Church in light of its place in God's saving design. The Church as a communion of the faithful, Rikhof concludes, is *Lumen gentium's* tacit, underlying principle.[68]

3.3. The Church as sacrament to the world—*Gaudium et spes*

I believe the pastoral constitution on the Church in the modern world, *Gaudium et spes,* is the crowning achievement of Vatican II.[69] With this work, the council embraced a vision of the Church as a full participant in the human community. Earlier visions of the Church, with their emphasis on the perfection of the Church, suggest that the Church had no need to enter into dialogue with the world, that contact with the world only somehow marred or soiled the Church. *Gaudium et spes,* however, called the Church a sacrament of salvation. The Church is a people of God, who walk along with all the peoples of the world. They are a leaven and a sign of God's good intentions for the world. *Gaudium et spes* represents a certain fullness of the mind of the council. The bishops in effect put their thumb on the scale in favor of an ecclesiology of communion.[70]

Gaudium et spes commits the Church to support the horizontal communion of human society, observing that the communal nature of human life is an essential part of God's design for us. "The human crea-

---

67. Rikhof, 3.
68. Rikhof, 38, 233–36.
69. Vatican II, *Gaudium et spes,* December 7, 1965; Tanner, vol. 2, 1069–1135.
70. Cf. Richard McBrien, *Church: The Continuing Quest* (Paramus, N.J.: Newman Press, 1970) 23f.

ture," the council wrote, "can attain its full identity only in sincere self-giv-ing."[71] The communal character of human nature "is perfected and com-pleted by the work of Jesus Christ. For the incarnate Word chose to share in human society." The communal characteristic of human nature expresses itself in solidarity with others (horizontal communion) yet has a tran-scendent dimension, what might be called an eschatological impetus. ". . . [I]t must continually increase until the day of its accomplishment. . . ."[72]

The Church, the council stated, "is now present here on earth and is composed of people who are members of the earthly city. . . ."[73] Though it will only find fulfillment in the day of God's reign, the Church cannot excuse itself from the human table. Instead, the council described a posture of engagement with the world. This engagement is aptly called a "real presence" of the Church.[74] The Church must engage in a sacrifi-cial mission on behalf of the world, as a saving presence in the world. The Church cannot afford to greet the world with apathy or contempt.

In *Gaudium et spes* the Second Vatican Council described a Church fully engaged in the exigencies of the human pilgrimage:

> Thus the church, as at the same time "an identifiable group and a spiritual community," proceeds on its way with the whole of humanity and shares the world's earthly lot, while also being a leaven and a sort of soul of human society, which is to be renewed in Christ and transformed into God's family. This interpretation of the heavenly and earthly cities can be grasped only by faith, and remains in fact the mystery of human history which will be disturbed by sin until the brightness of God's children is fully revealed.[75]

The Church is both part of the movement toward salvation and a cause of that movement. The Church, too, is being transformed through time. It penetrates human societies and has a mission to work with other men and women of good will to reconfigure human affairs more fully to ac-cord with the love and will of God.

3.4. The Church as sacrament continued— the contribution of Karl Rahner

For Catholic theologian Karl Rahner (1904–1984), the Church is the primordial sacrament. The Church, he said, symbolizes the grace of

71. GS, 24.
72. GS, 32.
73. GS, 40.
74. Cf. Henri de Lubac, "Christian Community and Sacramental Communion," in *Theological Fragments*, tr. Rebecca H. Balinski (San Francisco: Ignatius Press, 1989) 74.
75. GS, 40.

Christ in history.[76] The Eucharist and the other sacraments are effective symbols of the Church. The Eucharist is celebrated in local churches in real, yet humble acts of worship. In these acts the Church touches its highest actualization. The Church's highest act, Rahner said, is to represent God's redeeming grace for humankind "in the historical tangibilities of her appearance, which is the sign of the eschatologically victorious grace of God in the world."[77] The sacraments are effective signs of the deepest reality of the Church. They act like "lenses," for the Church experiences the sacraments as focal points for its own, innermost reality. The sacraments are signs of Christ received in the power of the Spirit. The Church sees itself in light of the divine work through the "lens" of the sacraments.

It is easy to see how worship and, particularly, the Eucharist lead to an idea of salvation from Rahner's perspective. The Church instantiates or represents to itself, in its actions, both an understanding of salvation and the grace which God gives to lead it toward salvation. The idea and the experience are received together. The idea of salvation and the doctrinal representations of the idea are nearly always inferior to the reality. Just as human love defies expression, so the divine love also transcends the Church's ability to describe it. Even the actions of the Eucharist do not contain, though they signify, the love of God. Still less do doctrinal propositions comprehend God's self-revelation.[78] The faith of the Church is not to believe one particular thing (rather than something else), or to do one unusual thing (rather than something else.) The faith of the Church is to be open to God's grace, wherever it is found. It is to be a freely flowing conduit of God's self-communication. The faith of the Church is to be wholly disposed to God's service to humankind.[79]

A splendid image for the Church's sacramental character is found in Rahner's 1972 essay, "Considerations on the Active Role of the Person in the Sacramental Event."[80] There Rahner described the qualities and exigencies of human life in liturgical metaphors. This he called the "liturgy of the world." He began describing a panorama of human aspiration from the birth-cries of the first human being to the dying breath of our

---

76. Rahner, *The Church and Sacraments*, tr. W. J. O'Hara (London: 1963) 18, 22. Richard Lennan, *The Ecclesiology of Karl Rahner* (Oxford: Clarendon Press, 1995) 27.

77. Rahner, *Church and Sacraments*, 70. Lennan, 27.

78. Rahner, "The Development of Dogma," in *Theological Investigations*, vol. 1, tr. Cornelius Ernst (New York: Seabury, 1982) 64–66. Lennan, 54.

79. Rahner, "On the Situation of Faith," in *Theological Investigations*, vol. 20, tr. Edward Quinn (New York: Seabury, 1986) 27f. Lennan, 186.

80. Rahner, "Considerations on the Active Role of the Person in the Sacramental Event," in *Theological Investigations*, vol. 14, tr. David Bourke (New York: Seabury, 1976) 161–84. Michael Skelley, *The Liturgy of the World: Karl Rahner's Theology of Worship* (Collegeville: The Liturgical Press, 1991).

species. The liturgy of the world is enacted in birth and death, in hunting and gathering, in praying for a good harvest, in maneuvering rush-hour traffic. The liturgy of the world reveals a world gasping for the breath of God. The body of the world comprises the whole of the human struggle for survival. The Church is the place where the liturgy of the world is transposed into the saving design of God.

The liturgy of the world, Rahner wrote, is both terrible and sublime. It is about death and sacrifice, freedom and slavery. It is sustained by God, because it will be subsumed into the liturgy of the Cross. For the liturgy of the Cross, the sacrifice of Jesus there, emerges out of the liturgy of the world. The Cross belongs "intrinsically to the world, emerges from it, . . . and constitutes the supreme point of this liturgy from which all else draws its life. . . ."[81] At the Cross, the liturgy of the world has reached its "high point." From the Cross, in its embrace by God, the liturgy of the Church begins.

For Rahner, therefore, the phrase "liturgy of the world" suggests that the world is an essential part of God's saving design. The world is not refuse. It may not be discarded. The liturgy of the Church is a subset of the liturgy of the world. The Church's worship is an instance, an articulation, an exemplar of the ongoing liturgy of the world, transposed by its participation in the paschal mystery.[82] Liturgy is thus something brought about in the human community by God's grace. Whether "merely human," like the liturgy of the world, or "truly sacramental," like the liturgy of the Church, both are signs of the Spirit at work in human life.[83]

If the actions of the world are already somewhat "liturgical," the communion of the world must be already somewhat "ecclesial." The interdependence of human beings may be a significant expression of that "primordial ecclesiality." Human children, unlike nearly every other mammal, depends on parent and tribe for an exceptionally long time. The Church is no less conditioned by such anthropological considerations.

If the actions of the world are already somewhat "liturgical," perhaps they are also somewhat "eucharistic." The liturgy of the world includes the sum of all human activity: giving birth, growing, eating, respiring, excreting, speaking, reproducing, dying. All of these actions are oriented to the survival of the organism. They maintain the biological systems required for life. Over the course of life, human beings respond to these acts. We experience them as life-giving, as confining, as restraining upon our desire for freedom or self-transcendence. They maintain us in our individuality and individualism, particularly when the actions of

---

81. Rahner, "Considerations," 169f.
82. Cf. Skelley, 93–99.
83. Cf. Skelley, 99.

one person threaten the survival of another. Our bodies symbolize our ability to enter into communion with one another (to form hunting parties, to gather seeds). They symbolize, also, our tragic inability to overcome isolation and alienation.

In the words of Orthodox theologian and bishop, John Zizioulas, the body is a "tragic instrument." It "leads to communion with others, stretching out a hand, creating language, speech, conversation, art, kissing." At the same time, it is the sign of our undoing. It is the "'mask' [*prosopon*] of hypocrisy, the fortress of individualism, the vehicle of . . . death."[84] We die so that our offspring may live.[85] In communion, the self-sacrifice and the self-offering of the "liturgy of the world," we perpetuate our species. Tragically and ironically, the very same events are experienced as sign and cause of our own undoing, our own inevitable *kenosis*. All of us participate in the "mere communion" of the world.

The Church is therefore a sacramental sign of the world's "outpouring." The Church must therefore be "worldly" in the sense that the Church brings the world before God. The Church epitomizes the world, because the Church is a sacrament of the body and blood of the world. The Church is the place where the world lays aside its cares to rest in confidence on God. The Cherubic hymn of the Liturgy of John Chrysostom eloquently expresses this idea. "Let us here . . . now lay aside all earthly care . . . So that we may welcome the King of the Universe . . . Alleluia."

The liturgy of the world, epitomized by the Cross, is radically changed by the resurrection of Jesus. The resurrection of Jesus is God's answer to the aspirations of the world. If the liturgy of the world is a plea for abundant life, the liturgy of the Church must answer that it is available in Christ who died and rose to new life. The constant groaning of the world has not been silenced. But it has become wed to the Holy Spirit's "groaning," the travail of a world that is being born. The eucharistic answer does not suggest that the Church can go away to dwell in splendid isolation, hoarding God's life for itself. The eucharistic Church must be prophetic and priestly. It must hear the voice of the world. It must respond with the voice of Christ. The Church is a sacrament, therefore, because the world can see in the Church a reflection of what it might become: the body of Christ, the people of God released from bondage.

To focus on the world is an important corrective for contemporary ecclesiology. From Vatican I until Vatican II, what Rahner named the "Pian era" after the popes who reigned during this period, church teach-

84. John Zizioulas, *Being as Communion* (Crestwood, N.Y.: St. Vladimir's Seminary Press, 1985) 50.

85. Sherwin Nuland, *How We Die: Reflections on Life's Final Chapter* (New York: Alfred A. Knopf, 1994) 255f.

ing focused on unchangeability and uniformity. Historical developments were naïvely construed by theologians and the magisterium. The entire Church, it was supposed, should mirror Rome in all things. The cultures and histories of the world's peoples would be overlooked in the attempt to unite the Church through centralization.

The Church of the future, Rahner believed, will eschew these two tendencies. Rahner's conviction rested on his faith in the Spirit, who, he said, works through all the members of the Church and not through the Church hierarchy alone. The churches of Africa, Asia, and South America have proper gifts or charisms. The churches of these places do not need to be poor imitations of Mediterranean Christianity. Variety, rather than uniformity, manifests the comprehensiveness of the Church. Variety symbolizes the ability of all people to respond in God's saving design.[86] Extending the ideal articulated by Möhler over a century ago, Rahner's idea embraces the conviction that the Church must embrace all permissible contraries in doctrine and practice. The ministry of the hierarchy is to maintain a fruitful tension and organize the dialogue of the Church. It is difficult to see how silencing opponents and suppressing difficult questions serve such a ministry.

The presence of the Church in the world, like the presence of Christ in the Church, must be seen as part of the divine mission of love. It is given by the Spirit. It is received in Christ's loving condescension to a thoroughly human estate. In itself, the Church does not exhaust the meaning of the divine mission to the world. It nonetheless originates in the desire of Jesus of Nazareth to establish the reign of God on earth, and in the power of the Spirit to raise up men and women of faith. The Church is given power to actualize and continue Christ's saving mission. Every act of the Church may be judged on the basis of how well it manifests Christ's power to save. The Church must always be structured and act in such a way that the coming reign of God may come and not be delayed.

4. The Church is a parable on salvation—the "soteriological norm"

The Church, I would argue, is always governed by a soteriological norm. The Church always acts out its hope for the coming salvation. Our ideas of salvation are always present in our work to construct and maintain the Church in truth. Hope for salvation and an idea of salvation always inform and motivate the social and cultural characteristics of the Church. Hope for salvation entails and proscribes certain types of behaviors—both personal and ecclesial. For example, Vatican II was remarkable as much for

---

86. Rahner, "Observations on the Factor of the Charismatic in the Church," in *Theological Investigations*, vol. 12, tr. David Bourke (New York: Seabury, 1974) 93f. Lennan, 216.

expanding the idea of salvation as it was for reconceiving the nature and mission of the Church. Vatican II was even more remarkable for the way in which it conducted its affairs than for the actual statements it made. The "opening of the doors of the Church," the *aggiornamento* called for by John XIII, made Vatican II a watershed for Roman Catholicism.

How does the Church express an idea of salvation when it performs the Eucharist? How is it governed by a soteriological norm? Paul believed the presence of Christ at the Eucharist was given for the sake of salvation. The unity of Christians is at the heart of the idea of salvation symbolized by the Eucharist and given with Christ's presence in Holy Communion. This idea is not new. Early Christian writers called the Eucharist a sacrament of unity *(mysterium unitatis)*, a sacrament of uniting *(sacramentum conjunctionis)*, and a sacrament of federation *(sacramentum federationis)*.[87] Thomas Aquinas equated the ultimate effect of the Eucharist (its *res tantum*) to the unity of the Church. Bonaventure, after calling the eucharistic body of Christ the *res media* (the "means"), went on to call the ecclesial body of Christ the *res ultima* (the "end") of the Eucharist. Finally, Augustine said that one is assimilated by the Eucharist more truly than one assimilates nourishment from the Eucharist. Receiving the body of Christ, one is made a participant in a reality far greater than one's self.

Summarizing the patristic authors, Henri de Lubac reminded his readers of these scholastic refrains. "One will say, for example, '*vesci corpore et corpus effici*' [to eat the body is also to become the body] or '*corpus Christi manducare, nihil est aliud quam corpus Christi effici*' [to eat the body of Christ is nothing other than to become the body of Christ]. . . ."[88] All these refrains contain the idea that Communion at the eucharistic table and communion in the Church are one and the same. Communion in one is mutually constitutive of the other. De Lubac epitomized the idea when he wrote: "Just as sacramental communion is at the same time *ecclesial* communion, so ecclesial communion at its culmination is sacramental communion."[89] To sit at the table with Christ is to sit at the table with the Church and vice-versa. This leads back to the idea of openness: All whom Christ has invited to the table, the Church "must" accept and "may not" exclude. Denying any member of the body of Christ, the Church denies itself.

In the history of Christian doctrines of salvation, one easily recognizes two strains. These strains of thought extend down into the deepest layers of the history of the Christian message, even into the Gospels themselves. The first strain: Salvation is the reconciliation of human be-

87. Lubac, *Corpus mysticum*, 27.
88. Lubac, "Christian Community," 72f.
89. Lubac, "Christian Community," 72.

ings to one another through the power and love of the Spirit of the risen Savior. The second strain: Salvation depends upon the atoning death of Christ as a propitiation of God who is offended by sin. Our eucharistic doctrines and practices tend to mirror these two strains of thought. We might understand the Eucharist as the place where men and women are united in loving communion, the first strain. Are these ideas not similar to the agapic theme identified by Lietzmann? On the other hand, we might understand the Eucharist as the place where men and women are united to the sacrificial and atoning death of Jesus, the second strain. Are these ideas not similar to the cultic theme identified by Lietzmann?

Usually, we cope with the inherent contradictions of these two strains, agapic and cultic, by calling them "mutually corrective" models, or something similar. An alternative approach, however, may be fruitfully considered. Both strains of thought about salvation are really about ideas of communion in Christ. Communion has both a sacrificial element and an agapic element. Christian ideas of sacrifice lead to agape. Likewise, Christian agape is based on our participation in the sacrificial love of Jesus. Both cultic and agapic ideas about salvation emerge from the Church's experience of the Eucharist. At the Eucharist Christians glimpse the salvation which Christ has prepared for us. It is a "foretaste of the feast to come."[90] The Eucharist is as much a sacrament of the death of the Savior as it is a rehearsal for life in the reign of God.

5. Conclusion

In this chapter I have outlined several key developments in ecclesiology and in eucharistic theology during the past century. For instance, the Eucharist can no longer be considered an act of a priest in isolation from the liturgical assembly. The proper role of the Christian assembly at the eucharistic table has emerged again because of the work of liturgical pioneers and others. The assembly itself is a sign and cause of Christ's presence and ministry to the world. This view is entirely consistent with Paul's doctrine of the Church as the "body of Christ." He used that metaphor explicitly to account for the legitimate diversity of ministries within the church at Corinth.[91]

Second, it is increasingly less satisfying for Roman Catholics to advert to ecclesiologies of church organization and power. As seen in recent ecumenical documents relating to ministry, Protestants and others have taken efforts to understand and appreciate the three-fold ministry of dea-

---

90. Offertory verse, Liturgy of Holy Communion, *Lutheran Book of Worship* (Minneapolis and Philadelphia: Augsburg Publishing House and the Board of Publication, Lutheran Church in America, 1978) 86.

91. 1 Cor 12:27-30.

con, priest, and bishop. Roman Catholics will wish to focus on the qualitative dimensions of the organization of the Church: how authority is exercised in the Church, how the Spirit is discerned, how baptized men and women are joined as partners in the Church's mission before the world. The mere fact of bishops ordained in apostolic succession does not, by itself, guarantee that those men are guiding the Church in saving paths. Neither does their collegiality with one another, nor their union with Rome. All of these factors work together, subordinate to their fundamental service to God's saving plan. Conservatism alone cannot guarantee the Church's fidelity to the Gospel. *Gaudium et spes* upheld the need to examine critically the qualitative dimensions of the Church's life. It directed the Church to be a servant of God within the human family. Through listening, speaking, garnering resources, organizing men and women of good will, resolving to order its own household in a just fashion, the council said the Church must assist in "building the world" and "leading it to its destiny."[92]

I have said that the Church is governed by a "soteriological norm." Under this concept, doctrines and practices of the Eucharist must be systematically related to the doctrine of salvation in Christ. In a word, the Eucharist and the manner in which we celebrate it cannot contradict the possibility of salvation. We cannot, like the Corinthians, say that we are a "body of Christ" and then gather at a table where a significant plurality of the baptized are uninvited by custom or by law. Paul's statements regarding the Eucharist in 1 Corinthians exhibit similar soteriological concerns. The entire thrust of his letter seemed directed at the establishment of an effective soteriological norm in the Corinthian church. Paul's aim was to enhance the *communion of their local church*. Their divided table was not a sign of salvation, he said, but of condemnation. Modern Christians are no less experts of dividing the table of Jesus than were those Corinthians of Paul's day.

Karl Rahner has helped us see the Church as a sacrament of salvation to the world. According to the traditional definition, "sacraments" are signs which cause what they signify. The Church causes and signifies the salvation which Christ is preparing for us. That is why the kind of salvation the Church elects to exhibit or obscure, the qualitative dimension, is so vitally important. When the Church obscures God's design for salvation, it undermines its own sacramentality and ceases to be what it is.

The argument of this book is that the chief way in which the Church exhibits or performs its sacramentality is in and through the Eucharist. The Eucharist must be a place in the Church's life where salvation is effectively signified and proclaimed. Whatever the Church understands "salvation" to mean must somehow be signified in the manner in which

92. GS, 93.

the Church approaches the altar. On this view, for instance, the history of eucharistic practices is accorded a higher status among sources for soteriology than may have been given previously. We might begin to see more clearly those times when the Church has thwarted itself in order to serve less than ultimate goals like colonialism, accumulating wealth, or subjugating people.[93] Eucharistic practices, indeed everything the Church or its ministers do as the Church or in the name of the Church, must be considered in light of their effect upon the coming age. Do they contradict the possibility of salvation in Christ? Do they hinder the day of the arrival of his reign of peace?

Human communion may be considered a subset of the absolute communion that exists in God.[94] At the Eucharist, human communion is touched by "communion" as such. The being or essence (the *ousia*) of the triune God, whose being is to exist as a communion of persons, is expressed in symbols comprehensible to human beings. Human communion, we believe, is not destroyed, but perfected as it approaches the communion of the new Jerusalem. Biblical scholar Rudolf Schnackenburg pointed this out when he wrote, "Human communion is included in the communion which comes from God."[95]

Therefore, when ceremonies or doctrines are twisted in favor of a "communion of self-interest," there is, strictly speaking, no Eucharist. When ceremonies or doctrines conceal a desire to eliminate or neutralize the beliefs or value of other human beings, a "communion of fascism," there is no Eucharist. Instead, if participants are immersed in a communion of dependence upon God in love for one another, a "communion of agapic sacrifice," our eucharistic rites and doctrines can be most effective agents for the building up of the Church and for the salvation of the world. The grace of God shines through them. Our Eucharists, our churches, are impoverished to the extent they do not exhibit the idea that Christ has redeemed us all, or is the savior of anything less than the entire world.

The Eucharist, de Lubac reminds us, is a "sacrament of hope." It does not only represent but also anticipates.[96] Some faint impression of

---

93. Cf. Tissa Balasuriya, *The Eucharist and Human Liberation* (Maryknoll, N.Y.: Orbis Books, 1979) 96–115. Colonialism and mission frequently warped the Eucharist. In Balasuriya's home country, Portuguese Catholics and Dutch Protestants imposed hateful policies on colonial subjects. The Mass and the Lord's Supper were made the tools and symbols for oppression.

94. Catherine LaCugna, *God for Us* (San Francisco: Harper Collins, 1991) 262.

95. Rudolf Schnackenberg, "Die Einheit der Kirche unter dem Koinonia-Gedanken," in *Einheit der Kirche: Grundlegung im Neuen Testament*, Einheit der Kirche, 84 (Freiburg: Herder, 1979) 71.

96. Lubac, *Corpus mysticum*, 79f. See also Yves de Montcheuil, "Signification eschatologique du Repas eucharistique," *Recherches de Science Religieuse* 33 (1946) 10–43. Geoffrey Wainwright, *Eucharist and Eschatology* (New York: Oxford University Press, 1981).

God's absolute future is seen or felt in the sharing of a humble, peasant meal like the Eucharist. Jesus promised to gather all people into a free relationship of love *(agape)*. Eduard Schillebeeckx has written, in another context, that "Eschatologically, church and mankind coincide fully."[97] Jesus' practice of open table-fellowship or open commensality likewise suggests that, eschatologically, the Eucharist and every human meal coincide.

97. Eduard Schillebeeckx, "The Church and Mankind," *Concilium* 1 (1964) 91.

Questions for meditation and dialogue on "Communion Ecclesiology"

1. *Ideas of the Church and the celebration of the liturgy.* One of the main ideas of this chapter is that our ideas of the Church are deeply influenced by our experience of the Church at worship. Does the way your congregation worships suggest the way it is governed? Can you describe your church's worship highlighting the way your church is organized and structured? Does your church emphasize the active role of all present or does it emphasize the role of the priest and ministers acting on behalf of the assembly?

2. *Mystical body of Christ.* Where do you most powerfully experience Christ's presence at the Lord's Supper or Mass? How do the members of your church signal to one another that they recognize the body of Christ at the Eucharist? For you and your church, is the presence of Christ more powerfully felt in the Word, in the preaching, in the minister, in the assembly, or in the consecrated elements of bread and wine? When you look at other churches and the way they celebrate Christ's presence in worship, are there practices or belief statements which you find either uncomfortable or compelling?

3. *Communion and* kenosis. How does your church view the "sacrificial" element of the Eucharist? When you are at worship, are you able to imagine the Church being "poured out" in love for others, or does your church sometimes seem more "bottled up"? Is your experience of the Lord's Supper nearer to the close, quiet intimacy of the Upper Room or to the public, open abundance of Jesus' meals with loaves and fish for everyone?

FOR FURTHER READING

Doyle, Dennis M. "Möhler, Schleiermacher, and the Roots of Communion Ecclesiology," *TS* 57 (1996) 467–80.

Hamer, Jerome. *The Church Is a Communion.* Ronald Matthews, tr. London: Geoffrey Chapman, 1964.

LaCugna, Catherine. *God for Us.* San Francisco: Harper Collins, 1991.

Lennan, Richard. *The Ecclesiology of Karl Rahner.* Oxford: Clarendon Press, 1995.

Lubac, Henri de. *Corpus mysticum: L'Eucharistie et l'Église au moyen âge,* 2nd ed. Paris: Aubrie, 1944.

McPartlan, Paul. *The Eucharist Makes the Church: Henri de Lubac and John Zizioulas in Dialogue.* Edinburgh: T&T Clark, 1993.

Rahner, Karl. "Considerations on the Active Role of the Person in the Sacramental Event." *Theological Investigations,* vol. 14. David Bourke, tr. New York: Seabury, 1976. 161–84.

Rikhof, Herwi. *The Concept of Church: A Methodological Inquiry into the Use of Metaphors in Ecclesiology.* London: Sheed & Ward/Patmos Press, 1981.

Zizioulas, John. *Being as Communion.* Crestwood, N.Y.: St. Vladimir's Seminary Press, 1985.

CHAPTER THREE

Church and Eucharist in Ecumenical Perspective

Many Christians think of the Eucharist as something the Church *does*, rather than as something the Church *is*. We think of the Eucharist in action words. We *bring* forward bread and wine, placing them on the table. By the power and words of the priest or minister we *transform* bread and wine into the body and blood of Jesus. Holy Communion is something done—we *extend* our hands, we *open* our lips, we *kneel* or *stand*, *eat* and *drink*.

These ideas are not entirely false. Gregory Dix, in his monumental book *The Shape of the Liturgy*, wrote extensively about the "four-fold shape" of the liturgy.[1] Dix's "four-fold shape" corresponds to the four main verbs of the Last Supper narrative: to take, to break, to bless, and to give. Never mind that there are several more verbs, such as the ones regarding the cup, Dix's four-fold shape has a certain interior logic that is attractive to this day. One would appreciate, however, an application of Dix's analysis of the history of the development of the Mass in light of the *eucharistic* nature of the Church. The person who "takes, breaks, blesses, and gives" is supposedly changed in a significant way for having performed those acts. Taking, breaking, blessing and giving at the Eucharist must somehow be at the heart of what the Church is, for they are the symbols by which the Church expresses its innermost reality to itself and to others.

One of the themes in the first two chapters was how individualistic conceptions of the Eucharist do not work from a biblical perspective. The Eucharist and the Church are corporate. We are not "saved" into isolation, but into a reconciled, agapic community. The meaning of salvation for the Christian is exhausted by the phrase: new life in the body of Christ by the power of the Holy Spirit. In this chapter on the Church and the Eucharist in ecumenical perspective, I want to show how our understandings of the Eucharist affect our understanding of the Church. The Eucharist is more than what we do, it is also who we are. If so, then each

---

1. Gregory Dix, *The Shape of the Liturgy* (New York: Seabury, 1982) *passim.*

time the Church gathers for the Eucharist it should remember what it is and what it ought to be. We find ourselves at the end of a nearly thousand-year history of divisions. I am convinced the Eucharist condemns this division. It threatens our communion with other Christians (in the "horizontal" plane) and with Christ our Savior (in the "vertical" plane).

1. Ecumenical method

I have chosen to focus on three statements on the Eucharist produced in ecumenical dialogue. The three statements are the "Windsor document" of the first and second Anglican-Roman Catholic International Commissions,[2] the "Lima document," *Baptism, Eucharist and Ministry* of the World Council of Churches,[3] and the "Theses on the Eucharist" of the Group of Les Dombes.[4] Each of the three statements has contributed greatly to ecumenical consensus on the Eucharist. In their discussion of the Eucharist each reveals fascinating assumptions about the nature of the Church.

It would be impossible to examine all the agreed statements and documents of the ecumenical movement for statements pertaining to our themes. Certainly there are other statements which could have been considered. For example, the Leuenberg Agreement of the Reformed Churches of Europe (1973) set the tone for several statements in BEM on the Eucharist.[5] More recently, the Porvoo Common Statement (1992) between the British and Irish Anglican Churches and the Nordic and Baltic Lutheran Churches, affirmed BEM and moved beyond it saying, "Celebrating the Eucharist, the Church is reconstituted and nourished, strengthened in faith and hope, in witness and service in daily life."[6] In light of these later agreements it is good to return to the earlier statements. We ask: what demands do our newly shared understandings of the Eucharist now make upon the churches?

As the number of sources to consider had to be narrowed, the ways in which we will consider the sources must similarly be limited. Our in-

2. Windsor, 1971, with Elucidations, 1979, and Clarifications, 1994. Apart from the 1994 Clarifications, the ARCIC-I Final Report , 1981, is found in *Growth in Agreement: Reports and Agreed Statements of Ecumenical Conversations on a World Level*, ed. Harding Meyer and Lukas Vischer, Ecumenical Documents 2, Faith and Order Paper 108 (New York and Geneva: Paulist Press and WCC, 1984) 61–130.

3. BEM, 1982. See *Growth in Agreement*, 465–503.

4. GLD, 1972.

5. Reformation Churches of Europe, "Leuenberg Agreement, 1973," in Kinnamon and Cope, 149–54.

6. Porvoo Common Statement: Conversations between the British and Irish Anglican Churches and the Nordic and Baltic Lutheran Churches, Occasional Paper no. 3 (London: Council for Christian Unity, General Synod of the Church of England, 1993), in Kinnamon and Cope, 154–56.

terest in these documents is not historical. There are many good historical studies available.[7] The responses of the churches to these statements
will not be considered. There exist several volumes of responses to BEM.
The official Roman Catholic responses to BEM and Windsor will be considered in the next chapter. The reception of doctrinal statements created
in ecumenical contexts is also an important problem, but has been considered in more detail elsewhere and will be deferred until chapter 6.[8]

Using ecumenical dialogue statements as sources for theology creates several interesting problems. For instance, Christians have used similar terms like "grace" to describe diverse experiences and concepts.
Words like "hypostasis" and "person" describe similar experiences and
concepts. The rules governing the combination of doctrinal words and
symbols vary from church to church. For instance a participant at a 1983
conference on BEM was reported to have asked, "How do you know that
when you use different words you are speaking with the same intentions?"[9] The preparatory commission to ARCIC-I expressed its desire to
examine dogmatic truths and "the means by which communions assent
to them."[10] When one writes or says "Eucharist" does one also include
the meanings of the words "Mass" or "Lord's Supper"? Do the various
terms admit significant differences or only shades in meaning?

Another problem facing the authors of ecumenical agreements are
the acceptable limits of diversity between churches and within churches.
Soon after the publication of the ARCIC I Final Report, Jean-Marie Tillard
wrote, "Pastoral differences often lead to ecclesial communities vastly

7. Polycarp C. Ibebuike, *The Eucharist: The Discussion on the Eucharist by the Faith and Order Commission of the World Council of Churches, Lausanne 1927–Lima 1982* (Frankfurt am Main: Peter Lang, 1989). Gerhard K. Schäfer, *Eucharistie im ökumenische Kontext: Zur Diskussion um das Herrenmahl in Glauben und kirchenverfassung von Lausanne 1927 bis Lima 1982* (Göttingen: Vandenhoeck and Ruprecht, 1988). Anton Houtepen, et al., *Bibliography on Baptism, Eucharist and Ministry (Lima Text) 1982–1987* (Leiden and Utrecht: Interuniversitair Instituut voor missiologie en Oecumenica, 1988). *Documentary History of Faith and Order: 1963–1993*, ed. Günter Gassmann, Faith and Order Paper, no. 159 (Geneva: WCC Publications, 1993). Michael Richards, "Twenty-five years of Anglican-Roman Catholic Dialogue: Where do we go from here?," *OIC* 28 (1992) 126–35. Alberic Stacpoole, "Pre-ARCIC Conversations between Anglicans and Roman Catholics, 1950," *OIC* 23 (1987) 298–323. Michael Fahey, "Genesis of the Lima Document," in *Catholic Perspectives on "Baptism, Eucharist and Ministry,"* ed. Michael Fahey (Lanham, Md.: University Press of America, 1986) 3–6.

8. Edward Kilmartin, "Reception in History: An Ecclesiological Phenomenon and Its Significance," *JES* 21/1 (1984) 34–54. The entire issue of JES 21/1 (1984) is devoted to the problem of reception.

9. Robert W. Bertram, "Chicago Theologians on BEM," *JES* 21/1 (1984) 66.

10. Anglican-Roman Catholic Preparatory Commission, Malta Report I, 5 *OIC* 5 (1969) 28. Jean-Marie Tillard, "The Deeper Implications of the Anglican-Roman Catholic Dialogue," *OIC* 8 (1972) 260.

diverse in their exterior aspect and cultural life . . ." Such diversity, he concluded, is "compatible with the common faith."[11] Modest diversity is nearly always accepted within churches. Churches are often less apt to accept diverse expressions of faith by members of other churches than they are to accept it among their own members.[12] Discussions of the so-called "acceptable limits" of diversity are less often about "unacceptable" doctrines than they are about excluding "unacceptable" groups of people. Trust and trustworthiness must be equal partners with theological precision in ecumenical dialogue.

Finally, ecumenical agreements have tried to speak to the vast range of Christian experience alive in the world today. Cultural, political, economic, sexual, historical, psychological, and technological differences affect and complicate ecumenical discussions, agreements, and steps toward unity. Ecumenism only became a problem when the old "state churches" of eastern and western Europe lost their hegemony at home and had to compete for "religious market-share" in the "new world" cultures of Africa, Asia, and the Americas. Doctrinal disagreements rarely touch upon essential doctrines (the Creed, Scriptures, belief in God, grace or faith) or the polemical subjects over which Churches originally divided. Listening to Christians speak about the faith of one another, one is easily astonished at the ease with which we paint caricatures of one another and argue with straw men. Learning to listen and learning to engage in discussion of real—as opposed to imagined—differences has been high on the agenda for the ecumenical movement.

When he convened Vatican II, John XXIII stated that none of the contents of faith should be allowed to slip away. They should be expressed in a form suitable to the spirit of the modern age. Human languages, at best, only approximate the pre-linguistic, substance of faith that is symbolized in doctrine. The principle received its most profound expression in the dogmatic constitution on divine revelation, *Dei verbum*:

> By [faith], a human being makes a total and free self-commitment to God, offering "the full submission of . . . intellect and will to God as he reveals," and willingly assenting to the revelation [God] gives . . . The same Holy Spirit constantly perfects faith by his gifts, to bring about an ever deeper understanding of revelation.[13]

Faith is the foundation for the deepest movements of the soul. It is the assent to God symbolized by verbal declarations of faith. Faith is entirely a gift of God's grace. Grace anticipates faith in human life, accompanies

---

11. Jean-Marie Tillard, "The ARCIC Report," *Ecumenism* 68 (1982) 12.

12. Jon Nilson, *Nothing Beyond the Necessary: Roman Catholicism and the Ecumenical Future* (New York: Paulist Press, 1995) 6.

13. DV, 5.

us in our expression of faith, and perfects faith through the gifts of the Holy Spirit and the correction offered in life's experiences.[14]

The council reaffirmed the ineffability of faith and defined its personal character.

> By divine revelation God has chosen to manifest and communicate both himself and the eternal decrees of his will for the salvation of humankind, "so as to share those divine treasures which totally surpass human understanding."[15]

The council thus affirmed that human utterance can scarcely contain what God has revealed to faith since revelation is, at its core, the self-communication of God, *Deus seipsum.* It is not merely information about God. The substance of faith is not the gnostic product of an arcane calculus. It is the chief product of communion between God and human beings in love with one another.

If the substance of faith is the relationship of human beings to a self-disclosing God, then the description of that relationship, its history, subtleties, meaning, and significance can be expressed only in always unsatisfying, less than adequate statements. One should not ask of faith and its doctrinal expressions, "Is this true?" Better to ask, "Is this an adequate description of the person we love?" Acknowledging the relative inadequacy of doctrine has opened many ecumenical possibilities. Christians easily share the same object of faith. They love the same God, are redeemed by the same Savior, and are sanctified by the same Spirit. Given this reality, could they not be forgiven for not being able, always and everywhere, to agree on the precise forms of words adequate to express this faith and love?

Ecumenical discussions have successfully followed a method which resolves difficulties caused by false polemicism, variant meanings and cultural differences. As a first step dialogue groups establish the ecumenical agenda. They focus on beliefs and practices which truly divide their churches. As a second step they may adopt an historical-critical method of study. Dialogue partners together examine and reappraise the historical and scriptural texts at the foundation of arguments made for and against such beliefs or practices. The next step might be to draft an ecumenical convergence statement. The reception and refinement of such statements by the partner churches concludes this process. In agreed statements, new language is used to express commonly held beliefs. Dialogue groups may suggest modifications to church practices in light of the faith they have both received. This final step represents the contribution of ecumenical dialogue, the creation of newly shared foundations for

14. *Ibid.*
15. DV, 6.

common belief and practice. Dialogue partners and commissions draft consensus statements in the hopes of clarifying remaining differences. The Windsor document and BEM are each the product of such processes.[16]

The success of modern ecumenism is premised upon the repudiation of an ecumenism of return. Prior to Vatican II, the ecumenical stance of the Roman Catholic Church could be called an "ecumenism of return."[17] Pius XI's 1928 encyclical *Mortalium animos* did not distinguish between essential and non-essential matters of faith.[18] Every article of faith, the Pope said, comes from God as its author. By a false inference, he thought every article of faith is equally binding on the believer. The Pope understood ecumenism as the conversion of the "separated brethren" to the doctrines and practices of the Roman Catholic Church.[19] On this view other Christian churches could only be considered schismatic. In *Mystici corporis*, Pius XII reaffirmed the views of his predecessor. The Church of Jesus Christ, he declared, is coterminous with the Roman Catholic Church. Until Vatican II, the official stance of the Roman Catholic Church was that those who desire Christian unity should seek it through union with Rome.[20]

Since Vatican II, the ecumenism of return has fallen by the wayside. According to the Vatican II decree on ecumenism, *Unitatis redintegratio*, Christian churches outside of the Roman Catholic Church may be effective, if partial, means of salvation. All who are baptized and justified by faith in Christ are members of his body, and so even "separated Christians" (i.e., non-Catholics) "have a right to be called Christian" and enjoy a communion—of varying degrees—with the Catholic Church. *Unitatis redintegratio* said that the Church of Christ "subsists in" the Roman Catholic Church. The means of salvation may be found in other Christian communities and churches. Stopping just short of recognizing non-Catholic churches as members of the one, true Church, the council declared the "Spirit of Christ has not refrained from using them as a means of salvation."[21]

Unitatis redintegratio described ecumenism as the restoration of full unity among Christians. This unity, the council said, will be constituted

16. Alan Clark, "ARCIC: Method in Credal Forms," *Theology* 78 (1975) 59–68. Gillian R. Evans, "The Genesis of the ARCIC Methodology," in *Communion et réunion: Mélanges Jean-Marie Roger Tillard*, ed. Gillian Evans and Michel Gourgues (Leuven: University Press, 1995) 125–38.

17. Wilhelm de Vries, "Communicatio in Sacris," in *The Church and Ecumenism*, ed. Hans Küng (New York: Paulist Press, 1965) 18–40. Nilson, 14.

18. Pius XI, Encyclical on true religious unity, *Mortalium animos*, Jan. 6, 1928.

19. Michael Fahey, "Twentieth-Century Shifts," in *Catholic Perspectives on "Baptism, Eucharist and Ministry,"* ed. Michael Fahey (Lanham, Md.: University Press of America, 1986) 28.

20. Nilson, 14.

21. UR, 3.

as a unity in essentials and charity in the estimation of differences among Christians. Everything which the Holy Spirit brings about in the hearts of Christians helps to build the Church as a whole and can also work for the building up of the Catholic Church. While the Catholic Church recognizes the fullness and unity of the Church of God in itself, it also recognizes that divisions among Christians prevent the Catholic Church from "realizing in practice the fullness of Catholicity."[22] This perspective was reiterated in a 1992 letter of the Congregation for the Doctrine of the Faith, *Communionis notio.* The congregation there affirmed that the Catholic Church also sustains a "wound" *(vulnius . . . iniungitur)* as long as divisions last.[23] One of the tasks for Catholics today will be to attend to the "woundedness" of the Catholic Church by gratefully receiving the gifts of the Spirit so generously bestowed on non-Catholic Christians: reverence for Scripture, their high estimation of the priesthood of the faithful, democratic systems in church governance and magisterium, and other gifts too numerous to mention.

2. Eucharist in ecumenical dialogue

Ecumenical agreements on the Eucharist have focused on the presence of Christ in the sacrament and on the Church's participation in Christ's sacrifice. Both problems touch the nature of the Eucharist as much as they touch the nature of the Church. What the Church is able to do in the Eucharist and the realities the Church is engaging at the meal are at the heart of the questions of communion. Different answers to such questions describe a spectrum among the churches. Communion may be merely secular and voluntaristic or it may signify participation in a far deeper reality. If we describe eucharistic communion as though God were only "watching us from a distance," as the popular song goes, then we are implying a nearly autonomous Church as well. The Church could do whatever it wants, because salvation would bear no meaningful relation to who we are as a people—the "church of the deist." However, if we describe eucharistic communion as though God continues to dwell among us, our conception of the Church would change accordingly.

2.1. Participation in the whole Christ

ARCIC's Windsor statement defined a strongly realist conception of Christ's eucharistic presence. Holy Communion signifies the reception of

---

22. UR, 4.

23. CDF, Letter to the bishops of the Catholic Church on some aspects of the Church understood as communion, *Communionis notio,* May 28, 1992; *AAS* 85 (1983) 840; *Origins* 22 (June 25, 1992) 108–12; *OIC* 28 (1992) 282–93.

an offer given unilaterally by Christ and grasped by the believer in faith.[24] The Church, the commission claimed, partakes of Christ's own body and blood in the Eucharist, which strengthens its identity as the "body of Christ." Partaking of the one loaf, they said, "we are one" in "commitment . . . to Christ," to one another, and to the mission of the Church in the world.[25] The commission saw participation in the Eucharist chiefly as a sign of human action. Participation unites Christians in mutual affection for one another.

The commission concluded that the Church participates in the Cross of Christ at the Eucharist. In the Eucharistic Prayer, they said, we participate in the benefits of Christ's sacrifice and we "enter into the movement of his self-offering."[26] Reception of the Eucharist "transmits the life of the risen Christ to his body," the Church.[27] Christ is present for the believer, they said, "awaiting his welcome." Full participation in the Eucharist results in a personal, ever-deepening relationship between Christ and communicant. Through receiving the Eucharist in Communion, Christ is known not only as a presence for the believer, but also as "a presence *with* him."[28] The theology of eucharistic participation in the Windsor statement sounds like an elegant gloss on Archbishop Cranmer's phrase from the Eucharistic Prayer of the *Book of Common Prayer*. The purpose for participation in the Eucharist is that Christ may "dwell in us, and we in him."[29]

The authors of the Windsor statement thus articulated an indissoluble connection between the presence of Christ in the Eucharist and the reason for his presence there. "The elements are not mere signs," the commission wrote. "Christ's body and blood become really present and are really given. But they are really present and given in order that, receiving them, believers may be united in communion with Christ the Lord."[30] In the 1975 Elucidations, the commission stood its ground on this principle: ". . . Christ gives himself to his people so that they may receive him through faith."[31]

The Group of Les Dombes is an ecumenical discussion group founded by the late Abbé Paul Couturier of Lyons, France, in 1937. The Group of Les Dombes has published numerous treatises on ecumenical

24. Windsor, 3.
25. Windsor, 4.
26. Windsor, 5.
27. Windsor, 6.
28. Windsor, 8, original emphasis.
29. "The Great Thanksgiving," Holy Eucharist, Rite I, *The Book of Common Prayer* (New York: Church Hymnal Corp., 1979) 336.
30. Windsor, 9.
31. Elucidations, 7.

concerns and issued its theses on the Eucharist in 1972. At that time many awaited the imminent opening of the churches to one another in eucharistic hospitality, or "intercommunion."[32] Under what conditions, they asked, may Christians from divided churches share a common Eucharist? The group began from the axiom that participation in the Eucharist and agreement in doctrine are linked. They believed that agreement in the meaning of the Eucharist is essential to inclusion at the Eucharist of another church. "One particularly important condition of this sharing of the Lord's table," they wrote, "is substantial agreement on what it is, despite theological diversities."[33] Because of their focus on the question of intercommunion, the Group of Les Dombes understood participation primarily in terms of eucharistic hospitality. They concurred that access to Communion should not be refused to a Christian of another denomination on the basis of their faith in the Eucharist alone.[34]

In one sense, the Group of Les Dombes expressed a norm similar to the one already established for valid ministers of baptism. In baptizing, the minister need baptize only with respect to the intention of the Church. In extraordinary circumstances, non-believers may validly baptize "in the faith of the Church." At the Eucharist, assent to the faith of the Church would seem to be sufficient for participation in the meal. The problem with this approach is that Communion in the table is not merely self-referential. Reception of Holy Communion does not signify assent to eucharistic doctrine by itself. Eucharistic Communion is a symbol also of commitment to the Church that performs those rites. In receiving Communion one has also made a simultaneous commitment to the people with whom one receives.

The Group of Les Dombes had no difficulty describing the Eucharist as an ordinary means of participation in Christ and in his body. "By giving himself to the communicants, Christ unites them in his body." Participation in the Eucharist, they stated, "makes the Church." Eucharistic sharing "makes the communicants one with the whole Christ, with one another, and with all other communicants at all times and in all places."[35]

They had difficulty, however, describing the Eucharist as a participation in the saving acts of Christ, in his self-offering on the Cross. There should be a self-evident connection between participation in the person of Christ and in his saving works. Our participation in the Eucharist mir-

32. Jean-Jacques von Allmen, "The Conditions for an Acceptable Intercommunion," in *The Future of Ecumenism*, ed. Hans Küng, Concilium 44 (New York: Paulist Press, 1969) 7–15.

33. GLD, 2.

34. GLD, 39.

35. GLD, 21.

rors Christ's self-offering through the paschal mystery of his life, death, and resurrection. Eucharistic participation is an act of Christ. It is a perpetuation of his self-offering, once made on the Cross.

Members of the Group of Les Dombes agreed that the consecrated bread and wine are sacramental signs, "a sharing of the body and blood of Christ."[36] The sacramentality of the bread and wine is "by virtue of Christ's creative word and by the power of the Holy Spirit." As signs, the purpose of the bread and wine is "to be consumed," yet that which Christ gives as his body and blood remains such, and, they said in conclusion, "requires to be treated as such."[37]

The group asked churches to consider aspects of their eucharistic practice on the basis of these principles. They asked Roman Catholics to reinforce the distribution of Communion to the sick and the absent as the primary reason for the reservation of the consecrated elements. They asked Protestants to adopt the best means for showing respect to the consecrated elements and not preclude their distribution in Communion to the sick.[38]

The text suggests the group was uncomfortable defining the connection between the significance of the bread and wine and the sacramentality of Christ's self-offering. "Christ's act being the gift of his body and blood, that is to say of himself," they wrote, "the reality given in the signs of the bread and wine is his body and his blood."[39] By stages, the statement established distance between the bread and the body of Christ, between the wine and the blood of Christ. The "reality given" in the Eucharist is not the "bread and wine," but it is, they say, "Christ's body and blood." The "*signs* of the bread and wine" are the vessels for the reality that is given, not the bread and wine themselves.

It is difficult to determine what this distance implies. It is easier to see what the introduction of ambiguity accomplished. The deliberate use of ambiguity in an ecumenical agreement broadens the possible community of assent. Even if participants could not agree that the bread and wine are the vessels of Christ's body and blood, they could agree that the reality given in the Eucharist, wherever that reality is located, is Christ's body and blood. An essential theological formula is asserted: "In the eucharist the reality of Christ's body and blood *is* given to communicants." Yet, the variant meanings of the formula remain open to discussion. The precise *nature* of the accessibility of Christ in the Eucharist is unresolved, while the *fact* of Christ's accessibility is unequivocally affirmed.

---

36. 1 Cor 10:16.
37. GLD, 19.
38. GLD, 20.
39. GLD, 19.

In response to some concerns raised by the theses on the Eucharist of the Group of Les Dombes, consider how the meaning of Christ is changed for us through his association with bread and cup.

Whatever symbols effectively signify Christ to us, because they are *sacraments* of his presence, they cannot signify a "partial Christ," but they must be taken to represent the *totus Christus*, the entire person and works of Jesus. If the sign did not signify the whole of Christ's person and works, then the person and works would not be accessible to us *in the way we need them to be* if Christ is our *savior*. Persons and actions inaccessible to human experience or faith cannot be considered "redemptive."

If the reality given in the Eucharist "*is Christ*," then who Christ is for us *is* "blessed cup and broken bread received in faith, in communion with all the baptized." There is not "a little bit more Jesus" apart from the bread we break or the cup we drink. The Eucharist is a participation in the whole Christ, head and members. The bread and cup exhaust the meaning of Christ for us. It would be wrong to say that the meaning of Christ in himself is *supplemented* or added on to by the meaning of his presence at the Eucharist. We may not *touch* the Christ of the Second Person of the immanent Trinity. The face of Christ which we *can* know, in this life, is the face we see at the eucharistic table, the gathered body of Christ, breaking his body and blessing the cup of his blood.

There is not some more of Christ *(illud extra Christi)* to be had outside the eucharistic table. Who Christ is for us cannot be the same as he was for those who knew him in the flesh. Christ *for us* can only be known sacramentally or eschatologically. He is known sacramentally in his Word, in his ministers, in our liturgical assemblies, and in the sacraments and especially at the eucharistic table in broken bread and blessed cup. This side of heaven, it is impossible *for us* to know Christ in an immediate, or non-sacramental fashion.

Is there "some more Christ" beyond these sacramental signs? Certainly, the Son of the Father enjoys an infinite intimacy in love with the Father and the Spirit (The Son is "begotten," "not-spirated," and so forth). Nonetheless, our Eucharist is not remote from the intimacy of the trinitarian persons. It is a full and complete expression of the love of the Father for the Son in and through the Holy Spirit. God is revealed to us in the eucharistic communion *as Communion itself*, for the word "communion" fundamentally signifies who God is. Catherine M. LaCugna epitomized this in her statement, "God *for us* is who God is *as God*."[40] The face of Christ revealed to us in the Eucharist (or in the Word, or in the Church) is the whole Christ revealed for us as Redeemer. The Lima document presents a conception of participation farthest on the spectrum of the three documents from this point.

40. LaCugna, 305.

The Lima document of the World Council of Churches, *Baptism, Eucharist and Ministry*, presents participation as the sharing of bread and wine by members of eucharistic assemblies. There is no notion of participation for the sake of union with Christ. Rather, BEM uses the word "participation" in a secular and voluntaristic sense. Participation here implies human solidarity in a world of actions taken to meet a common goal. The authors of BEM did not translate the *koinonia* of 1 Corinthians as "participation," but as "fellowship."

Like the Theses of the Group of Les Dombes and the Windsor statement, BEM expresses the idea of communion in Christ with reference to the Eucharist. "In the eating and drinking of the bread and wine," the document states, "Christ grants communion with himself."[41] The unanimous emphasis of these three ecumenical sources points up the possibility that there is a genuine movement away from considering the Eucharist chiefly in terms of objects mysteriously conjoined to the body and blood of Jesus of Nazareth. Rather, the Eucharist is being viewed as an action of the Church, performed in concert with the intention of Jesus to unite us to himself and to one another by means of these actions taken with bread and wine. *Actions* also have their place in the sacramental economy. It is not enough to obtain bread and wine, one must also *do something* with them if they are to become the sacrament.

It is curious that the various commissions supposed the most important act the Church performs with bread and wine is to eat and drink them. For Paul, we noted, the main verbs were not "to eat" or "to drink." In 1 Corinthians 10:16 he called the bread "that thing which we break" and the cup "that thing which we bless." For Paul, the bread and wine acquire their meaning through "breaking" and "blessing." "Eating" and "drinking" appear only later, in 1 Corinthians 11:26. Those acts proclaim the death of the Lord and must be done with a view to the entire body.

Paul linked communion in Christ to the Church's actions of blessing and breaking. Communion in Christ is more closely related to the elements of the bread and wine and to the actions of the Church blessing and breaking them. It is less easily identified with the solidarity that members of the Church might feel for one another. In the Christian context, solidarity—as a type of communion—is a solidarity in Christ to the exclusion of all others. For Paul, at least, fellowship in the Church could only have meant communion with the whole Christ, therefore a communion with one another *in Christ*. One may not validly move, therefore, directly from the reception of bread and wine to the solidarity of the Church in communion. The communion of the Church depends upon

41. BEM, 2.

the sharing of bread and wine, only in so far as they are themselves already a communion in Christ.

The authors of BEM described the eucharistic actions of the Church in relation to the redemptive work of Christ. "The incarnation, life, death, resurrection and ascension of Christ," the works of Christ, BEM asserts, ". . . can neither be repeated nor prolonged." Instead, the Church benefits from the *results* of those events. The Church offers thanksgiving and intercession at the Eucharist "in communion with" the now risen and ascended Christ, "our great High Priest."[42] The Eucharist signifies "universal communion in the body of Christ" as "what the world is to become" at the end of time.[43]

One might have desired to see the Church drawn close to the redemptive works of Christ in the Eucharist. Instead, BEM maintained their distance. Christ's work of salvation was projected into the past as an event closed and inaccessible to future ages. It was projected into an equally remote future as events for the close of time. The "mighty works" of Christ scarcely touch the present in BEM's presentation. BEM asserts a communion with Christ through prayer alone, a participation of the Church in sharing Christ's intentions for the world. Such a desire is not, in itself, a bad thing. The churches must, through prayer, always draw closer in conforming their will to Christ for our world's salvation. Yet, one doubts whether the Lima document's idea of participation as shared prayer and intercession is sufficient to sustain the soteriological value of the Eucharist.

As shown in our sample of ecumenical statements on the Eucharist, Christians share a common readiness to speak of participation in Christ through the Eucharist. They envision that participation differently. For ARCIC, through the eating of bread and wine, one participates in the death of Christ and all of his redemptive works. For the Group of Les Dombes, bread and wine are signs of the reality of Christ's body and blood, given in the Eucharist. For the authors of BEM, participation is primarily expressed in an ongoing ministry of intercession. It is one of the effects of Christ's redemptive work in history. Authors of the three documents connected participation in Christ to eucharistic communion in varying degrees. Few Christians doubt the value of solidarity with Christ and conformity to his intentions and will for the world. In its fullness Christian communion ought to touch saving realities on a deeper level than this. Christians legitimately describe the Church's participation in the work of Christ at the Eucharist with varying terminology. I believe the discomfort some traditions feel applying the term *sacrifice* to the Eucharist underlies the more ambiguous statements in the ecumenical agreements.

42. BEM, 8.
43. BEM, 4.

2.2. Sacrifice—past and present

The "sacrificial" character of the Eucharist has provoked many harsh words between Catholics and Protestants since the Reformation. The doctrine of the sacrificial character of the Eucharist speaks not only to the nature of the Eucharist but also to the nature of the Church that celebrates the Eucharist. To say that the Eucharist is a communion in the sacrifice of Christ or to refuse to say so depends very much on how one evaluates the Church and the actions it takes in worship. Any new consensus in eucharistic doctrine will need to face this issue squarely.

The parties to ecumenical dialogue have engaged this question on several levels. First, they have tried to broaden the list of things in which the Church participates through the Eucharist. For instance, they have said that the Church participates in Christ's service and mission, in his priestly ministry of intercession, in his body and blood, and in the community of God's people. The sacrificial character of the Eucharist, on this view, must be seen as part of the whole earthly ministry of Jesus. Second, they have tried to redefine the nature of Christ's sacrifice and to clarify how the Church has a communion in an event that has been already accomplished in the past whose effects are still unfolding in the present.

The Scriptures never refer to the Eucharist as a *thusia*, the Greek word for sacrifice. Paul's discussion of the Eucharist in 1 Corinthians indicates, however, that he may have understood the Eucharist as a *communion* in the sacrifice of Christ. He believed that the Eucharist is the ordinary means by which many participate in the one and once-only death of Christ. Christians can know the sacrifice of Christ in only one of two fashions. They may know it *immediately* had they been present at the crucifixion as was the Roman centurion.[44] They may know it *sacramentally* through the proclamation of the Gospels, in the Eucharist and other sacraments, or through martyrdom. Barring the unlikely invention of time travel, most Christians know the Cross sacramentally. That is, they know the death of Christ by means of efficacious symbols like words, bread and wine, baptismal water, hymns, crosses and icons.

The Cross is one part of the entire picture of salvation. To focus too exclusively on the sacrificial character of Christ's death therefore runs the risk of ignoring other facets of the mystery of salvation. The paschal mystery does not consist of a death for death's sake. It includes also the gift of new life, the promised resurrection, and the mysterious power and the gifts of the Spirit which transform life today through love, hope, joy, wisdom, etc. The consequences of the Cross must not be lost in our discussion of the eucharistic sacrifice. The Eucharist is not a communion in the

---

44. Mark 15:39.

death of the Savior for death's sake. It is communion in the death for the sake of a promised resurrection, a communion in a place where the Spirit's transforming power and gifts are most prominently received.

If the sacrifice of Christ on the Cross is necessary for salvation, then it must be somehow *accessible* to those who are going to be saved. The Cross and its consequences (new life, the gift of the Spirit) must be known by Christians as something actively shaping their lives in the present moment. The Cross cannot be something "over and done with," or "encapsulated in the past." Christians must know the Cross in a sacramentally mediated fashion. The ecumenical problem is not whether Christians must know the sacrifice of the Cross. The problem is whether the Cross is known *eucharistically*. Is the Eucharist a "salutary gift" as Archbishop Cranmer wrote? Is it "a holy and living sacrifice?" Is there a connection between the two?

BEM states that the Eucharist is the "living and effective sign of [Christ's] sacrifice." The sacrifice of Christ was accomplished "once and for all on the Cross," yet is "still operative on behalf of all humankind." When celebrated in the liturgy, the "present efficacy" of God's work on the Cross, they said, is covered by the biblical term "memorial" or *anamnesis*.[45] According to BEM, the memorial of the Cross at the Eucharist both *represents* the past and *anticipates* the future. *Anamnesis,* they write, "is not only a calling to mind of what is past and of its significance. It is the Church's effective proclamation of God's mighty acts and promises."[46] For the authors of BEM, the Eucharist is like the Word. It proclaims the gospel of the Cross of the past and foretells the salvation of the future. In the present, however, we may only speak of access through *anamnesis* or "memorial."

The authors of BEM had no difficulty calling the Eucharist a memorial of Christ's sacrifice. Ecumenical agreement on the *anamnetic* character of the Eucharist is one of the great strides made in the past several decades. The Eucharist, according to BEM, is "the sacrament of the unique sacrifice of Christ."[47] The very next statement, however, plunges BEM headlong into rougher waters: What God accomplished in the "incarnation, life, death, resurrection, and ascension of Christ, God does not repeat . . . [They] can neither be repeated nor prolonged."[48] BEM had profitably associated the Eucharist with the saving works of Christ through *anamnesis*. In the next statement the profit is lost, because it is withdrawn from the very same events. First, the claim denies the christology of Chalcedon which understands the incarnation as having been

45. BEM, 5.
46. BEM, 7.
47. BEM, 8.
48. *Ibid.*

prolonged eternally because of the resurrection. Christ did not "lose" his humanity at the ascension, nor did the mystery of God's becoming flesh, the incarnation, grind to halt on the day after Christmas. Second, it is improbable that the Greek term *ephapax* may validly be extended to mean "neither repeatable nor prolongable."[49] The first problem is self-evident. The second problem merits further explanation.

The "once-and-for-all" or *ephapax* character of the Cross is an important component to the debate surrounding the sacrificial character of the Eucharist. On the one hand, the "non-repeatability" of historical events is a simple consequence of living in time. In human experience, time does not turn back upon itself. What is done is done and cannot be undone. Events do not recur. The *consequences of* certain events may allow us to speak of an event as though it had been sustained through time, much like the damper pedal prolongs the tones of a chord played on the piano. Initial events, like the striking of a chord, resonate through time and space. They have an acoustical quality.

The mysteries of God, played out in the life of Jesus of Nazareth, have such an acoustical quality. They continue to resonate in their effects through time and space. Yet, the events of Jesus' life, death, and resurrection are not strictly historical events. They also have a mysterious character which suggests their consequences are not limited to time and space as we experience them. Insofar as the death and resurrection of Jesus are *historical*, they are non-repeatable. Resurrection refers to the relationship which Jesus now enjoys—eternally—with God and offers to humankind through his Holy Spirit. This aspect of the resurrection does not and cannot exist *in time*. It transcends both time and place because, like the hub of a wheel, it draws all times and places into relationship with itself.

To suggest, as BEM did, that the mysteries of Jesus' life, the incarnation, the crucifixion, the resurrection, the ascension and so forth, may not be prolonged comes perilously close to denying their ability to work for our salvation. If they are not prolonged in space and time, they are not accessible to us. If they are not accessible, we can have no communion in them. If we deny the possibility of communion, there is no salvation in the Christian sense. The authors of BEM were legitimately concerned to protect the *ephapax* quality of Christ's sacrifice as described in Romans 6 and Hebrews 7. However, they may have gone too far in that concern. The meaning of the term *ephapax* as it is applied to the sacrificial character of the Eucharist must be redefined if it is to become useful in an ecumenical context.

The Greek *ephapax* does not designate the punctual quality of Christ's sacrifice in time. Rather, it describes the *universal sufficiency* of

---

49. Scripture cited in the text include: Rom 8:34; 12:1; Heb 7:25; and 1 Pet 2:5.

Christ's sacrifice to save. None of the four most important passages in the New Testament using this word suggest that Christ's actions may not be "prolonged."[50] Rather, all imply that Christ's saving works are sufficient by themselves for the forgiveness of the sins of all. The arguments were crafted to explain why Christians no longer need to participate in the sacrificial worship of the Jerusalem Temple. The texts do not speak, in any meaningful sense, about the saving effect of the Eucharist or of its relationship to the death of the Lord. From this perspective, the arguments the New Testament authors constructed using the term *ephapax* are no more remarkable than any other arguments they made for the relaxation of the Jewish law. Christians should not be required to constrain their claims about the saving effect of the Eucharist on the basis of scriptural arguments against the efficacy of worship in the Jerusalem Temple. Correctly understood, the *ephapax* character of the paschal sacrifice is the basis of an argument for the limitless power of Christ's acts to save the world.

The Windsor statement moves in this direction with its more nuanced statement on the connection between Christ's sacrifice and the Eucharist. In paragraph 5, the document asserts the singular character of the death and resurrection of Christ, "which took place once and for all in history." Christ's sacrifice is the "culmination of his whole life of obedience." It is "one, perfect, and sufficient" for "the sins of the whole world."[51] Unlike BEM, Windsor did not limit the extent of the sacrifice of the Cross in order to preserve its historical uniqueness. The commission did not shrink from describing the *ephapax* or all-sufficient character of the sacrifice either. Windsor does not deny the possibility of the prolongation of Christ's sacrifice as did BEM. The commission concluded that "what was then accomplished once for all by Christ" cannot be "repeated" or "added to." Like all human beings, Christ can only die one time with respect to his humanity. Universally, Christian doctrine does not allow one to claim that any other sacrifices, offerings, deaths, or human deeds contribute to the saving effect of the paschal sacrifice of Jesus. At the most, we may assent to our salvation and cooperate with it, or we may act to reject God's love and work against it.

Reminded of these limits, the commission then moved to consider the relationship between the Eucharist and the Cross. The Eucharist, they wrote, is a "means through which [the sacrifice of Christ] is proclaimed and made effective in the life of the church." The eucharistic memorial is "no mere calling to mind." It is an "effectual proclamation" in the present of the entirety of "God's reconciling action in [Christ]."[52]

50. Rom 6:10; Heb 7:27; 9:12; 1 Pet 3:18.
51. Windsor, 5.
52. *Ibid.*

The Eucharist as a proclamation of the Gospel remains at the forefront, as it did for the authors of BEM. Through proclamation, we remember. The Church does not *add* to the sacrifice of Christ, but partakes in its fullness through *anamnesis*. *Anamnesis* is essential to the possibility of the Church's sacramental communion in the saving deeds of Christ. The commission unfortunately focused too exclusively on the eucharistic prayer in their discussion. They failed to consider how other acts which comprise the Eucharist, like breaking the bread, pouring the wine, and sharing the cup, have an anamnetic quality. Human beings remember with their bodies and not with their minds alone. If we could not remember motions as much as concepts, we would never acquire skills like riding bicycles or dancing. If anything, *anamnesis* is *more* like remembering how to dance than it is like remembering a little bit of information.

The official response of the Roman Catholic Church to BEM in August 1987 confused this issue. In its response, the Catholic Church criticized BEM for not affirming "unambiguously that the Eucharist is in itself a real sacrifice, the memorial of the sacrifice of Christ on the cross."[53] If BEM did not go far enough, Rome had gone too far. The Eucharist can be called a "sacrifice" only with reference to *communion* in the sacrifice of the Cross. The Eucharist is a communion in the sacrifice because each Eucharist is a real participation in the one and only truly effective sacrifice that has ever occurred.

The sacrificial character of the Eucharist is real, but it is twice-removed from the *ephapax* sacrifice of the Cross. First, it is a *communion* in the death of the Lord. Second, only as much as the death of the Lord is a sacrifice, is the Eucharist a *communion* in the sacrifice. The Eucharist today bears little resemblance to the holocausts of ancient Israel or to the sacrifices of breads, grains, meats, animals, or human beings in other religions. The main resemblance between the Eucharist and other religious sacrifices is chiefly in the similar effects men and women seek in performing them: to establish communion between themselves and the divine.

The Church's performance of the Eucharist may be called sacrificial in a derivative and limited sense. The "sacrifice" of the Church is its actions of praise, thanksgiving, and intercession offered before God. The ability of the Church to perform this limited kind of sacrifice entirely depends upon its communion in the paschal sacrifice at the Eucharist. In another sense, because it is the body of Christ, the Church may offer itself sacrificially in the Eucharist. The Eucharist resembles the Cross if it is the place where the Church as the body of Christ spends its life com-

---

53. *Churches Respond to* BEM: *Official Responses to the "Baptism, Eucharist, and Ministry" Text*, vol. VI, ed. Max Thurian, Faith and Order Paper 144 (Geneva: WCC Publications, 1988) 22.

pletely. The Eucharist is the place where the Church offers its own life for the salvation of the world.

A study group of the Evangelical-Catholic theological dialogue in Germany, the so-called "Anathema Study," came to nearly such a conclusion in the early 1980s. They stated that, in the Christian context, sacrifice always means the "giving over of oneself out of love." They further concluded that the loss of the sacramental and anamnetic understanding of the eucharistic sacrifice underlies Reformation era disagreements on this issue. The rediscovery of the "communion structure" of the Eucharist, outlined above, enabled the group to sweep aside centuries of polemicism to arrive at a new agreement on the sacrificial character of the Eucharist.[54] The Eucharist is a sacrifice *sacramentally*. As a sacrament, the Eucharist is an anamnetic participation, a communion, in the Cross of Christ. It is a "sacrifice" only because it has a communion in the sacrifice.

The sacrifice of the Eucharist differs in several ways from the sacrifice of the Cross. The sacrifice of the Eucharist has no *ephapax* character, as the Cross does. It is performed many times and in many places. The sacrifice of the Cross occurred once. The Eucharist may be applied to particular intentions. The Cross had a universal and comprehensive effect. Whenever Catholics and others have sought to apply the "fruits of the Mass" to the situations of their lives, they usually do so in particularly local terms—"for a good harvest," "for the health of Aunt Sally," "for the conversion of Russia." The Eucharist is prolonged, the Cross is punctual. If the Eucharist is an iteration, the Cross is an exemplar.

Because Roman Catholic doctrine affirms the identity of the Church with the body of Christ, it is not surprising to see the sacrifice of the Eucharist and the sacrifice of the Cross similarly equated. The equivocation is analogous. Both the Eucharist and the Cross are acts performed by Christ. One was performed in history by Jesus of Nazareth. The other is performed through time in the person of his Church. The identity of both bodies—Jesus' earthly body and the Church's mystical body—depends upon the unity of the person of Christ. The identity of both deeds—the Eucharist and the Cross—likewise depends upon the unity of the person performing them. While the paschal sacrifice of Christ is a singular act of ultimate self-surrender, it is known in two modalities. The one act of Christ once performed on a Cross in his physical body is performed on many altars in his ecclesial body, the Church.

---

54. Ökumenisches Arbeitskreis evangelischen und katholischen Theologen, "Das Opfer Jesu Christi: Abschliesender Bericht," in *Das Opfer Jesu Christi und seine Gegenwart in der Kirche*, ed. Karl Lehmen and Edmund Schlink (Freiburg: Herder, 1982). Jenson, 38ff. Cf. John Reumann, *The Supper of the Lord: The New Testament, Ecumenical Dialogues, and Faith and Order on Eucharist* (Philadelphia: Fortress Press, 1985) 104f.

The sacrifice or *kenosis* of Christ touches upon a central theme in the eucharistic understanding of the Church. For the Church to be a communion in the body of Christ it must have entered into the *kenosis* of Christ. The Cross, and the Eucharist as a memorial of the Cross, is at the heart of communion. The reconciliation of humankind with God comes by means of the *kenosis* of Christ in the incarnation, in his death, in the resurrection, and in the outpouring of his Spirit and is described in several traditional ways. We speak of the "forgiveness of sin," "propitiation," "right relationship," "atonement," "reconciliation," etc. For Christians the Cross is not important because it was the location of a death *per se*. The Cross is valuable because Christ's matchless love was expressed there, whose triumph was vindicated by the resurrection and whose grace is made available in the gift of the Spirit. Christ's sacrifice is aptly called a satisfaction for sin. The legal jargon, though, sounds strangely hollow. The Cross "satisfies" only because the division between God and humankind has been healed there by the establishment of a new communion.

Life in communion does not steal us away from the human condition. As Michael Bouttier remarked, "It does not enrich [us]—on the contrary, it deprives [us]. [We] believe without touching, [we] love without seeing [and we live] *in Christo* away from Jesus."[55] *Kenosis* animates the heart of Christian communion, and is its distinguishing feature.

The horizontal communion of the secular sort was possible and remains possible outside of the "bursting forth" of new life in Christ. On the other hand, ecclesial communion of the vertical sort depends entirely on the continuing dynamics of Christ's self-giving. Thus, in Paul's glorious hymn to Christ in Phillipians 2, our ability to acknowledge "Christ as Lord" is one outcome of Christ's self-surrender. Our eucharistic doctrines and practices must always be transparent, therefore, to Christ's act of self-surrender. This seems to lie at the core of Paul's consternation with the Corinthian Christians. Their practice of separate eating and drinking, with hoarding and failing to share, gives no evidence of self-offering.

Contemporary churches bar access to the Eucharist on the basis of policies that are sometimes antithetical to Christ's *kenosis*. In history and today, confession, catechism, polemic, culture, class, ethnicity, and mutual estrangement have all been used to excuse other Christians from the table. These norms may derive from sociological concerns that are similar to those for which Paul rebuked the Corinthian Christians. "Party spirit" and "fractiousness" are not dead. Divisions of the human community motivated by self-preservation, group survival, power, and control bear little similarity to the kenotic self-offering of Christ in love. Such divisions do not create or even pretend to simulate the "open commen-

---

55. Michael Bouttier, 37.

sality" of the meals of Jesus. The churches that continue to erect and patrol barriers between themselves and other churches act as though Christ's sacrifice were sufficient for some, but not for all. In their eucharistic practices as in their self-distinction, as a church or as a confession, they exhibit little faith in the *ephapax* character of Christ's sacrifice. Their actions suggest Christ's ability to save us is both remote and weak.

Christian communion and Christian sacrifice must be held together as a single act of Christ.[56] By his Spirit Christ creates communion in the world by plunging human beings, together, into the movement of his own self-offering, into his own agapic love. The sacrifice of the Word was to give up its exclusive claim to the love and being of God and to draw humankind near in communion with God. As Paul states, our lives are "hidden with Christ in God."[57]

The authors of BEM and the Windsor document spoke of the Church "entering into" the sacrifice of Christ or into the "movement of his intercession." A slightly more robust expression seems called for. The Church participates in the sacrifice of Christ through the Eucharist, because, in breaking the bread and blessing the cup, the inestimable force of Christ's sacrificial love is brought to bear on those who would receive its consequences in faith, hope, and love. Paul's rhetorical aim was to convince Corinthian Christians that they shared a communion in Christ's vulnerability whenever they gathered for the Lord's Supper. To depend entirely upon the sacrifice of the Cross is the sacrifice of the Church. It is proclaimed, rehearsed, and received in every Eucharist.[58] The Church does not *possess* communion in Christ. It is *possessed by Christ in communion*. The sacrifice of the Mass is not something the church *performs*, it is something the Church *undergoes*.

If the Eucharist is a sacrifice, it is an act of ecclesial powerlessness before God. At the altar, the entire Church, in a certain sense, "genuflects" before the saving and loving will of God. If the Cross was the location of the passion of Christ, then the Eucharist is the location of the passion of the Church. It is the place where the Church rests in self-abandoning faith on the saving deeds of Christ. The sacrificial character of the Eucharist is the worst possible basis for a triumphalist ecclesiology. If the Church is a communion in the sacrifice of Christ, it must also be a communion in his powerlessness. The Church must be the place where humankind is emptying itself in complete accord with the kenotic design of God's love.

---

56. Cf. Jenson, 40.
57. Col 3:3.
58. Cf. Joanne Pierce, "The Eucharist as Sacrifice: Some Contemporary Roman Catholic Reflections," *Worship* 69 (1995) 394–405.

2.3. The presence of Christ

The Church that is in communion with the sacrifice of Christ, that is a communion in his powerlessness, is a sacrament of the presence of Christ in the world. We had said, in chapter 2, that the Church is the "mystical body of Christ," and the Church is a sacramental sign of Christ's ongoing incarnation. In the Eucharist, the Church receives the presence of Christ as sign, symbol, and cause of its own identity.

Communion with Christ in the Eucharist, according to the Windsor statement, presupposes his presence "effectually signified by the bread and wine." Christ is given, Anglicans and Catholics agree, "through bread and wine."[59] The bread and wine, they concluded, do not merely signify Christ's presence, but also, "in mystery, [they] become his body and blood." The commission affirmed the eucharistic presence of Christ is subordinate to Christ's entire redemptive works. That is, Christ's presence is offered in the context of the entire movement of salvation. Christ's presence is given for a reason, to transmit "the life of the crucified and risen Christ to his body, the Church."[60] The presence of Christ is not passive, but active. Christ is present as an invitation. Christ presides in the actions of the minister. Christ "gives himself sacramentally in the body and blood of his paschal sacrifice."[61]

BEM adopted several principles similar to those found in the Windsor statement. Christ's presence, the authors said, is *anamnetic*. Christ is wholly present with "all that he accomplished" on our behalf.[62] The Eucharist, BEM affirmed, is the "sacrament of [Christ's] real presence."[63] Christ makes his presence known to us in preaching, in the Word, and in baptism. However, the presence of Christ at the Eucharist is unique. It is "real, living, and active." The affirmation of Christ's eucharistic presence depends upon his promise to be present. Christ's words, "This is my body . . . This . . . is my blood," are true.[64] BEM continues, "and this truth is fulfilled every time the Eucharist is celebrated." The presence of Christ is self-authenticating. It depends upon his promise of presence and authenticates this promise. Although Christ's presence does not depend upon human faith, it is only discernible in faith.

BEM section 13 notes that Christians do not usually disagree on the fact of Christ's presence in the Eucharist. More often they disagree on the manner in which Christ becomes present (e.g., through transubstan-

---

59. Windsor, 3.
60. Windsor, 6.
61. Windsor, 7.
62. BEM, 6.
63. BEM, 13.
64. 1 Cor 11:24 and parallels.

tiation) or on the consequences of Christ's presence for liturgical practice. In the commentary to section 15, the authors of BEM noted several incompatible theologies of real presence, but did not attempt to reconcile them.

Christ is present in the Eucharist as a sacrament of the communion of the triune God. Christ's presence is effected by the work of the Holy Spirit. Christ's presence is not only sacramental and anamnetic, it is also epicletic. That is, the real presence of the Spirit must also be part of our doctrine of the eucharistic communion.[65] The Spirit, BEM states, makes "the historical words of Jesus present and alive."[66] The communion of the triune God is known in the communion of the Christian eucharist. The Father, BEM states, "is the primary origin and final fulfillment of the eucharistic event." The Son "is its living centre [*sic*]," and the Spirit is "the immeasurable strength of love which makes [the Eucharist] possible and continues to make it effective."[67]

The Lima document is first among attempts to organize an ecumenical doctrine of the "real presence of the world" in the Eucharist. The Eucharist is a sacrament given for the renewal of the world. It "brings into the present age a new reality which transforms Christians into the image of Christ and therefore makes them his effective witnesses."[68] The Eucharist is the anticipation or *prolepsis* of the kingdom of God. It is a meal of reconciliation and "an instance of the Church's participation in God's mission to the world."[69] The Church, according to BEM, "possesses a eucharistic mission to the world." That mission is to be a catalyst for the reception of God and God's love. Insofar as Christians remain unable "to unite in full fellowship around the same table to eat the same loaf and drink from the same cup," our ability to succeed in that mission is weakened.[70]

The eucharistic presence of Christ persists through time. The persistent quality of Christ's presence is both an ecumenical problem and an ecclesiological problem. It is an ecclesiological problem for the presence of Christ in the Eucharist touches upon the persistent quality of Christ's presence in the Church. It is an ecumenical problem for the churches do not agree on the question. BEM states that Christ's presence at the Eucharist is for the purpose of receiving him in Communion. The bread and

---

65. "Epicletic" comes from the Greek word *epikaleo*, which means "to call down upon." A concise treatment is found in Herbert Vorgrimler, *Sacramental Theology* (Collegeville: The Liturgical Press, 1992) 149–51. Peter Fink, ed. *Dictionary of Sacramental Worship* (Collegeville: The Liturgical Press, 1990) s. v. "Epiclesis," 390.

66. BEM, 14.

67. *Ibid.*

68. BEM, 26.

69. BEM, 25.

70. *Ibid.*

wine, they said, are "sacramental signs for Christ's body and blood," and they "remain so for the purpose of communion."[71] The authors acknowledge that some churches stress "Christ's presence in the consecrated elements . . . [continuing even] after the celebration [concludes]," while others "place the main emphasis on the act of celebration itself and on the consumption of the elements in the act of communion."[72]

The Group of Les Dombes agreed that the eucharistic presence of Christ fulfills his promise to be present "always, even until the end of the age."[73] The presence of Christ, they agreed, may be *discerned* only "in faith." The reality of the presence of Christ does not depend upon discernment.[74] Christ *is* present, even for those who do not comprehend it. The group agreed, while the presence of Christ is given in order to be consumed, "that which is given as body and blood remains body and blood."[75]

If one allows that the eucharistic elements are the body and blood of Christ for the purpose of extending communion to those who are absent, on what basis do some Churches conclude that the elements somehow cease to be the body and blood of Christ following the communion of the faithful? If the communion of the broken bread and blessed cup in the body and blood of Christ is only temporary, on what basis has one said that bread and cup have *become* the body and blood of Christ? "It is distressing to acknowledge," Robert Jenson writes, "that the question of the temporal *extent* of the eucharistic presence can undo consensus, when that presence itself has been agreed in such seemingly clear language. Yet it turns out so in all dialogues but that of the *Groupe des Dombes*."[76]

The denial of the persistence of the presence of Christ after the celebration has been a problem for Roman Catholics.[77] Catholics maintain that the extension of time between the consecration of the elements and the communion of the faithful is legitimate and that forms of worship appropriate to the enduring presence of the Lord in the elements can also be legitimate. The idea of "sacramental sign" evidenced in the official Roman Catholic response to BEM depends upon the idea of an "intrinsic change" in the elements. There is a "unity of being" that is realized between the "signifying realities" of bread and cup and the "reality that is being signified," Christ's body and blood. There is more than a "change of meaning" for the bread and cup. The change effected in consecration

---

71. BEM, 15.
72. BEM, 32.
73. GLD, 6.
74. GLD, 18.
75. GLD, 19.
76. Jenson, 41, original emphasis.
77. Kilmartin, "Lima Text on the Eucharist," *Catholic Perspectives on BEM*, 156.

is not the change of extrinsic relationships. Rome's response relies upon classical definitions of matter and form.

One may wonder whether a doctrine of real presence absolutely requires the "unity of being" that the Vatican supposes. Could "real presence," from a simply biblical perspective, not be sufficiently described as a "real communion" between the eucharistic elements and the body and blood of Christ? From another perspective one may speak of the relational character of being itself. Relationships are never solely extrinsic and may not be dismissed or discounted. Relationships impinge upon the essential qualities of a thing. If the Roman Catholic Church is to adhere to a doctrine of transubstantiation, as opposed to other possible doctrines of real presence, how does the doctrine contribute to the possibility of salvation? If transubstantiation (and not a more generic doctrine of real presence) were suppressed or denied, how would the possibility of salvation in Christ be undermined?

On the other hand, some statements of Protestant theologians do little to allay Vatican suspicions that their churches' doctrines of the eucharistic presence of Christ are deficient. For example, commenting on the Windsor statement for the Evangelical Council of the Church of England, John Stott lamented.

> If only the commission had had the wisdom of Hugh Latimer before his judges! [Saying:] "that which before was bread now has the dignity to exhibit Christ's body. And yet the bread is still bread, and the wine still wine. For the change is not in the nature, but the dignity.[78]

Likewise the response of the Presbyterian Church of Wales to BEM does not illumine: "'Consecration' signifies the setting apart of the elements for the purpose of communion, with the result that the method of disposal is an irrelevance."[79]

BEM addresses these issues by exhorting the churches to avoid offensive practices. BEM asks Catholics to emphasize reservation of the Eucharist for the purpose of the communion of the sick and the dying. BEM urges Protestants toward greater care for the disposal of elements that have been consecrated for the purpose of communion in Christ. Citing the French Protestant theologian André Birmelé, Robert Jenson has challenged this type of response. "Mere mutual avoidance of offensive practice," he writes, "'does not resolve the theological problem [which is] the posit of a thing-like . . . presence of Christ, separate from the sacramental celebration itself.'"[80]

---

78. John Stott, *Evangelical Anglicans and the* ARCIC *Final Report: An Assessment and Critique* (Bramcote: Grove Books, 1982) 8.

79. Cited in Jenson, 29.

80. Jenson, 29. André Birmelé, *Le Salut en Jésus Christ dans les dialogues oecuméniques* (Paris: Cerf, 1986) 145.

The saving effect of the Eucharist is also at stake, and the question may not be made to hinge solely upon the fact of Christ's presence. From a classic Protestant perspective, the extended devotion (the *latria*) of the Eucharist among Catholics is idolatrous. It attributes an absolute and divine value to finite things, to these creatures of bread and wine. From a classic Catholic perspective, one wonders what can be meant about presence when "someone who denies the persistence of the real presence . . . asserts its occurrence at all"?[81] If Christ and the Spirit cause bread and wine to become sacramental signs of the body and blood of Christ for the purpose of our communion in him, should one suppose that they cease to be sacramental signs only because several portions of bread or wine were not immediately consumed?

The entire question of the meaning of the presence of Christ remains open until the problem of the temporal extent of that presence is resolved. What do Christians mean when they speak of the presence of Christ's body and blood at the Eucharist? First, they must speak of the bodily presence of a person. The body is an original symbol of a person's accessibility to others. As Jenson writes, "A person's body is the person him- or herself, insofar as the person is available."[82] Bodies are vulnerable. They *can* be abused. The eucharistic body of Christ is no different in this respect. One does not deny the presence of the body, then, in order to continue abusing it in another way. The bodily presence of Christ in the Eucharist *can* be abused. All the more reason to reconsider both Protestant and Catholic critiques of one another's eucharistic practices.

There can be no "subjective" presence, no "change of meaning," unless there is first an object. Subjects are things in relationship to other things. The eucharistic presence of Christ, from this perspective, must refer to the establishment in various times and places of a certain critical mass of relational factors which make the thing to become *him* and not just any other thing. When those factors are in place, faith discerns his presence: "He is here and present with us and for us, not as a thing, but as a Savior."

Writing on Paul's theology of the body, John Robinson said that "Man [*sic*] does not *have* a body, he *is* a body."[83] The bodiliness and the incarnation of Christ do not end with the ascension. The mystery of Christ's eucharistic presence will always be "thing-like." One must be careful, then, to avoid treating the "holy things" like mere "things" and not like Christ. Christ is accessible to us *in communion* with his body and

---

81. Jenson, 29.
82. Jenson, 126.
83. Robinson, 14, original emphasis.

blood, in the elements of the bread and cup which the Church has blessed, broken, and poured.

The accessibility of Christ in his body and blood is the chief aim of the doctrine of the presence of Christ in the Eucharist. Doctrines of eucharistic consecration and the epiclesis of the Holy Spirit further clarify the doctrine of Christ's eucharistic presence. When the gathered Church performs the Eucharist in the power of the Spirit, an entire constellation of relationships is established which, here and now, allow faith to perceive Christ present in our communion. The doctrines of eucharistic consecration and the epiclesis of the Holy Spirit, when rightly expressed, allow us to depend on the reliable establishment of that constellation of relationships each time the Church is gathered about the altar. The doctrines of consecration and epiclesis place the conditions of Christ's presence firmly outside the grasp of any human power or authority. Christ's presence is a result of *Christ's* desire to remain with us, by the power of his Spirit, in the manner he has chosen until the end of time. The doctrines do not describe the power of the Church or of its ministers. The Church can never "make Christ appear." The Church can only humbly and confidently receive the gift of Christ's presence. These doctrines demand the Church confess its powerlessness to know and to love God except through the intervention of God's Word and the work of the Holy Spirit.

3. The Church in ecumenical dialogue

The ecumenical dialogue statements considered here have led us toward interesting connections between the Church and the Eucharist. What kind of Church do these dialogue statements envisage? Participants in the ecumenical dialogue groups and commissions assumed that the Church originates in the Eucharist. They agreed that the Eucharist propels the Church outward in mission as a sacramental presence of Christ in the world until his coming again. The Church receives its identity from the Spirit of Christ at the Eucharist as a gift for the world. The communion of the Church thus takes on the character of a sacrament.

Vatican II led the Roman Catholic Church to re-discover the ecclesial dimension of the Eucharist and the eucharistic nature of the communion of the people of God. In a certain sense, *Lumen gentium* and *Sacrosanctum concilium* embraced the principle once voiced by Henri de Lubac: "The Eucharist makes the Church and vice-versa." By the time the council had concluded, the bishops had described a Church fully engaged in the human pilgrimage. This is the legacy of *Gaudium et spes*. The mission of the Church begins with Jesus of Nazareth and continues until the full establishment of the reign of God. The Church can no longer be sufficiently defined with reference to its structural elements alone. Ecclesial structure is a means to the service of God's grace and love. Structure is not an end in itself. It is not enough that a Church have bishops in union with one another and with Rome. They must, in concert, serve the saving mission of Jesus Christ *for the life of the world*. Their ministry must be both prophetic and charismatic. The Eucharist is at the foundation for these claims upon the structure and ministry of the Roman Catholic Church. We should now consider such claims from an ecumenical perspective.

The Group of Les Dombes also concluded that "if the church makes the Eucharist, the Eucharist makes the Church."[84] Such statements, though powerful, must be read carefully. The verb "makes" in the statement must be read equivocally. The Church's "making" of the Eucharist is not the same as the Eucharist's "making" of the Church. The Church performs the actions and speaks the words which comprise the Eucharist. The Church bakes bread and makes wine. The Church brings them into the liturgy. The Church hears God's word and responds in thanksgiving and prayer. The Church blesses, breaks, pours and receives from God's table. In the sense that human actions comprise a ritual performance, the Church "makes" the Eucharist. In the sense that Christ and the Spirit create communion around the eucharistic table, the Eucharist "makes" the Church. Christ, by the Spirit, consecrates the bread and the wine. Christ, by the Spirit, unites communicants to one another in his body. Christ reconciles communicants and so in each Eucharist "re-establishes" his Church here and now, in each locale, at each time. Christ, by the Spirit, enables the Church to fulfill his mission to the world.[85]

Missing from de Lubac's and the Group of Les Dombes' simple slogans is the third, divine element. By the divine mission of Word and Spirit, both the Church and the Eucharist "are made." It happens that they "are made" in the same instant, in the moment of human reception of the divine love, in the "Amen" of each communicant as they receive. ARCIC-I made a similar claim. "Christ through the Holy Spirit in the eucharist," they said, "builds up the life of the church, strengthens its mission, and furthers its mission."[86] The Eucharist and the Church are both effects of the work of Christ and the Spirit on human beings. God's gift of the Word and the Spirit effectively "consecrates" the body of the Church into the body and blood of Jesus Christ. Whether one adopts the "low ecclesiology" of the Church as a voluntary gathering of believers or the "high ecclesiology" of a Church continuing to manifest the incarnation of Christ through time and place, the result is the same. The Church

84. GLD, 21.
85. GLD, 13.
86. Windsor, 3.

is not separable from the saving mission of God through Christ and the Spirit. Every ecclesial structure such as the council, the primacy, the episcopate, the diocese, or the assembly must either serve that soteriological end, it must be reformed, or it must be abolished.

From a purely human perspective, the Church is sociological and voluntary. From a sacramental perspective, the Church is divine in origin and it must be ordered toward the reconciliation of God with humankind. The ritual acts which comprise the Eucharist have both a human and a divine purpose. They signify in both directions establishing horizontal and vertical dimensions of communion. The Church, too, comprises both horizontal and vertical dimensions of communion. The Church is an historical and sociological extension of the table-fellowship *(haburah)* of the earthly Jesus as much as it is a location of the divine love breaking in once again upon human life.[87]

Some Catholics and others may want a stronger guarantee. They might wish us to say that the Eucharist makes claims upon God, that our ritual acts always and everywhere can "do their work." They might want to be certain the Church is always in communion with God. They might want to know that the rites we perform at the altar always point to and participate in the divine reality. Who can be so sure?

At least the actions and words of the Church which comprise the liturgy nearly always represent a human community drawn together in sacrificial love. However, one cannot leap from that statement to claim that the actions and words of the Church by themselves establish a relationship with God. The Eucharist may always *signify*—by intention if not in reality—the love and grace of God. Yet it is God alone who uses the Eucharist—"as an instrument," according to Thomas Aquinas—to *effect* the love and grace that exist among us. The *sign-value* of the Eucharist may depend upon *human beings* and may change with reference to time and place. The *effectiveness* of the Eucharist depends entirely on *God* who does not change and who desires to draw all humankind, indeed all of creation, into communion with God's self. The Church depends upon God for its communion in Christ.

The Eucharist is a collective act and is not the act of an individual. The Eucharist may have once depended upon the acts of an individual person, Jesus of Nazareth. Jesus invited people into table-fellowship with him. He shared a final meal with his disciples. After his resurrection, he made his presence known among them "in the breaking of the bread." Today, the Eucharist is an act of the Church. When the Church proclaims God's word, receives the gifts of the earth transformed by human labor, remembers Christ's passion, death, and resurrection. When the Church

---

87. BEM, 1.

welcomes Christ and the stranger to its table, the Church acts as a whole, even if these acts are performed by a few people, or by one person. Collectively the Church looks forward to Christ's final appearing. Together the Church is united in commitment to God and, in solidarity, to one another.[88] The minister does not perform these actions in isolation, but with the consent of the Church.

Catholics and Protestants can affirm the collective agency of the Church in the Eucharist. Acting together in worship, the Church finds itself entangled in a new relationship with God and the world. Performing their worship and receiving the Eucharist, Christians find themselves drawn into a personality which extends beyond the horizon of their experience, faith, and understanding. In very technical language, this larger thing is sometimes called the "ecclesial consciousness," or the ecclesial being. It is the *hypostatization* of the communion of the Church. That is to say, the ecclesial being *is* Christ, insofar as Christ is the consummation of the Church—both head and members. At the Eucharist our solidarity in commitment to one another, our mutual remembrance of Christ, our participation in the holy meal are all the acts of the Church and *as such* they are acts of Christ. Having enacted the Eucharist, the Church is aware of having been "acted upon" and "acted through." Contemplating its own actions, the Church encounters a reality that challenges and appears to transcend its finitude.

Arguments against the eucharistic sacrifice are nearly always ethical or soteriological. Few deny that the Church *could* offer sacrifices to God. With a word we could erect hundreds and thousands of bloodied, smoky altars tomorrow. The real question is ethical: *should* the Church be offering sacrifices at all? The soteriological question is similar. Is the Eucharist the kind of sacrifice that God finds *acceptable*? For Protestants the problem is not that the Church is unable to offer sacrifice, but that it cannot *ethically* offer a sacrifice to a saving effect. It has been a common mistake, however, to argue from the inability of the Church to offer an efficacious and ethical *sacrifice* to the Church's impotence to do *anything at all* on its own behalf before God. Quietism was the historical result of such arguments.

From a Roman Catholic perspective, to speak of the Church's sacrifice in the Eucharist is possible only because the Eucharist is already part of the one, sole sacrifice of Christ—of which the Church, as Christ's body, is a partner. The Catholic response is to identify the acts of the Church with the acts of Christ, because the acts of the Church are acts of those who live in communion as Christ's body.

---

88. Windsor, 4.

In his monograph on the ARCIC Final Report, John Stott rejected this view and categorically distinguished the acts of the Church from the acts of Christ. " . . . [T]o respond to [Christ's] self-offering and to 'enter into its movement' are two quite different concepts. Indeed, . . . [they] move in quite opposite directions."[89] The Church, Stott was claiming, is able to respond to Christ's self-offering; it cannot identify with him in his saving work. Whether the Church can act as Christ finally reduces to this question: Can the Church act *sacramentally?* Can we "see" the saving work of Christ within and through the work of the Church? The answer churches provide to this question profoundly affects their understanding of ministry.

The Group of Les Dombes stated that the eucharistic assembly "receives [the Eucharist] from Another."[90] The origin of the Eucharist outside of the Church, they said, is signified in the person of the minister, who, "remaining a member of the congregation . . . is at the same time the man [*sic*] sent to signify God's action and the link between the local community and the other communities in the universal Church."[91] The group believed that the minister signifies the presidency of Christ who "gathers together and feeds his Church."[92]

Many Christians may agree it is fitting or apt for the Church to delegate and ordain presiding ministers. They do not necessarily agree on the consequences of such delegation. Some may dissent from the view that the minister represents Christ over against the Church. One may respond that the Church is less confronted by "Another" in the Eucharist than it is offered an image of its own true "Self." The Eucharist, as the site for the encounter with Christ, is more like a "mirror" or a "lens." Should the Church encounter Christ as a "foreigner" or an "outsider," that should be a signal for pastoral action. It should not be considered the status quo.

Theologies of ministry, I believe, cannot presume that ministers always represent Christ over and against the Church. They also represent the Christian community to itself—in its best and in its worst aspects. Ministers signify the faithfulness (or unfaithfulness) of the entire communion. They symbolize the Church's sense of mission (or apathy toward mission). Ministers are rarely effective when they impose their will on Churches with the alienating power of a tyrant. Ministry, as evidenced in the prophetic ministry of Jesus, is more effectively exercised by intimates, in vulnerability, to the point of failure. If Christian ministry follows an incarnational and sacrificial model, if it is a ministry in service to *communion*, it will be a ministry of powerlessness among the powerless.

89. Stott, 7.
90. GLD, 14.
91. *Ibid.*
92. GLD, 32–33.

The *eucharistic* ministry of a *eucharistic* Church will enter (and always seek to enter more deeply) into the *kenotic* movement of Christ's sacrificial love.

Martin Buber's classic formulation of the "I-Thou" relationship may assist in the description of ecclesial communion. The Church is called to conform to its nature as the body of Christ. Christian communion presupposes that the existential chasm between Self and Other is bridged by Christ in the Spirit. The Church ("Self") and Christ ("Other") are conjoined in a communion of love. The Church becomes the opposite of alienation and the self-awareness of the Church blurs into its awareness of itself-as-Christ by the Spirit's power.

In communion, "I" and "thou" are joined in the dance of divine love. The ancient Greek writers called this the *perichoresis* of the divine persons. The root word *-choresis* is similar to the English word "choreography," meaning dance. With its prefix "*peri-,*" *perichoresis* means "to dance around." In the sacramental order, there is not one person, Christ, over against another person, the Church. They are united in a dance of *kenotic*, sacrificial love and the gestures of one are freely and gracefully matched by the gestures of the other. Both partners give themselves over to one another's movements *for the sake of the dancing*. So the Church and Christ unite *perichoretically*. They freely move together *for the sake of the saving mission*.

Catherine LaCugna summarized this view in a remarkable passage. "The starting point in the economy of redemption . . . locates *perichoresis* not in God's inner life but in the mystery of the one communion of all persons, divine as well as human. . . ."[93] Communion in human life is not different from the communion in God. All our knowledge of the communion in God wells up from the communion we experience in human life. There is only *one* dance, God's dance and we are part of it. "The one *perichoresis*, the one mystery of communion," according to LaCugna, "includes God and humanity as beloved partners in the dance."[94] Even in the horizontal communion of the secular society, God may not be excluded but joins in the dancing, an "unknown partner." In effect, there is no "vertical" communion with God, except within and through the "horizontal" communion of the Church. The "way to God," says Orthodox theologian John Zizioulas, "has to pass *through* the relationship with the neighbour."[95]

---

93. LaCugna, 274.

94. *Ibid.*

95. John Zizioulas, "The Early Christian Community," in *Christian Spirituality: Origins to the Twelfth Century*, ed. Bernard McGinn, John Meyendorff, Jean Leclerq (London: Routledge and Kegan Paul, 1986) 37. McPartlan, 276.

Catholicity is the result of the *perichoresis* of God with humankind in the communion of the Church. Too often, well-meaning and intelligent men and women confuse "catholicity" with "universality." The universal character of the Church is not the same as its catholicity. The word "catholic" comes from the Greek, "*katholou*" and means, roughly, "according to the whole." The word "universal," suggests that the Church exists "everywhere and for all times." Instead, to be "catholic" means to exist in relation to the whole. In ecclesiology, it refers to the way in which the whole body of Christ is manifest in each local church. Very simply, because of their catholicity local churches are not "defective," they are not a mere "part" of the Church. In the sacramental economy, whenever the body of Christ is encountered, the *whole* Christ is encountered. Whenever Christ is met in a particular place and time in whatever form (eucharistic, ecclesial, natural), the *whole* Christ is met.

The Group of Les Dombes described the "catholicity" of the Eucharist. "The sharing of the one bread and the one cup in a given place makes the communicants one with the whole Christ, with one another, and with all other communicants at all times and in all places."[96] The authors of BEM expanded this definition.

> The sharing in the one bread and the common cup in a given place demonstrates and effects the oneness of the sharers with Christ and with their fellow sharers in all times and places. It is in the eucharist that the community of God's people is fully manifested. Eucharistic celebrations always have to do with the whole church, and the whole church is involved in each local eucharistic celebration.[97]

Communion in Christ is therefore never partial. This idea is similar to the communion of partners in marriage. Partners in marriage are always in "communion" with one another. Their communion of love may be expressed more or less completely in certain times and places than in others. Partners in love may not *know* their spouse entirely. Spouses remain mysteries to one another, even in their golden years. It is a good thing they do, else they would too easily bore one another. We ascribe the love of partners, even when they can only express their love partially, to the *whole spouse*. The signs a woman enacts in love of her husband express or signify the *entirety* of her love for the *entire* person of her husband. The signs of her love are *catholic*, even though she can never love him *entirely*.

Similarly, the local church is always in "communion" with Christ. Its communion of love may be more fully expressed at certain times and places than in others. Christ remains a mystery to the Church. None can

96. GLD, 21.
97. BEM, 19.

know Christ in fullness. While the Church's signs, expressions, and knowledge are never capable of conveying all of its love for Christ, they do express or signify the *entirety* of the Church's love for the *entire* person of Christ.

In each Eucharist, Christ is wholly accessible. The Eucharist is *catholic* because Christ expresses the entirety of his love for the Church at this meal. Catholicity is a result of Christ's desire and ability to remain present by his Spirit with the Church, wherever and whenever it is gathered. There is a catholicity with respect to place—Christ present in the Upper Room, as at Emmaus, as in Antioch or in Rome. There is a catholicity with respect to time—Christ present in 50 c. e. as in 1050 as in 1950. The catholicity of the relationship between Christ and the Church bears important ramifications for ecumenism and for the nature of the Church itself.

All three of the ecumenical dialogue statements considered here affirm the Eucharist as a sacramental anticipation of the communion of saints. The Windsor statement called the Eucharist an anticipation of the "eschatological banquet," "the first fruits of the new heaven and the new earth."[98] The Group of Les Dombes called the Eucharist a "banquet of the kingdom."[99] The Eucharist is always a "sign of the kingdom."[100] The Eucharist signifies "what the world is to become."[101] The Holy Spirit is the agent of this signification.

Ecumenical dialogue has been content to describe salvation in eschatological terms. The Final Report of ARCIC-I gives no sense that salvation will be ecclesial or collective. Yet, it stands to reason that, if the Eucharist anticipates the "eschatological banquet," then the eschatological banquet will be in some sense "ecclesial" and "eucharistic." BEM claimed that the Eucharist creates the unity of all believers both synchronically, right now, and diachronically, throughout the flow of time.[102] The unity of the Church is not limited by time because Christ possesses the whole of the Church in a communion that transcends time. The unity of the Church is not limited by space because Christ possesses the whole of the Church in a communion that transcends geography. This lack of limitations is not primarily a quality of the Church. It is first a quality of the risen Savior, who is not limited with respect to space or time. It is second a quality of the Eucharist, by the communication of idioms. *Christ's* accessibility and presence in the Eucharist is not limited with respect to space or time. Finally, it is a quality of the Church. *Christ's* accessibility

98. Windsor, 11.
99. GLD, 29–31.
100. BEM, 1.
101. BEM, 4.
102. BEM, 18.

and presence in the Church is not limited with respect to space or time.[103] The Church does not possess this quality in a simple sense, because the *Church is* limited. It is not everywhere. It has not occurred in every time. However, wherever the Church has been, Christ has been there too. This claim only makes sense if Christ is, as Paul believed, "all in all."[104]

4. Conclusion

Ecumenical dialogue on the Eucharist has profoundly challenged our traditional understandings of the Church. Communion ecclesiology depends on the identity in distinction of the "body of Christ" in the Church and in the Eucharist. Communion ecclesiology will always emphasize the local eucharistic assembly as the primary location of the Church. The local church is the place where Christ and the Church are known and experienced in faith and worship. The local church is the place where the Word is preached and heard. Every sacrament is enacted and received in the local church. The local church, in openness, is established as a communion with every other local church and with the local churches of all times and places.

Communion ecclesiology is challenged to describe the relationship between the local church and the whole Church. The relationship between local churches and the assembly of all Christians from every time and place must be assessed with great precision. In the absence of a principle of unity between local churches, communion ecclesiologies tend to be indistinguishable from congregationalism, with its emphasis on local autonomy.

Congregationalism poses unique challenges for communion ecclesiology. If local assemblies are sectarian and isolationist, their relationship with nearby churches may be strained or non-existent. Such isolated churches cause serious ecclesiological problems. In their life and practices, they exhibit the idea that salvation is almost inaccessible, or that it is primarily available to their own members. Their church may also exhibit the individualist's creed that each church can work out salvation on its own terms. The individualistic piety of "me and Jesus" can infect the group consciousness. The isolated church suggests that "we and Jesus" are enough. Communion ecclesiology by contrast must strongly insist on an expansive rhetoric of inclusion. "We and Jesus" must mean everyone. The Church is not identical with any small group, even if the small group is a bona fide local church. Catholicity is no excuse for sectarianism.

Local eucharistic assemblies will successfully embrace their identity as the people of God only to the extent that they view themselves in an

103. Cf. Jenson, 137.
104. Eph 1:23.

open rather than closed fashion. The image of the Church as people of God suggests that Christ's body is in a process of cultivation. We are "being built up into Christ." Christ's redemptive work, because it is *epha-pax*, is happening whenever there are people whom Christ desires to save.

Communion ecclesiology helps us see how Christ and the Church are first known and experienced in closeness and intimacy. The Church will always be "local" and "particular," because it will always be "incarnate" and "inculturated." But this intimacy and closeness must also be transparent to a wider vision of the Church's situation within the people of God as a whole. Tillard gives this wider vision a name. The "Church of God," he calls it, "from Abel the just."[105] Can contemporary Christians see their way through the intimacy of local assemblies and base communities, to a universal vision of a united Church? Will they be able to embrace a vision of the Eucharist as invitation to open table fellowship? Will the Church know again the ineffable intimacy of the messianic banquet, the festal *haburah* which Jesus once shared with disciples?

The eucharistic table is aptly called a "borderless board" because it was prepared by God to be the place where Christians dine with enemies in order to become their friends. In a powerful essay, Lauree Hersch Meyer called the Church's failure to acknowledge salvation wherever it is found "Christian idolatry." "Christian idolatry," she writes, "is a posture that subverts the gospel of Jesus Christ. . . ."[106] Christian idolatry treats salvation as a possession, whereas salvation is more properly understood as being possessed by Christ in love. If salvation were a possession, then the powerful in Church and society could try to manage it. She observes that when the powerless and "others" nevertheless receive the "crumbs that fall from our table, we rage when 'they' enjoy what *we* do not bestow."[107]

Communion ecclesiology must not become a shill for the maintenance of ecclesial power-brokers and clerical prestige. If the Church is truly focused on the Eucharist, it should avoid this error. Our power is in weakness, Paul wrote; our strength is in mutual vulnerability. The doctrine of the sacrifice of the Eucharist tells us that eucharistic communion is first and foremost a communion in the paschal mystery, in Christ's powerlessness and servant-nature.

In themselves as human societies, the churches possess no inherent unity. There is nothing in human society, in human nature, in our cul-

---

105. EDE, 114f. CofC, 83ff.
106. Lauree Hersch Meyer, ". . . And Then Turn South . . .," *Women and Church: The Challenge of Ecumenical Solidarity in an Age of Alienation,* Faith and Order Series / USA, National Council of Churches of Christ in the USA, ed. Melanie A. May (Grand Rapids: Eerdmans, 1991) 26.
107. *Ibid.*

tures, that impels us toward a world without borders. The churches, however, are a countersign of this centrifugal tendency. Where do the churches acquire this countercultural, *unnatural*, characteristic? They are gathered into one through Christ and the power of his Spirit. The churches could be no more united than Parliament or Congress, the European Union or the United Nations, if they were not the creation and expression of a single person who transcends them all and collects them into a living body. If the churches are to manifest unity and not obscure it, then all of their actions and structures, their doctrines and ministers must be grounded in their dependence upon the Spirit and Word of God. The clarity with which the image of Christ is seen in any local church will vary in direct proportion to that community's collective dependence on God. God's *kenosis* in love creates our communion; our communion is a *kenosis* in God's love. The communion of churches is a direct outcome of this dynamic.[108]

108. Cf. Francine Cardman, "BEM and the Community of Men and Women," *JES* 21/1 (1984) 88.

Questions for meditation and dialogue on "Church and Eucharist in Ecumenical Perspective"

1. *Substance of faith.* What, for you, is the "substance of faith"? When you describe faith for others or express faith in action, are you able to touch the central core of Christian faith? How do you handle differences in the expression of faith with other Christians—in your family, in your church, with members of other churches?

2. *Ecumenism.* What do you imagine will be the outcome of the ecumenical movement as you understand it? Is this outcome desirable or undesirable? Do you believe the union of the churches will be the result of Christians having agreed "on everything" or their having determined to "tolerate one another's differences"?

3. *Eucharistic presence of Jesus.* Does your church emphasize the presence of Jesus *in* the elements of bread and wine or *in* the actions of the Church? What word best describes your understanding of Jesus' presence—memory, thing, person, friend, judge, sacrifice, or forgiveness? Does anyone ever treat Jesus' presence in the Eucharist like a mere thing?

4. *Sacrifice and Eucharist.* Does your church ever talk about the Eucharist as a "sacrifice"? Why or why not? Could you possibly experience the Eucharist as a "self-offering?" How do you or the members of your church feel about the phrase, "in the Eucharist we enter into the movement of Christ's self-offering"? In what ways do you recognize the Cross and sacrifice of Jesus in the Eucharist?

5. *Eucharist and the Spirit of God.* Many Christians and churches share powerful experiences of the Spirit in special gifts, like speaking in tongues or "Spirit baptism." In many other churches, the Eucharist is a highly structured, ritualized event. How do you make sense of the presence of the Spirit at the Eucharist? Do you think it is possible to reconcile the "highly structured" character of the Eucharist with the "freely given" experience some associate with the outpouring of the Holy Spirit? For you, is the Church more "charismatic" or "institutional?"

FOR FURTHER READING

Cardman, Francine. "BEM and the Community of Men and Women," *JES* 21/1 (1984) 83–95.

Dix, Gregory. *The Shape of the Liturgy.* New York: Seabury, 1982.

Fahey, Michael, ed. *Catholic Perspectives on "Baptism, Eucharist, and Ministry."* Lanham, Md.: University Press of America, 1986.

Jensen, Robert. *The Unbaptized God: The Basic Flaw in Ecumenical Theology.* Minneapolis: Fortress Press, 1992.

May, Melanie A., ed. *Women and Church: The Challenge of Ecumenical Solidarity in an Age of Alienation.* Faith and Order Series/USA, National Council of Churches of Christ in the USA. Grand Rapids: Eerdmans, 1991.

McPartlan, Paul. *Sacrament of Salvation: An Introduction to Eucharistic Ecclesiology.* Edinburgh: T & T Clard, 1995.

Meyer, Harding and Lukas Vischer, eds. *Growth in Agreement: Reports and Agreed Statements of Ecumenical Conversations on a World Level.* Ecumenical documents 2, Faith and Order Paper 108. New York and Geneva: Paulist Press and WCC Publications, 1984.

Nilson, Jon. *Nothing Beyond the Necessary: Roman Catholicism and the Ecumenical Future.* New York: Paulist Press, 1995.

Thurian, Max, ed. *Churches Respond to BEM: Official Responses to the "Baptism, Eucharist, and Ministry" text.* 9 vols. Geneva: WCC Publications, 1988.

CHAPTER FOUR

Ecumenism at Risk

I wish to say a few words about the official Vatican response to the ecumenical statements considered in the previous chapter. The Catholic Church has issued official responses and preliminary observations to the Windsor statement, the ARCIC-I Final Report with Elucidations. There is the recent response of Cardinal Cassidy to ARCIC-II regarding the 1994 Clarifications on the Final Report which went a long way to soothe disappointment over the official responses. The official response of the Roman Catholic Church to BEM is also an important document. Finally, there is John Paul II's encyclical on Christian unity, *Ut unum sint*.[1]

In all these statements the Vatican speaks in two voices. One voice praises the participants of ecumenical progress. This voice applauds the many substantive points of agreement that have been reached. Another

---

1. For further commentary see David Brown, "The Response to ARCIC-I: The Big Questions," *OIC* 28 (1992) 148–54. George Carey, "Comments of the Archbishop of Canterbury on the Response of ARCIC-I," *OIC* 28 (1992) 49–50. Gillian R. Evans, "Rome's Response to ARCIC and the Problem of Confessional Identity," *OIC* 28 (1992) 155–67. Howard Root, "Some Remarks on the Response to ARCIC-I," in Evans and Gourgues, 165–76. Francis A. Sullivan, "The Vatican Response to ARCIC-I," *OIC* 28 (1992) 223–31. Jean-Marie R. Tillard, "Roman Catholics and Anglicans: Is there a future for ecumenism?" *OIC* 32 (1996) 106–17. George Tavard, "Considerations on an Ecclesiology of *Koinonia*," *OIC* 31 (1995) 42–51. Catherine Clifford, "Reception of the *Final Report*: Beyond Strengthened Agreement," *OIC* 32 (1996) 130–48. Jon Nilson, *Nothing Beyond the Necessary: Roman Catholicism and the Ecumenical Future* (New York: Paulist Press, 1995). Konrad Raiser, *Ecumenism in Transition: A Paradigm Shift in the Ecumenical Movement?* (Geneva: WCC Publications, Inc., 1991).

Official responses to Windsor, Elucidations and Clarifications: CDF, "Observations on the ARCIC Final Report," *Origins* 11 (May 6, 1982) 752–56; *AAS* 74 (1982) 1060–74. CDF and PCPCU, "The Official Response of the Roman Catholic Church to ARCIC-I," December 1991. Reprinted in *OIC* 28 (1992) 38–48. President of PCPCU, Cardinal Edward Cassidy, Letter to the co-chairs of ARCIC-II, March 11, 1994, *Origins* 24 (October 6, 1994) 299f.

Official response to BEM: CDF and PCPCU, "Official Response of the Roman Catholic Church to *Baptism, Eucharist and Ministry*," in *Churches Respond to BEM: Official Responses to the "Baptism, Eucharist and Ministry" text*, vol. VI, Faith and Order Paper 144, ed. Max Thurian (Geneva: World Council of Churches, 1988) 20–25.

John Paul II, Encyclical on ecumenism, *Ut unum sint*, May 25, 1995; *Origins* 25 (June 8, 1995) 49–72.

voice sounds more harsh. The second voice, critical of what it terms "ambiguities" and "imprecisions," sometimes sounds as though non-Catholics are being asked for one-hundred percent agreement to the doctrines and practices of the Catholic Church. This combination of two voices would not be a problem except for the absence of a third voice. A third voice might announce the actions Catholics will take to answer the doubts and concerns of non-Catholic Christians. The combination of the first two voices too easily sound like a milder, toned-down version of the "ecumenism of return." The addition of a third voice along with some modest, yet genuine, movement toward other Christians, might have ensured a warmer reception for these Vatican responses.

Perhaps the most harsh of the official statements was the first. The CDF statement, "Observations on the ARCIC Final Report," March 29, 1982, criticized the Windsor statement for its treatment of eucharistic sacrifice, the real presence of Christ in the Eucharist, and the reservation and adoration of the Eucharist. The CDF's responses referred to an interpretation of Catholic doctrines, quoting sources in the acts of the Council of Trent, Paul VI's encyclical on the Eucharist, *Mysterium fidei*, and John Paul II's apostolic letter on the Eucharist, *Dominicae coenae.*[2]

Addressing the issue of eucharistic sacrifice, the CDF was concerned to protect the propitiatory value of the Eucharist.[3] The desire to protect the power of the priest to effect the eucharistic sacrifice of Christ seems to lie at the heart of this problem. An ecclesiology of communion enhances the entrance of the Church—the entire Church, not just the minister—into the *kenosis* of Christ. The leadership and ministry of the priest is to serve this movement, to model the *kenosis* of Christ, so that the Church as a whole may enter into this movement of powerlessness and *ascesis.*

Addressing the issue of real presence, the CDF voiced the genuinely deep commitment of Roman Catholics to the doctrine of transubstantiation.[4] One wonders what is gained, after committing to the doctrine of the real (corporeal, personal, and saving) presence of Christ in the eucharistic elements, as had the authors of the Windsor statement and Elucidations, by further insisting that the broken bread and blessed wine are no longer bread or wine? The presence of Christ in, with, and through the Church is an essential part of an ecclesiology of communion. We do not suppose, however, that the Church has abandoned its human condition, or that Christ cannot subsist within the human condition of our earthly communion. Proponents of a doctrine of transubstantiation must

2. Paul VI, *Mysterium fidei.* John Paul II, Apostolic letter to all the bishops of the Church about the mystery and worship of the Eucharist, calling for a continuation of the renewal, *Dominicae coenae*, February 24, 1980.

3. Observations, B.I.1.

4. Observations, B.I.2.

be challenged to consider why bread must abandon its "breadness" and wine its *vinitas* in order for the earthly creatures to become fitting vehicles for Christ's presence. What does the doctrine accomplish *soteriologically* that is otherwise at jeopardy?

Addressing questions related to the reservation and worship of the Eucharist, the CDF seemed to fear the loss of a metaphysical warrant for such practices.[5] If the elements remain in any sense creaturely, then does the worship which is offered to Christ before them become idolatrous? The CDF Observations cite the Council of Trent, concluding that the worship of the eucharistic elements was a matter of dogma.[6] Yet if one reads the decrees carefully, the council did not *require* devotional practices and devotional practice was not among the reasons given for the worship of Christ in the Eucharist. The canon relating to this point does not condemn those who do not take part in eucharistic devotions. It condemns only those who hold the practices idolatrous on the grounds that Christ should not be worshipped in the Eucharist. The authors of ARCIC neither condemned eucharistic devotion nor did they require it. Communion ecclesiology might be less interested in the eucharistic elements as objects of worship than it might be interested in redefining the nature of worship as such. Need worship continue to imply distance, fear or awe? May worship be reconsidered in light of our relationship to God and one another? What does eucharistic worship say about justice, love, mutual respect? How does it build communion?

In its response to BEM, the Vatican congregations raised many of the same points. For Catholics, they stated, "the conversion of the elements is a matter of faith and is only open to possible new theological explanations as to the 'how' of the intrinsic change. The content of the word 'transubstantiation' ought to be expressed without ambiguity."[7] The paragraph continues, "there is a unity of being . . . realized between the signifying reality and the reality signified." Yet, the authors contend that BEM remains open to an interpretation of "change" which implies that the gifts only undergo a change of meaning through nothing more than the establishment of an extrinsic relationship.[8] The authors write, "Tran-

5. Observations, B.I.3.

6. Council of Trent, Decree on the eucharist, *Sacrosancta oecumenica*, October 11, 1551; Tanner, 695. Chapter 5, " . . . [I]t is not less worthy of adoration because it was instituted by Christ the Lord in order to be consumed." See also Canon 6, "If anyone says that Christ, the only-begotten Son of God, is not to be adored in the holy sacrament of the Eucharist by the worship of adoration, including its outward expression; . . . *anathema sit*," Tanner, 698.

7. Response to BEM, 20.

8. Response to BEM, 23.

substantiation is a central mystery of faith," and Catholics "cannot accept expressions [of that mystery] that are ambiguous."[9]

1. To hear the voice and wisdom of non-Catholics

In each of these three cases, the CDF authors seemed to have missed the point. Non-Catholics do not doubt that these are the official Catholic positions. The majority of non-Catholic Christians do not doubt the real presence and other eucharistic doctrines. Non-Catholics are far more interested in hearing Catholics once again consider and question their tradition for its conformity to fundamental issues of faith. In an ecumenical context it is insufficient proof to advert to authoritative Church statements. Even if the decrees and canons of Trent are true, one hardly expects Protestant and Orthodox Christians to be persuaded to agree because Vatican authorities reassert them. Non-Catholics are far more interested in the reasons Catholics produce in support of their beliefs and practices. "Because Trent says so," or "Vatican I," or "Vatican II," or "the pope" are not reasons. They sound more like excuses for maintaining division.

The response of non-Catholics to developments in doctrine since the Great Schism and the Reformation should be heard sympathetically, for they represent a part of the "mind of the Church" on such questions. Their resistance to Catholic definitions suggests that at least parts of the standard formulations of Catholic doctrines may, however unintentionally, lead to unacceptable consequences. The inability of Catholic Church leaders to hear the voices and receive the wisdom of non-Catholics is part of the "wound" the Church suffers for its divisions. The substantial agreements reached in ecumenical dialogues should not be lost because Catholics are allowed to accept only exact quotations of authoritative teachings.

The reader's indulgence requested if I have emphasized the second voice of the Vatican responses at the expense of the first. It remains that the "two voices" sound very much like a dialogue internal to the Roman Catholic Church at this point in its history. These "two voices" can be seen in the documents and revisions of the decrees of Vatican II and in the various documents implementing the liturgical and other reforms following the council. The official responses suggest that some Vatican authorities consider Roman Catholic doctrine on the Eucharist and the Church a "closed book," while others are eager to hear the wisdom of non-Catholics. The responses suggest that some authorities have not sufficiently considered how the dialogue statements challenge and enrich the Catholic tradition on the Eucharist. The new statements forged in ecumenical dialogue provide the churches with the vocabulary needed to

---

9. Response to BEM, 22.

develop doctrines and establish practices more likely to unite the Church than to solidify divisions.

In a 1980 article, Jean-Marie Tillard described the temptation to read Catholic doctrine like a closed book among the easiest temptations for Roman Catholics.[10] There is, he observed, a desire to find the whole of the "catholic datum" in the convergence and agreed statements even on those points of doctrine only made explicit after ecclesial divisions had occurred. To confuse contemporary Roman Catholicism with the fullness of the apostolic faith, he warned, will not aid but will hinder ecumenical endeavors.[11] Roman Catholics must begin to recognize and trust the apostolic faith as it subsists in the communions of other Christians.

2. Ut unum sint—*the unity of truth*

John Paul II's encyclical on Christian unity, *Ut unum sint*, touches specifically upon the question of the ecclesial status on non-Catholic churches and it advocates redefining ecumenism as the outgrowth of a communion in truth. In the encyclical the Pope focuses on and seeks to create a definitive interpretation for this key phrase from *Lumen gentium*, "the church of Christ . . . subsists in the catholic church, governed by the successor of Peter and the bishops in communion with him."[12] Overall, the tone of the encyclical is warm and gracious. Major portions of the letter reaffirm the ecumenical perspective of Vatican II, and the Pope especially encourages ecumenical initiatives between Roman Catholic, Orthodox, and other Eastern churches. He calls upon Catholics to deepen their commitment to ecumenism "on all levels."[13]

John Paul addresses the ecclesial status of other Christian churches in section 11. The "one Church of Christ" is "effectively present" within other Christian communities and churches and they possess, he writes, a "certain, though imperfect communion" with the Roman Catholic Church.[14] This imperfect communion is constituted by the 'elements of sanctification and truth" which are present to varying degree in the other churches. It is important to note that John Paul did not say that the ecclesial deficiency exists in the other churches. Deficiency exists in the *relationship between* the other churches and the Roman Catholic Church. The communion of the churches is deficient, not the communion in the other churches as such. John Paul states there is no ecclesial boundary

10. Tillard, "Preparing for Unity," *OIC* 16 (1980) 9.
11. *Ibid.*
12. LG, 8. The original reads "Haec est unica Christi ecclesia . . . in hoc mundo ut societas constituta et ordinata *subsistit in ecclesia catholica*, a successore Petri et episcopis in eius communione gubernata . . .," emphasis added.
13. UUS, 80.
14. UUS, 11.

"beyond the boundaries of the catholic community." He continues, "Many elements of great value are also found in the other Christian communities."[15]

In the Catholic Church, however, the Pope claims that these "elements of great value" are "part of the fullness of the means of salvation and of the gifts of grace which make up the church."[16] Sins and deficiencies caused by members of the Catholic Church "cannot destroy what God has bestowed on the [Catholic Church] as part of his plan of grace."[17] In a particularly bold statement, the Pope describes the Catholic Church in light of the eschatological fullness of the Church given by Christ and the Spirit:

> The Catholic Church believes that in the Pentecost event God has already manifested the Church in her eschatological reality, which he had prepared 'from the time of Abel, the just one.' This reality is something already given. Consequently we are even now in the last times. The elements of this already-given Church exist, found in their fullness in the Catholic Church and, without this fullness, in the other Christian communities.[18]

In section 18, John Paul writes that unity among Christians is a result of adherence to the truth. "The unity willed by God," he writes, "can be attained only by the adherence of all to the content of revealed faith in its entirety." He adds, "a 'being together' which betrayed the truth would thus be opposed both to the nature of God who offers his communion and to the need for truth found in the depths of every human heart."[19] "Full communion," he declares, "will have to come about through the acceptance of the whole truth into which the Holy Spirit guides Christ's disciples."[20] There are few objections one can raise to such claims. To suggest that the Catholic Church *already* adheres in the "unity of truth," and that it has already accepted "the whole truth," but that other churches do not and have not—such suggestions *would* be a great obstacle to Christian ecumenism.

In the next paragraph, John Paul cites a recent declaration of the CDF which may be interpreted by some as making such a claim. In its declaration in defense of catholic doctrine on the Church, *Mysterium ecclesiae*, the CDF makes four claims. (1) Revealed truth is distinct from changeable conceptions of it. (2) Declared doctrine is sometimes expressed in terms which "bear the traces of such changeable conceptions." (3) Dogmatic

15. UUS, 13.
16. *Ibid.*
17. UUS, 11.
18. UUS, 14.
19. UUS, 18.
20. UUS, 36.

formulas are suitable for conveying revealed truth, or at least they are not *a priori* unsuitable. (4) When dogmatic formulas are interpreted correctly they remain suitable vehicles for revealed truth.[21] There is little to object to in this argument. However, the Pope and the CDF authors commit a fallacy should they use this argument to make a blanket statement about the truth-value of any particular magisterial statements.

The content of faith, I contend, is relational. It is not propositional. The content of faith does not consist of the mere assent to a series of statements. It must consist of the adherence of a whole person to Christ as Christ reveals himself to that person over the course of a lifetime. Adherence to Christ, who is the Truth, must be sufficient for Christian unity. Adherence to Christ is established in baptism. Assent to doctrinal propositions is not, in itself, the cause of unity.

In the sacraments the whole Christ is received. Even the Christ who remains hidden from the intellect, the *Christus absconditus*, is received by faith in communion. Communion in truth cannot mean adherence to a closed set of propositions. It must remain open to the encounter with the whole Christ, *even the Christ which the Church does not yet entirely comprehend*. Communion in truth must therefore consist of the will to live in communion with all who seek the truth wherever that path leads. The communion of the Church must not be limited only to those who presume to possess the truth in its entirety because they do not question the historical formulations of truth.

The Pope suggests that the results of bilateral discussions must become part of the "common heritage."[22] They must be judged, at all levels, by "the whole people of God." Their reception requires, he says, a "universal consent." Ecumenism, therefore, must consist of a dialogue of conversion. The relationship among Christians, he says, must be "something more than a mere cordial understanding or external sociability. The bonds of fraternal *koinonia* must be forged before God and in Christ Jesus."[23] The success of ecumenism depends, the Pope concludes, upon obedience to the will of the Spirit who gives us the ability to become one.

One may reasonably ask how John Paul's idea of ecumenism differs from Pius XI's ecumenism of return. The subtleties of the Pope's considerations do not allow one to equate the two. The ecumenism of return assumes that non-Catholic Christians and their communities ought to converge on a predetermined set of truths, truths enshrined in doctrines which the Catholic Church already possesses. It presumes a full awareness of the deficiencies in the faith of those with whom the Catholic Church

---

21. CDF, Declaration in defense of Catholic doctrine on the church, *Mysterium ecclesiae*, June 24, 1973, 4; *AAS* 65 (1973) 402–03.

22. UUS, 80.

23. UUS, 82.

is engaged in dialogue. The ecumenism of return further presupposes that the doctrinal positions of the Catholic Church are self-sufficient, adequate, and final. John Paul's position may differ from an ecumenism of return if later history shows that his legacy actually led Catholics to receive non-Catholics in Christian charity. John Paul's position may also differ from an ecumenism of return if what he means by "the fullness of the means of salvation" can be affirmed of any church not presently in communion with Rome.

Ecumenism, John Paul reminds us, will never succeed if it does not lead to communion in truth. Yet, the documents of Vatican II effectively reveal that the Church does not proclaim an undifferentiated set of unrelatedly true doctrines. The doctrinal statements of the Church are always situated within a hierarchy of truth. Any given doctrinal statement carries weight relative to more central doctrines. The churches make many statements which do not touch on the possibility (or non-impossibility) of salvation. Those that do certainly rank among the central truths of the Christian faith.

History shows that the Church's doctrine has grown and developed over the ages. The Church has contradicted itself as new historical and cultural conditions arose. The Church has occasionally been side-tracked by conflict over issues such as the divinity of Christ, the nature of the Trinity, the necessity of circumcision, or the date for the celebration of Easter. In determining those issues, the Church has stepped forward to claim its heritage with greater precision. At this time, is it not possible that the churches are being asked to live with ambiguity or to make their claims to truth with more humility and modesty?

On the other hand, it may be that a certain church will decide, in good conscience, that it does not need to grow in truth. Perhaps that church has decided that it does not need to amend historical expressions of doctrine. Perhaps that church supposes that God has not allowed it to err or wander. Then, one must ask a further question of that church. Is that church, the church that does not believe it needs to be converted, a true image of the Church which Christ intended?

3. Catholic or confessional?

Recent Roman Catholic responses to ecumenism exhibit a desire to see Roman Catholic doctrines unambiguously expressed in ecumenical dialogue statements.[24] The effect is one of a church that is hesitant to retire the ecumenism of return. Is it impossible to consider how Catholic doctrines and practices might be changed or set aside in the interests of meeting the legitimate concerns and fears of fellow Christians?

24. Nilson, 11.

To the extent that the Roman Catholic Church and its authorities have been unwilling to change in response to ecumenical dialogue, our church appears sectarian. To the extent that we are sectarian, one hesitates to speak of our church as "catholic," as a "full expression" of the Church of Christ.[25] By focusing on Christian basics, in Scripture, in the early Christian writers, and in the councils of the undivided Church (before the Great Schism and the Reformation), Roman Catholic authorities will serve ecumenism well. On the other hand, to reassert doctrines developed since the divisions of the churches, many of them heavily imbued with polemical symbolism, is less acceptable to other Christians and will impede the day of the churches' reunion.

Recent Roman Catholic responses to ecumenism may reveal an inflationary dogmatism which seeks to "level the hierarchy of truths." Roman Catholics, we are told, cannot accept ambiguity on nearly every matter of doctrine. The essentialist mindset consists of the desire to assert control over a group by the reinforcement of distinctive, though unimportant, characteristics. Present sociological conditions do not allow the Catholic Church to speak with the same degree of authority it once enjoyed. In the past the Catholic Church may have been able to articulate its positions and they were not questioned. Even though the Church possesses the ability to speak the truth infallibly, that does not mean the Church *should* ever again so speak. Nor does it imply that, *when* the Church speaks, modern women and men will listen.[26]

When I first became Roman Catholic, I once walked past several churches in the small Michigan city where I lived and indulged the fantasy of a massive "return to Rome." What, I thought, if all these churches could once again become Catholic? This fantasy, I admit, involved the revision of church architecture and liturgical styles (prayers and music) more than an authentic reunion of hearts and minds. The idea reflected my conviction at the time that, when I became Roman Catholic, I had found "the Truth." I wondered then what I could do to convince the people in these churches of the same "truth." My thoughts, I am afraid, displayed a typically adolescent ignorance of the "truth" I was receiving, of the nature of truth itself, and of the way that men and women receive the truth and participate in truthful societies, like their churches.

I look back on this post-conversion fantasy with embarrassment and I reveal it to make one point. To expect Christians of other churches to move beyond their ecclesial heritage in the interests of full, visible communion is audacious, though such movement is necessary for successful

---

25. Cf. Tillard, "The Church is a Communion," *OIC* 17 (1981) 122.
26. Karl Rahner predicted this situation. Rahner, *The Shape of the Church to Come*, tr. Edward Quinn (New York: Seabury Press, 1974) 21–22.

ecumenism. However, should one expect Christians of other Churches to make such changes, without making an equally profound commitment to engage the same process to the same depth in one's own Church, is grossly unfair and will defeat ecumenism.

Questions for meditation and dialogue on "Ecumenism at Risk"

1. *Ecclesial boundaries.* John Paul II has said that there is no ecclesial boundary "beyond the boundaries of the Catholic Church." What do you suppose he means by this? Is it possible for the churches to exist in an "imperfect communion"? Is anything more than baptism required for "full communion" with other Christians? If so, could you make a list of those requirements?

2. *Many voices in the Church.* The Roman Catholic Church sometimes sounds like it is speaking in two or three voices. It is fair to ask members of other churches whether their churches also speak in multiple voices. Do the churches—Catholic, Orthodox, and Protestant—ever use doctrines to remain separated for less than legitimate reasons? Can you imagine a church that speaks in several voices on doctrinal and moral issues? What might that church sound like? Could you imagine worshiping in a church that was not merely silent in its disagreements, but worshiped and preached possibly contradictory messages? Could such a church preach the Gospel of salvation?

FOR FURTHER READING

Clifford, Catherine. "Reception of the Final Report: Beyond Strengthened Agreement," *OIC* 32 (1996) 130–48.

Rahner, Karl. *The Shape of the Church to Come.* Edward Quinn, tr. New York: Seabury, 1974.

Tavard, George. "Considerations on an Ecclesiology of *Koinonia*," *OIC* 31 (1995) 42–51.

CHAPTER FIVE

Church of God—A Communion of Local Churches

The writings of Jean-Marie Tillard provide excellent examples of the current state of Roman Catholic communion ecclesiology. In his books Tillard follows an expository approach. Significant passages from patristic authors are quoted at length in support of each point. The conclusions he draws, however, do not evade modern questions. One always sees that he is working toward rapprochement between modern Christianity and Christian antiquity, between Catholic and non-Catholic perspectives. Tillard's expositions point the way to a new appreciation of the ancient writings. By helping his readers hear the ancient writers with fresh ears, Tillard's work suggests that many key problems facing those in ecumenical discussion can be more easily resolved.

In the background of Tillard's writings stands his experience as member of numerous ecumenical commissions. In his service to the Anglican-Roman Catholic International Commission, Tillard's preparatory paper for the Windsor statement had untold influence on the depth of agreement expressed there. An official Roman Catholic delegate to the Faith and Order Commission of the World Council of Churches, he was involved in the writing of BEM. Tillard has served in official capacities on ARCIC-I and ARCIC-II, the Joint Commission for Theological Dialogue between the Roman Catholic Church and the Orthodox Church, the Disciples of Christ-Roman Catholic Dialogue, and the Faith and Order Commission of the WCC. He is also an official observer of the Roman Catholic Church to the WCC.

1. Jean-Marie Tillard's contribution

Tillard has written extensively on the Eucharist, ecclesiology, and ecumenism.[1] His works include six major books in French: *Eucharistie: Pâque de l'Église*; *Le Salut: Mystère du pauvreté*; *L'Évêque de Rome*; *Église*

---

1. For a bibliography complete to 1994 see, "Bibliographie de J.-M. R. Tillard," in Evans and Gourgues, 5–20. See also the bibliography in my dissertation, *The Eucharist as*

d'Églises, Chair de l'Église, Chair du Christ, and *L'Église locale*.[2] All except the last two have been translated into English. Tillard has published hundreds of articles in French and English. His essays appear frequently in *Irénikon, Sobornost, One in Christ, Mid-Stream, Ecumenical Studies*, and *Ecumenical Review*. Tillard's theology shows the strong influence of his ecumenical involvement and his ability to communicate Roman Catholic perspectives with sensitivity for his Orthodox, Anglican, and Evangelical dialogue partners. Tillard's convictions remain solidly rooted in Roman Catholicism.[3]

This study of Tillard's contribution to the ecclesiology of communion will focus on four of the major works: *L'Église locale* (The Local Church); *Chair de l'Église, Chair du Christ* (Body of the Church, Body of Christ); *Église d'Églises*, and *Eucharistie: Pâque de l'Église*. For the last two books, I will refer to the English translations: *Church of Churches* and *Eucharist, Pasch of God's People* exclusively.

The four major works suggest a progression in Tillard's thoughts on communion ecclesiology. The first book, *Eucharist: Pasch of God's People*, treats the Eucharist in light of salvation for the individual and for the Church. In this book, Tillard develops his conception of the "two moments of grace" in the Eucharist. The second book, *Church of Churches*, describes the structures of the Church from the perspective of communion ecclesiology. In this book Tillard describes the entire Church as a communion of local churches. The local church is the focus for ecclesiology, while the communion of local churches ensures the "unity in diversity" of the entire "Church of God." The third book, *Chair de l'Église*, is a sequel to *Church of Churches*. In it, Tillard describes the "structures of grace" which flow in and beneath the ecclesial structures. The Church is a structure of grace and a creation of the Holy Spirit. Tillard wrote this

---

Sacrament of Ecclesial Koinonia with Reference to the Contribution of Jean-Marie Tillard to Ecumenical Consensus on the Eucharist, Ph.D. diss. (University of Notre Dame, 1996) 369–77.

2. Tillard, *The Eucharist: Pasch of God's People*, tr. Dennis L. Wienk (Staten Island, N.Y.: Alba House, 1967); *Le salut: Mystère du pauvreté*, Lumière de la foi 36 (Paris: Cerf, 1968); *The Bishop of Rome* (London: SPCK, 1982); *Church of Churches: The Ecclesiology of Communion*, tr. R. C. DePeaux (Collegeville: The Liturgical Press, 1992); *Chair de l'Église, Chair du Christ*, Cogitatio fidei 168 (Paris: Cerf, 1992); *L'Église locale*, Cogitatio fidei 191 (Paris: Cerf, 1995).

3. For commentary on Tillard's writings on ministry: John J. McDonnell, *Communio, Collegiality, Conciliarity: A Comparative Analysis of These Concepts Drawn from Certain Catholic and Orthodox Theologians*, L.T.D. thesis (Rome: Pontificias Universitas Gregoriana, 1990); Thomas E. Esselman, *The Principle of Functionality in Ecclesiology (Church Structures)*, Ph.D. diss. (Toronto: University of St. Michael's College, 1990); Conrad T. Gromada, *The Theology of Ministry in the 'Lima Document': A Roman Catholic Critique*, Ph. D. diss. (Philadelphia: Duquesne University, 1988).

book as a remedy to an overly one-sided emphasis upon church hierarchy. The most recent book, *L'Église locale*, is the third in Tillard's "trilogy" on the Church. In it, he describes the local church in light of its relationship to the universal Church. The local church is not "part of the Church." It is not "a deficient church." The local church, in its catholicity, is the Church gathered "here and now" in communion with all the other local churches.[4]

On more than one occasion Tillard reminds his readers of St. Augustine's injunction to the newly baptized: "Become who you are." In his sermon, Augustine was enjoining new Christians to look at the eucharistic bread and cup, to receive Christ in them, and receiving Christ, to receive a new identity. They are to *become* the Christ whom they will receive. The Church, receiving Christ in the bread and cup, is challenged to receive its identity. It must *become* the Christ whom it has received. The challenge of sanctification is to allow one's self and one's community to be conformed, over time, to God's saving plan by grace. This challenge, "to become who you are," was fully revealed by Jesus in his paschal mystery, in the pouring out of his being, for the sake of others. Tillard called this movement *dessaisissement*, or self-abandonment. The term plays an important role in Tillard's discussion of sacramentality. The movement of the soul in self-abandonment is mirrored in the life of the Church. Communion is made possible only because the self has been "poured out," as God poured out God's self in the Word and the Spirit.

It would be impossible in one chapter to adequately summarize and restate Tillard's ecclesiology. Instead, I will focus on four themes in Tillard's works. First, Tillard sees in the Eucharist two unique moments of grace, consecration and communion. The two moments exist in the order of salvation, though they are sacramentally expressed in the Eucharist. Second, we wish to see how the Church is affected by its communion in the "two moments" of grace. Third, we wish to explore how Tillard links the Eucharist with the constitution of the Church. Finally, as described so thoroughly in *L'Église locale*, the local church—where the Eucharist takes place—is constituted in communion with the entire Church.

1.1. Two moments of grace

The Church exists in tension between unity and diaspora. The Church is united in Christ, but dispersed with respect to time, place and hundreds of other qualities. Therefore, unity and diaspora are united in God's saving plan. Tillard has called the two moments of God's saving plan "offer" and "acceptance;" "creation" and "recapitulation." These

---

4. Cf. David Carter, Review article, *L'Église locale* by J.-M. R. Tillard, *OIC* 32 (1996) 378–85.

two moments are crucial to understanding Tillard's conception of the Eucharist and the Church.

According to Thomas Aquinas, the world of grace may be considered according to two movements in God's saving design. These two movements are the *exitus* and *reditus*. The *exitus* refers to God's offer of salvation to the creature. The *reditus* refers to the reception of salvation by the creature in freedom. Salvation does not consist of an offer from God alone, neither does it consist of the creature's acceptance of that offer alone. The two moments together form a conceptual pair on every level of the sacramental economy. Thus, "two moments" can be identified in every sacramental act. It can be seen in baptism, Eucharist, reconciliation, preaching, orders, the reception of Scripture, prayer, even in the singing of a hymn. The Eucharist has a consecratory moment which signifies God's *exitus* or offer. It has a receptive moment which signifies the acceptance of God's offer, the *reditus*, or return into communion with God.

Tillard's theology of the two moments is developed in his first book, *Eucharist: Pasch of God's People*. There, he describes the structure of the Eucharist in terms of the "two moments:" offer and acceptance. These two moments of salvation are rooted in the life and being of God. The possibility of salvation as Christians conceive it depends on the doctrine of the communion of the triune God, who limitlessly offers and receives itself in love for eternity.[5] The results of God's limitless self-offering and self-reception are observed, up and down, on every level of the economy of grace. These dynamics are seen in the incarnation, in the creation of the world, in the anthropology of the human person. They are seen in the paschal mystery, in the life of the Church, in the sacraments, and they will be seen in the parousia. The principle of "incarnation" implies that, in creating the world, God does not "overwhelm" the world with love and self-giving, but God does not "abandon" the world either. The missions of Christ and the Spirit are means through which God elects to be present to the world in limitless love.

The dynamic of the two moments begins in a "word of promise." God posits an "offer" to the recipient (the Word, the Spirit, the creature, the Church). This word of promise is answered by a "word of acceptance." The Word accepts begottenness in the Father's image and likeness. The Spirit accepts the love of God for the Word and the world. The creature accepts the love of God's Word in the Spirit.

In the order of human experience, however, the two moments are often experienced in reverse order. Recipients must speak a word of "acceptance" before they can perceive the word of "promise" as "promising" rather than as "bondage" for instance. In the experience of the

---

5. Tillard, "What is the Church of God?" *Mid-Stream* 23 (1984) 371.

human condition, Christ may be known and received as an offer from God, as a definitive "word of promise." Yet, Christ cannot be known and loved as the Word of God unless he is received as such. Christ's "promise" remains unfulfilled to the extent he has not been "received." The "word of promise" becomes promising only to the extent that it is received "as promise." An "offer," however well intentioned, that is incomprehensible is, strictly speaking, no offer at all. Christ speaks his word in a mode and manner that can be heard. In the order of divine grace, however, the word of promise is considered prior to the word of acceptance. Therefore, some classical theologies have tended to emphasize God's act of condescension at the expense of the ability of human beings to respond to God.

Christians know and love Christ *only as much as* he has been "received." There may exist a little bit of Christ which is hidden from our knowledge. There may exist among us differences in our abilities to know and receive Christ—the Spirit helps us in our weakness.[6] Therefore, we should not think that our salvation depends on either the catechism's knowledge of Christ or those unknown and hidden qualities of Christ we cannot know, such as his infathomable love for the Father. Instead, we should focus attention on the knowledge and love of Christ as we actually receive it. In the Eucharist the whole Christ is offered. Yet, the whole Christ is not receivable. In each Eucharist, the whole Christ is received *in part.* The communicant need only intend to love and know the whole Christ, by means of their love for the part they know. They must trust that the limitations of their knowledge are no obstacle to God's love, which works even when and where it is hidden and obscure.[7] We arrive at a simple affirmation. God is eternally offering creatures a surplus of love and knowledge, more than they are capable of receiving.

In Tillard's theology, the first eucharistic moment is known in the forgiveness of sins. Forgiveness is not an end in itself, but offered in excess, points toward sanctification and life in nearness to God. Forgiveness does not leave the creature isolated and forlorn. Forgiveness draws the creature, through reconciliation, into communion with God in Christ Jesus.[8] If God forgave our sins, but left us to stew in the consequences of our misdeeds, that would be unnecessarily cruel. Instead, Tillard suggests that salvation consists of a "redemption opening into the communion of Life, in a communion of Life, rooted in redemption."[9] The life of the Church originates in forgiveness for the sake of God's tender intimacy. Divine life is already a communion, when it is offered to human beings it

6. Rom 8:26.
7. Cf. CofC, 126.
8. Col 3:3.
9. Pasch, 40.

is offered as life in communion. The communion of the Church is a sacramental reflection, an expression or sign, of the communion of "Life" which God offers to those God elects to save. The movement of grace culminates, Tillard writes, "in the projection of [humankind] into the very bosom of the world of the resurrection, the new world inaugurated in the Lord Jesus."[10]

If the first moment of grace is directed from God toward the creature, the second moment appears initially to be an autonomous act of the creature, directed toward God. However, the two acts, the act of God toward the creature and the act of God within the life of the creature, originate in the same reality of grace.[11] Both moments of salvation originate with God. Both are experienced as "grace." In words from John's Gospel, salvation is indeed a "grace upon grace."[12] The proclamation of forgiveness and its reception in the faith are two sides of a single act.[13] Reception is an act of the Spirit, accomplished in the Spirit.

For Tillard, reception is consummated in the "yes" of faith by which each person and the entire assembly replies to God's offer of salvation. This "yes" exists on a level beneath doctrine, for doctrine depends on the movement of the soul and does not precede it. That is, the "yes" is prelinguistic. It is, as Thomas Aquinas called it, a *habitus*, or "habit." Doctrine, by contrast, is linguistic, or at least symbolic. In written and spoken words, good doctrine is formulated in an attempt to articulate the inchoate movements of the soul.[14]

One commentator suggested that Tillard's method is "convergent" rather than "linear."[15] In Tillard's description faith and the description of faith in doctrines converge. But if one were to graph the convergence, the lines would appear nearly parallel. The convergence of doctrine toward faith is asymptotic. Faith is more or less constant, yet doctrine, being ever more refined, will never approach a full and adequate description of faith. Because of this, the theologian is free to examine the relationship between expression of faith and the substance of faith, between the description of faith and the existential assent of the soul to God. There is the "amen" of the soul and the "amen" of the lips. The "amen" of the lips (or the pen) is a true sign of the "amen" of the soul, but never adequately encompasses faith.

Tillard's concept of the "two moments" derives from his analysis of the Eucharist. In the Eucharist, the two moments of grace are sacramen-

10. Pasch, 211.
11. Tillard, "Spirit, Reconciliation, Church," *ER* 42 (1990) 240.
12. John 1:16.
13. CofC, 125.
14. Cf. Tillard, "One Church of God," *Mid-Stream* 20 (1981) 286.
15. Michael O'Connor, "The Holy Spirit and the Church," *OIC* 28 (1992) 331.

tally reenacted. Forgiveness originates in the event of which the Eucharist is the memorial (the paschal mystery) and is given for the sake of our communion in the eschatological banquet of which the Eucharist is the foretaste (the kingdom of God).[16] Only because we experience the life of communion in symbol, at the Eucharist, do we suppose that we will experience the offer and reception of communion in finality, at the end of time. Christians infer their idea of salvation by extrapolating from their experience of the "little salvations," the graces, they receive each day.

In the Eucharist the first moment of grace is the consecration. The Eucharist is given, "for the forgiveness of sins."[17] The Eucharist is a sacrament of forgiveness because it is a memorial of the passion. Thomas Aquinas taught that the Eucharist has the power to "forgive every sin without exception" because it is the sacrament of the passion of Christ, the "source and cause of the remission of all sin."[18] Forgiveness, therefore, does not come from the Eucharist itself, rather through its "anamnetic" character as memorial of the passion. The communion of the Church is a "redeemed" and "forgiven" communion.[19] It is given as a sign of the communion of love which God is establishing in the midst of humankind.

The second moment of the Eucharist touches upon the disposition of communicants. Not every communicant is prepared to receive the fruits of the sacrament in their fullness. The faithful Christian, Tillard writes, must "enter freely into the movement of grace."[20] This phrase, which appears so prominently in the Windsor document, suggests that Christians enter into grace under their own power. However, the Church does not possess grace, but is freely possessed by God in grace. The Church is so flooded by forgiveness, it freely chooses generously to bestow everything it receives from God upon the human community.[21] God's infinite generosity is the origin of *kenosis*.

For Tillard, the Eucharist must bring about the progressive pardoning and destruction of sin. It must strengthen and repair "the bonds of charity and unity in Christ."[22] The Eucharist, he writes, must first be a "sacrament of pardon," if it is to be a "sacrament of hope."[23] The Eucharist builds up the Church by strengthening the union between Christ

16. "The Bread and Cup of Reconciliation," in *Sacramental Reconciliation*, ed. Eduard Schillebeeckx, Concilium 61 (New York: Herder and Herder, 1971) 52.

17. Matt 26:28. Pasch, 130–34.

18. Thomas Aquinas, *Summa theologiae* III.79.3.

19. Cf. Pasch, 202f.

20. Pasch, 189.

21. GS, 40.

22. Pasch, 202.

23. Tillard, "The Eucharist, Gift of God," in *Ecumenical Perspectives on Baptism, Eucharist and Ministry*, ed. Max Thurian, Faith and Order Paper 116 (Geneva: WCC Publications, 1983) 110.

and Christians. The Church is built up by "snatching [the people of God] progressively from the world of sin" and by strengthening and intensifying their movement toward their "decisive entrance into . . . communion with the goods of the Father in the day of the Son of Man."[24] Tillard calls the hatred of humanity for itself a symbol, the "opposite of a sacrament," of its hatred for God.[25] Hatred, he says, is the anti-type of the Eucharist. It is the "anti-sacrament" of salvation and destroys the Church. The local church in the eucharistic assembly is not a gathering of "friends." It is, Tillard states, a gathering of former enemies, now reconciled in Christ.[26] The two moments of salvation have not yet been decisively accomplished in time, yet their decisive outcome has already been determined. This places the Church in a situation of tension between what God has already accomplished in Christ by the Spirit and what God is accomplishing in human lives, one person at a time.[27]

1.2. The Church in light of the two moments

The "two moments" of the Eucharist correspond to the "levels of communion" which exist in the divided Church. Tillard states that participation in the Eucharist represents a phenomenon of "ascesis," the "Amen" of the communicant, on two levels.[28] The Eucharist is therefore a sacrament also of the confession of faith, for it represents an assent to the faith in general and in particular.[29] The "ascesis" represented by the "Amen" of the communicant constitutes the Church as an acceptance of salvation in Christ *as such*, the "first Amen." It also constitutes the Church as an acceptance of *the faith of this church* in particular, the "second Amen," implied by the first.

Confession of faith is more than oral affirmation of dogma, the answering of a catechism question, or the recitation of a creed. Confession of faith, Tillard says, is the unique way in which believing communities, having received God's offer of salvation, communicate that offer to others in this world now and in the future. Confession (also contained in acts like proclamation, preaching, sharing, giving) is a sign of the "surplus" of God's generosity shown the Church. It is a sign of the Church's decision to freely bestow all the goods of God at its disposal upon others. Confession of faith is *performed* in words and in deeds.

---

24. Pasch, 195, 211.
25. Eph 2:16. CofC, 47.
26. CofC, 48.
27. Pasch, 211.
28. Pasch, 144.
29. CofC, 164.

Tillard says that confession of faith is the ultimate foundation of the existence of any given Christian community. Particular acts of confession, in a sermon, in the Eucharist, at prayer, in gifts to the poor, imply the source of a community's "obedience to God."[30] Confession arises from the depths of the heart. At bottom, it is an expression of the movement of grace within the Christian community. Confession is not separate from human temperament and is radically conditioned by cultural and historical contexts. Confession of faith is inherently risky, for confession is as likely to constitute the Church in union as it is to divide Christians from one another.

To receive the Eucharist represents an assent to the Church as a whole and to the local church in which one stands. To receive the Eucharist in communion with Christ and the Church implies a dual solidarity. This dual solidarity is expressed in each of the two "Amens" of the eucharistic liturgy. There is the "Amen" with which one responds to the eucharistic prayer, "Yes, this is my prayer," and there is the "Amen" one performs in the reception of the eucharistic meal, "Yes, this church, this bread, this cup is Christ's body and blood."[31] The dual solidarity is first an assent to the deposit of faith confessed by the whole Church, "Jesus is Lord." It is second an affirmation that the deposit of faith is discernible here and now, in the faith of this local church.

The first "yes" is part of the movement of faith at the heart of the person. It represents their free acceptance, their *ascesis*, to Christ by the Spirit. This first "yes" is the *id quod requiritur et sufficit*, "that which is both required and sufficient," the minimal grounds of faith. Tillard argues that this first "yes" is sacramentally signified by each "Amen" spoken or sung in the Eucharist. The accumulation of such Amens over time signifies a lifelong, renewable covenant.[32] Tillard writes that we believe "personally," but only within the context of a given church. One may believe "in the depths of one's heart," but only within the context of a history of committed actions affirming such faith.

The second "yes" represents the fullness of faith "in confessional clarity." The second "yes" represents an acceptance of faith "put into practice and put to the test daily in the rough struggle of fidelity."[33] One never may confess a "generic" faith, a "naked" faith. Confession is always particular and sometimes even peculiar. Words and deeds accumulate over the course of one's life to describe a unique history of struggle between sin and the Spirit, between willfulness and obedience, between slavery and freedom. Individuals and local churches do not escape this dynamic.

30. CofC, 146.
31. LL., 258.
32. CofC, 234.
33. *Ibid.*

The Eucharist is the preeminent place where confession of faith is experienced and enacted.[34] In the local church, Tillard believes, one is assured that all the "Amens" are said in the same faith.[35] Here I suggest a slight adjustment to Tillard's already subtle approach. The local church, I suggest, is where one is assured that all the "Amens" are said in the same *communion* of faith.[36] In order to live in communion with others, one need never believe that one's faith is *identical* with everyone else's around the table. One must rather be content with the particularities, the individuality, of each person gathered there. One should assent to the conviction that the Spirit is working in these others, perhaps even to greater effect than in one's self. One assents to the *people* gathered there, for God has chosen them in love.

Confession of faith is not only assent to a catechism or to a distinctive way of life (for Amish, riding buggies; for Orthodox, growing beards). It involves saying "Amen" to the entire company of people who say "Amen" to God. Confession of faith is first a communion with people who have been led by the Spirit to set their hearts on Christ. These people will say "Amen" and mean their assent to Christ differently, perhaps far more profoundly and deeply than my own. To say "Amen" *with them* is to say that I rely on their faith, for their "Amen" supplements and strengthens my own.

The mystery of *solidarity* in communion would be destroyed by the requirement that partners at the table be *identical*, mere "clones" in faith. Instead, it requires partners at the table knit together in the performance of an "Amen" greater than any one of them is able to say alone. "Within the church every *concrete* form of human solidarity can be realized," Tillard concludes, "though the church itself is not limited to the human social condition."[37] We need not understand God as, he puts it, "limited to hanging over" human history. Rather, because of the Spirit, God encompasses our history, even the most horrendous episodes, and "invades it" with love.[38]

According to Tillard, the first "yes" is required for eucharistic sharing. The second "yes," "for the sake of charity," cannot be required.[39] In a word, the Eucharist must be a communion *in faith*, the first "yes," but it need not be a communion *in identical expressions* of faith, the second "yes." Without a unity in the first "yes" the gospel of salvation would be falsified. With respect to the second "yes," however, there must be a

34. CofC, 164.
35. CofC, 167.
36. LL, 152.
37. CofC, 31.
38. CofC, 7.
39. Tillard, "Preparing for Unity," *OIC* 16 (1980) 10.

healthy respect for the diversity and great pastoral finesse.[40] Without such finesse, Tillard fears the ecumenical movement would either soften into an ecumenical *laissez-faire* or harden into an ecumenism of return. The ecumenism of return does not respect diversity in the expression of faith. *Laissez-faire* ecumenism does not respect unity within the substance of faith.[41]

In the face of the two extremes, Tillard proposes to Catholic theology what amounts to a doctrine of *adiaphora*. *Adiaphora* was Martin Luther's term for those practices which are neither contrary to the Scriptures nor required by them. In using the term to describe Tillard's contribution, a slightly broader application is intended. Tillard would not necessarily equate the essentials of faith with Luther's *sola scriptura*. There are items from the first centuries of the Church which the churches now recognize as *essential* to faith, the Creed, the primacy, the episcopacy and so forth. The churches, he says, must be united in *essentials*. They must complement and enrich, but not harm, one another by their diverse expressions of faith. Union, he states, is not the same as "fusion."[42] The Church is constituted as a unity in diversity.

The diversity of the Church, he says, is the result of God's implanting communion in diverse human circumstances.[43] Salvation does not "level-out" or destroy human differences. The Spirit is no melting pot, but perfects our diversity, in effect, "harmonizing" our differences. The Genesis story of the Tower of Babel has long been read as the anti-type of the Church. The outcome of Babel is the diaspora of humankind symbolized in the story by people's inability to communicate with one another. Babel represents an "unharmonized" diversity, the diversity of existential loneliness, isolation, and alienation.

The Church, unlike the men and women at the mythical tower, expresses a diversity in unity. Luke's story of Pentecost represents the reversal of Babel. The many languages, outcome of the Babel story, were not abolished but were transformed into the substance of a common faith.[44] Peter's Pentecost Day homily, spoken in his own language, was heard by thousands in their mother tongues. His audience was enabled to receive the message as though it had been couched entirely in their own cultural and social idioms. The glossolalia of the apostles was not the greatest miracle of the Pentecost story. Of far greater consequence was how the Holy Spirit progressively opened the primitive Christian community to receive

---

40. "Preparing for Unity," 11.
41. "Preparing for Unity," 12.
42. See Tillard, "The Ministry of Unity," *OIC* 33 (1997) 98.
43. Tillard, "Communion and Salvation," *OIC* 28 (1992) 7.
44. Acts 2:1ff. CofC, 8.

the Gentiles as part of the comprehensiveness and universality of God's plan for salvation.

Tillard's schema of two moments of grace, in offer and in acceptance, raises interesting questions about the relationship between God's desire to save creation and the redemption and sanctification of real people who dwell in particular places and times. Christ has created salvation *once and for all (ephapax)*. Individuals and the Church are given a share in the paschal mystery of Jesus, not one time only, but many times over the course of a lifetime. Thus, the paschal mystery is not "once and for all" in the sense that it is finished and ended, trapped like an isolated event in first-century Jerusalem. The paschal mystery is also accessible and tangent to all places and times.[45] When we describe the *ephapax* character of Christ's sacrifice, we may not do so in a way that traps it like an insect in amber. The paschal mystery is accessible to us, not because we want it, but because the Holy Spirit has inserted us into its saving power. Thus communion is not only a reality uniting us to Christians of the present time. The "openness" of the Church is a reflection of its participation in the *ephapax* mystery of Christ's sacrifice. The Church's openness does not end with those alive today, but includes all times and places, "wherever" Christ has been or will be.[46]

The communion of the Church is both "vertical" and "horizontal."[47] The Eucharist cannot be a sacrament of communion with God (vertically) if it is not first a real, human communion (horizontally)—with everything that implies. Our Eucharists are therefore always somewhat marred by the finitude of human love and are marked by our weaknesses and vulnerabilities. The sacramental quality of the Eucharist is ironically linked to its limitations. Our sacraments reveal salvation as much as they reveal our imperfections. The Eucharist is a sign of God's absolute salvation, received in weakness. This tension lies at the heart of every sacrament, even the sacrament of the Church. This tension does not falsify the sacrament, for it illumines the contradictions at the heart of human being.

1.3. The eucharistic constitution of the Church

In *Chair de l'Église*, Tillard calls the Church the communion of humanity reconciled with God and itself in Christ. "By the Word and the Spirit," he wrote, the Church "is the osmosis of the sacrificial body of the Lord and the concrete tissue of the life of the baptized."[48] The Church is the sacramental expression of Christ, whose human and divine natures

---

45. Pasch, 126.
46. This leads to the mystery of inculturation, LL, 176.
47. Pasch, 48f., 51ff., 53.
48. CdlE, 155.

share a single being. The Eucharist is the *sacramental* medium for this exchange of being, the "osmosis" he calls it, between Christ and the Church.

Were one to select the single most influential contribution Tillard has made to ecumenism, it would be this. He reconfigured the problem of the nature of Christ's presence and sacrifice in the Eucharist. The presence of Christ, he wrote, is given for the purpose of salvation. The sacrificial character of the Eucharist is found within its sacramentality.[49] These two insights paved the way toward a more profound consensus among the members of ARCIC-I in the Windsor statement.[50]

In the preparatory paper for the Windsor document, Tillard states that *sacramentality* is a mode of being. To exist sacramentally is to exist in a certain sort of way. Sacramentality is not just another quality among the qualities of a thing. It rather defines what a thing is at a fundamental level. So, every other quality of the Eucharist is affected by its being a sacrament. Thus, consider the sacrificial quality of the Eucharist. The Eucharist is a sacrifice. But the Eucharist is not *simply* a sacrifice. This was demonstrated in an earlier chapter. The Eucharist is *sacramentally* a sacrifice, or it is "sacrificial" to the extent that its communion in the sacrifice of Christ is effectively signified.[51]

In the preparatory paper, Tillard writes that Christ is present "for the purpose of salvation,"[52] a phrase inserted, verbatim, into the eucharistic agreement. The Eucharist does not include the presence of Christ for its own sake. The presence "accomplishes the gift of God," salvation.[53] Christ is present as a gift and an offer and corresponds to the "first moment" of salvation. In the Eucharist, consecration is analogous to the divine offer of salvation. Consecration cannot be divorced from the "second moment" either. Consecration therefore is accomplished for the purpose of reception in faith. It is given for the sake of communion.

The presence of Christ is neither arbitrary nor is it taken away when faith is weak or lacking. As Windsor states: "Christ's presence does not depend upon the individual's faith in order to be the Lord's real gift of himself to his Church."[54] Through reception, however, the purpose for Christ's presence is fulfilled. The statement thus answers evangelical objections that, for some, the presence of Christ in the Eucharist is made to seem like an end in itself. The statement also answers Catholic objections

---

49. "Roman Catholics and Anglicans: The Eucharist," *OIC* 9 (1973) 137f., 164.

50. "Liturgical Reform and Christian Unity," *OIC* 119 (1983) 249. Julian Charley, "Friendship: The Forgotten Factor in Ecumenism," in Evans and Gourgues, 113f.

51. Jenson, 35.

52. "Roman Catholics and Anglicans," 164.

53. Tillard, "The Eucharist, Gift of God," in Thurian, *Ecumenical Perspectives on BEM*, 105.

54. Windsor, 8.

that, for some, the emphasis on the need for a subjective relationship between Christ and the communicant calls into question their confidence in the objective promise of Christ to be present for the Church "in the breaking of the bread." Tillard deals with this tension through application of the term "sacramental." The presence of Christ is always a qualified, as opposed to absolute, presence. It is always a "sacramental" presence. The "sacramental presence" of Christ always describes a "presence in absence." Sacramentality describes the limitation of creatures to convey the realities of God. It does not describe a limitation with respect to God.

The presence of Christ must always be qualified as a "sacramental presence."[55] The Council of Trent declared that the presence of Christ in the eucharistic species was "true," "real," and "substantial" according to the "sacramentality of his presence," a mode of existing not incompatible with his "natural mode of existing" at the right hand of God the Father. [56] The sacramental elements of bread and wine thus contain *(continere)* Christ himself who is not contained by them. The sacramental presence of Christ should not be explained in such a way as to deny the doctrine of his ascension. If Christ were located in the sacramental elements, he could not be said to be seated at God's right hand. The sacramental species must *contain* Christ, but they do not *limit* him, who is free with respect to all created things.

Sacramentality describes a "presence in absence."[57] For Tillard, "sacramentality" describes a mode of existence. Sacramental things are present in a way that is not "connatural to it, yet excludes the merely figurative."[58] To say that Christ is "present in absence" means that the totality of who Christ is may lie beyond our comprehension and, only insofar as he is "comprehensible," he is available. Sacraments represent God's saving reality and the mysterious, efficacious presence of that reality. Sacraments are thus symbolic, soteriological, and accessible with respect to the limitations of those who receive them. Sacraments are oriented toward our salvation, our redemption and our sanctification. They are not "locked up in the past." They are not a mere "calling to mind." Sacraments change participants by inserting them into new relationships with Jesus Christ, sending them forth to relate in new ways to others.[59]

---

55. "Roman Catholics and Anglicans," 160.

56. Council of Trent, Decree on the most holy sacrament of the eucharist, *Sacrosancta oecumenica*, 1; Tanner, vol. 2, 693f.

57. "Roman Catholics and Anglicans," 138.

58. *Ibid.* See Ernst Käsemann, "The Pauline Doctrine of the Lord's Supper," *Essays on New Testament Themes* (London: 1964) 106–35.

59. "Roman Catholics and Anglicans," 137f.

Sacraments thus represent a limit with respect to creatures. They do not limit God. God is continuously and eternally offering the whole of God's self to the whole of creation. Always and everywhere the divine offer of salvation is infinitely poured out. In any given Eucharist, however, believers are able to receive this divine self-giving only *partially*. The human communicant, acknowledging her finitude, desiring the entirety of salvation, remains limited with respect to what she is able to receive from God at any given time. Receiving the *part* she can, she is also drawn into relationship with the *whole* she cannot. She is woven into that network of living fibers which concretely constitute the Church's communion.[60] The Eucharist is thus a sacrament of the whole Christ and of the entire salvation he has accomplished, even if, at the Eucharist, individuals and local churches only experience part of him and that part may at times seem obscure.

The mystery of communion is that by faith, Christ, who is present "for the believer," becomes also a presence "with the believer."[61] Over the course of a lifetime, the life and love of Christ is knit together into the lives of those who receive him.[62] To receive Christ is to have a communion in his love. To receive Christ is to participate in his saving mission. To receive Christ is to receive all who have this relationship with him. The Church is the body of Christ only because Christ desires, in love, to continually unite himself to its conditions and limitations.[63] The Christian community, Tillard concludes, is the people of God brought to its fulfillment as the body of Christ.[64] The body of Christ exists as a communion of the redeemed, in a network of loving relationships established by God. There are not two incarnations of God, one in Jesus and the other in the Church. There is one incarnation expressed in two modalities.[65]

Tillard claims the Eucharist is the source of the "network of mutual relationships and exchanges that . . . the community weaves together in order to be the Church which God wills."[66] This "network of mutual relationships" is the Church of God. For this reason the Eucharist may be called the "sacrament of ecclesial communion." The Eucharist, establishing people in relationship through reconciliation by Christ and the Spirit,

---

60. Tillard, "La mémorial dans la vie de l'église," *La Maison-Dieu* 106 (1971) 31, my translation.

61. Windsor, 8.

62. "Roman Catholics and Anglicans," 165.

63. CdlE, 76.

64. CofC, 85.

65. See David N. Power, "Sacramental Celebration and Liturgical Ministry," in *Liturgy: Self-Expression of the Church*, ed. Herman Schmidt, Concilium 72 (New York: Herder, 1972) 40–42.

66. CofC, 155.

creates the Church; the Church, receiving God's offer of salvation in Christ by the Holy Spirit, makes the Eucharist.

If the Church is a sacrament of Christ's presence, it must also be a sacrament of Christ's saving acts. The sacrifice of Christ is also given sacramentally. The Church's eucharistic sacrifice, if we may be allowed to speak of it, is always a "sacramental" sacrifice. This sacrificial character of the Eucharist depends on the memorial character of the meal. Because the Eucharist is a memorial *(anamnesis)* of Christ's sacrifice, the tradition was able to arrive at an understanding of a "sacramental presence of the historic sacrifice" of Christ in the Eucharist.[67] Following the work of Max Thurian, formerly a brother of Taizé, Tillard believed that a renewed understanding of the biblical term *anamnesis* would fill out and strengthen the otherwise insufficient eucharistic theology of Trent.[68] The idea of the eucharistic sacrifice excludes the idea of a repetition of the event of the Cross or of the Mass possessing powers separate from the Cross. The Eucharist, Tillard writes, is no "hollow image of the Passover." It is not something simply appended, an afterthought, to Christ's sacrifice. The Eucharist signifies the transformation of slaves into a community, by a passage from tribulation into hope. It is analogous to the passage of Israel through the Reed Sea.[69]

Participation in these saving deeds by way of the sacraments represent the ordinary means by which human beings have a part in the saving plan of God.[70] The anamnetic dimension of the Eucharist evokes in us the memory of a saving event in the past, such that the original grace is replicated in the present.[71] Past deliverance is liturgically symbolized in a cultic act in the hope that present participants may be similarly delivered by the saving deeds of God, into the fullness of the life to come. The liturgical principle of *anamnesis* allows us to maintain the unity of God's saving plan. The Passover, the meals of Jesus, the Cross, the resurrection, the gift of the Spirit. All such events are, in the sacramental order, identical, for they all participate in the single, saving plan of God.

The Eucharist is an extension of the *ephapax* event of the Cross from one time and place into many times and places.[72] Because the body of

---

67. "Roman Catholics and Anglicans," 144.

68. Pasch, 212f. See Max Thurian, *L'Eucharistie, Mémorial du Seigneur* (Neuchâtel, Paris: 1959); tr. *The Eucharistic Memorial*, 2 vols. (Richmond, Va.: John Knox Press, 1961). F. J. Leenhard, *Le sacrement de la Sainte Cène* (Neuchâtel, Paris: 1948). P. Benoit, "Les Récits de l'institution et leur portée," *Lumiere et Vie* 31 (1957) 49–76. Anamnesis rescues Trent from some of Trent's more difficult points. "Sacrificial Terminology and the Eucharist," *OIC* 17 (1981) 306–23.

69. Exod 15; 1 Cor 10:1-5. CdlE, 48f.

70. "Roman Catholics and Anglicans," 144.

71. "Roman Catholics and Anglicans," 143–55. Cf. Robert L. Brawley, "*Anamnesis* and Absence in the Lord's Supper," *Biblical Theology Bulletin* 20 (1990) 139–46.

72. "Sacrificial Terminology and the Eucharist," 319.

Christ always belongs to Christ, there exists an identity of persons between the Church and Jesus. So the sacrifice of Christ from the Cross is "laid over" the sacrifice of Christ at the Eucharist. The sacrifice of the members, their *kenosis* to one another in love, is recapitulated in the sacrifice of the head.[73] At the Eucharist, Tillard concludes, the sacrifice of Christ and the sacrifice of the Church are "not only united, Christ 'inserts' the members of his body into his sacrifice."[74]

Such language understandably makes some Protestants restless. What must be remembered, however, is that the "sacrifice" of the Eucharist has already, occurred once-and-for-all in the sacrifice of the Cross. Yet every future Eucharist was, in a sense, contained in or implied by the cross. The Scottish Presbyterian theologian, John McIntyre, expressed a similar idea in his recent book, *The Shape of Soteriology*. Remarking on the fact that "Christ died for our sins," McIntyre observes that the phrase, "for our sins," implies that every sin *in particular* must have been related in some sense to the death of Christ—or we could not be saved. He writes, "It was as if they were each and all already, from the beginning, embraced within the salvation accomplished in the death of Christ."[75] The sacrifice is not *performed* over and over again. Its saving effect is *applied* over and over again to new sins, to new situations, to new relationships. The only place where Christians may wish to argue is whether this *application* of the sacrifice is itself "sacrificial."

Taking bread, breaking, and giving it, the human gestures which comprise the Eucharist, are only one instance of the complete, once-and-for-all sacrifice of Jesus. These actions converge and blend into the saving acts of Christ. They were his actions to begin with. The ability to see, in and through our actions, the saving deeds of God enriches our understanding of the sacramental character of the Eucharist. It enriches our understanding of the sacramental character of the Church as well, for we are not only looking at the deeds that are being performed but also at the one who performs them.

Nothing intrinsic to the human actions of the Eucharist accounts for their efficacy—except to satisfy a little hunger. So, if we are going to make claims about their saving effect, we must advert to the role of the Holy Spirit in these actions. The human community must rely on the Spirit to accomplish the saving work of God in its midst. We pour ourselves out in confident trust of the Spirit. Tillard remarks, "Only in the Spirit can the gift of God be delivered."[76]

73. CdlE, 58.
74. CdlE, 127. See Augustine, *City of God* 10, 6.
75. John McIntyre, *The Shape of Salvation* (Edinburgh: T&T Clark, 1992) 94.
76. "The Eucharist, Gift of God," 106.

The Church depends on the Holy Spirit for its unity. For Tillard, the unity of the Church originates in the Spirit because communion in Christ is the result of the reconstitution of the human community by the Spirit.[77] Through the work of the Spirit, the mere communion of human society is reconstituted as a living body.[78] Within the lives of men and women the Spirit establishes conditions necessary to draw them into relationship with one another. The Spirit likewise establishes within the lives of churches the conditions necessary to draw them into communion with one another. By the Spirit, men, women, and the human community as a whole, are painstakingly transformed into the image of Christ, the body of Christ, from whose side "flowed blood and water . . . for those whom he loved."[79] Tillard reminds us, the Spirit made Jesus the Christ, the "anointed one," by "joining him to the humanity over which he will reign."[80] In each Eucharist, the Spirit makes the Church the body of Christ by "joining him to the humanity over which he will reign." Because the Church is constituted by the Spirit, it is constituted as the body of Christ. The body of the Church is the body of Christ.

By the Spirit, many unlikely people are converted to the Gospel. Consider two such stories from the book of Acts: the Ethiopian eunuch or the Roman centurion.[81] The conversion of a eunuch (and Ethiopian at that) greatly troubled Philip, who could only remember Israel's law against eunuchs. The conversion of the Roman centurion Cornelius and his household astounded Peter, who had great difficulty accepting its veracity. These unlikely conversions created a problem for early Christians. Could *everyone* who had been converted by the Spirit and the Gospel, be received by the Church? The Spirit prepares men and women to receive and respond to the word of God. The Spirit has also to prepare the Church to receive the men and women whom God has chosen.

The human acts that comprise the Eucharist and constitute the Church as a society in "horizontal" communion must be performed in confidence that "God will provide." There is a natural "helplessness" which human beings face when they come into relationship with God. It is a leap we take, a sacrifice we make, to recognize our incapacities before the "incomprehensible God" to whom we must capitulate, and whom we must trust.[82] Our participation in salvation requires that we be made to trust in God. If we experience that conversion as a "sacrifice," as a loss of self, then we are within reason to call it so.

77. CofC, 312.
78. 1 Cor 12:12-13.
79. CdlE, 39.
80. CofC, 20f.
81. Acts 8:34-40, 10:1-33.
82. Cf. CofC, 126ff. Karl Rahner, *The Shape of the Church to Come*, 70.

This dynamic holds true no less for the individual person than for the Church. The Church, too, must trust in God and sacrifice itself. The communion of the local church is called upon to become a communion "in communion" with other local churches. Thus, the sacrificial character of the Eucharist is expressed, not only in the lives of individuals, but also in the lives of the local churches and in their relationships to other local churches. This is where a "high doctrine" of eucharistic sacrifice effectively challenges many Roman Catholics. A genuinely eucharistic church will shun self-distinction, for it has fully entered into the *kenosis* of Christ's love. A genuinely eucharistic church will reach out to every other church in table fellowship.

As Tillard writes in one of his harshest assessments of the current ecumenical situation, "The scandal of some juridical ecclesiologies is that they have offered a quiet conscience on the cheap." Obedience to a juridical conception of the Church, however time-honored or traditional, he says, does not satisfy the ecumenical destiny of the Church. The Church must continue to pray for the power of the Holy Spirit to transform the world, but it must also add a prayer for the transformation of itself: "Come, Holy Spirit, renew your Church!"[83]

Christians believe the Lord's act of self-abandonment is the basis for the reconciliation of humankind with God. Should we believe that anything less than the Cross will be necessary to reconcile the divided churches? Tillard spoke of this act as Christ's *dessaisissement*, his "letting go."[84] Christ's "letting go" effected his passage into the fullness of resurrected life. The Church's entrance into resurrected life, into a revivified communion, will it not require a similar "letting go?" The Church has communion in the sacrifice of Christ and therefore also in his paschal mystery. The Church's communion, however, only goes as deep as its entry into Christ's movement of self-abandonment into God. Tillard calls this "self-abandonment" the "similitude of a holocaust."[85]

When churches and church authorities are more concerned to maintain control and power, to sustain division than to extend love and hospitality, are they still fulfilling the office to which Christ ordained them? Ecumenical discussion will need to move from the sacrificial character of the Eucharist to consider whether any churches today exhibit the *kenotic* love of God around their table and in their relationship with other churches.

83. Tillard, "The Church of God is a Communion," *OIC* 17 (1981) 131.
84. CdlE, 109ff., 113.
85. CdlE, 114.

1.4. Communion at the heart of the Church and between each church

Tillard refused on more than one occasion to call his ecclesiology of communion an "ecclesiological model." Perhaps he was obliquely referring to Avery Dulles's important book on the models of the Church.[86] Communion is a model for the Church, but it is also far more than a "model" because it extends far beneath other explanatory systems. Communion reaches down to the existential core of the Church. Tillard therefore claims to be describing fundamental structures of grace. Every valid ecclesiological model must take these primordial structures of grace into account.

Were one asked, however, to describe Tillard's "model" or "definition" of the Church, one could do no better than to quote the following passage from *Church of Churches*. The Church, he says, is the "*communion of communions* appearing as a *communion* of local churches, spread throughout the world, each one itself being a *communion* of the baptized gathered together into communities by the Holy Spirit, on the basis of their baptism, for the eucharistic celebration."[87]

By local church, Tillard means the *diocese*. In this he follows the definition of Ignatius of Antioch.[88] The communion of these local churches is not additive. That is, there is not one church after another. But there is one Church, in which all the churches have their being. The multitude exists in communion *as a communion* by the power of the Holy Spirit. By turning toward one another in love, the churches are bound to one another, their salvation.[89] The Church is collected "from the roots upward," in the many concrete relationships which exist between each local church. It is collected "by the Spirit downward," as the fullness of Christ, given so abundantly, "spills over" into the whole Church, into the communion of the local churches.[90] The Eucharist, he says, is the "sacrament of the Church of God," because, on this earth, only the local church can celebrate the Lord's Supper. In the Eucharist, the local church anticipates and reflects the entire movement of Christ's sacrifice of love.[91]

Just as one finds the whole sacrifice of Christ in each Eucharist, so also one finds the whole Church of God in each Eucharist. Recall, because it is a communion in the body of Christ, the Eucharist is a sacrament of the Church as much as it is a sacrament of Christ. So the local church is a sacramental expression of the entire Church in one place and time. The entire Church is constituted in the local church as the com-

86. Avery Dulles, *Models of the Church*, 2d ed. (New York: Crossroads, 1987).
87. CofC, 29.
88. CofC, 29.
89. CofC, 23.
90. LL, 104.
91. CofC, 230. Cf. CdlE, 145.

munion of the local church with the entire Church. This is symbolized in the person of the bishop, in the collegiality of bishops, and in the synodality of churches.[92] The communion of the Church exists as a communion of reconciliation with God.[93] That communion does not end with the local gathering. The reconciliation of God in Jesus Christ is truly borderless. It has a universal extension. So the Church celebrates this reconciliation *in communion with* "all the churches of God, from every place and time."[94]

One of the best analogies for the "Church of churches" comes from nature in the "compound eye." The insect's eye is an "eye of eyes." Each individual eye is an entire eye and sees the world wholly and independently. Yet the entire eye, the mind's eye, depends upon the synergy of vision produced when every eye contributes sight to the whole. The function of the eye, "to see," is distributed holistically to every eye within the eye. The contribution of each eye, a unique perspective on the world, must be recapitulated and synthesized in the mind of the creature in order to create a unified vision of the world. Tillard's conception of the Church of churches suggests that the diaspora of the Church into local churches and the unity of the Church, "its unified field of vision," are mutually dependent. Each local church contributes a unique perspective on the world and must be recapitulated, holistically, within the mind of the whole Church. But the so-called "mind of the whole" is also distributed, for it exists in the relationships between each and every other local church.

The Church is the place where diversity and unity are conjoined *perichoretically.* The two principles are not simply held in tension. They process together to form a harmonious whole. The diaspora of the Church in place and time *constitutes* and *does not destroy* the unity of the Church. The diaspora is necessary, for without it, God's offer and promise, the first moment of salvation, would remain foreign and unknown to many. The unity is equally necessary, for it represents the reception of God in signs and symbols of human love.

2. Conclusion

Like most Catholic ecclesiologies of communion, Tillard's term "Church of churches" relies on an extension of the communication of idioms. Whatever can be said of Christ in his humanity can also be said of Christ in his divinity and vice versa. If the Church, constituted by the Spirit, is an extension of the person of Christ, then whatever can be said

92. LL, 251.
93. LL, 256.
94. LL, 257, my translation.

of Christ *in his ecclesiality* must first be true of Christ in his humanity and his divinity. "Catholicity" therefore is an ecclesial category because it is first a quality of Christ in hypostatic union with his humanity. Tillard states that, by the work of the Spirit, Christ is recapitulated in the communion of the Church.[95] Citing Irenaeus, he writes that the Church is not the mere aggregation of individuals. They are not simply packed together. There is a necessary structure given to the Church by its relationship to Christ. The communion of God, constituted in the *perichoresis* of the triune persons, is sacramentally recapitulated in the communion of human beings.[96] If he is the savior, Christ must be accessible to all times and places. "Catholicity" is a quality of the Church, because it is possessed in communion by the Lord. Therefore, "catholicity" is not simply the result of a limitless expansion of Christ's power into the world, a "rising tide of grace," as it were. Rather, catholicity represents the actualization of the paschal mystery, Tillard says, in every human condition without exception.[97] Catholicity does not represent the imperial pretensions of the tyrant, but the *ephapax* ability of Christ to touch each person, each culture, and each church, with an abundance of love. It represents also his ability to teach every person, every culture, and every church how to turn toward one another in love and, by the Spirit, he gives them the ability to do so.

Tillard's "Church of churches" comes from the letter to the Ephesians. Tillard intends it to denote the catholicity of the Church with respect to place and time. He emphasized the phenomenon of multiple local churches is not simply a matter of accumulation or addition. There is not just "one church after another." Rather, churches exist as *churches in communion* with one another. No church exists on its own *as a church.* Autocephaly or schism are anomalies in Tillard's system. Every church must remain open to every other church. This openness is no mere convenience. It is not easy. It is no mere "pastoral consideration." The church that is not "open," because it refuses to live in communion with all the others, is no longer a Church of churches. It is no longer "catholic." Inasmuch as they refuse to recognize any part of Christ's body, those churches refuse to recognize their innermost self.

Tillard subordinates the doctrine of the Church to the doctrine of salvation. The Church, he writes, "is only to be understood in relation to salvation."[98] Salvation is not simply the product of God's benevolence, a "nice reward" that God gives to good people after a virtuous life. Salvation is, Tillard reminds us, a "cosmic enterprise." It involves the whole

---

95. Cf. CofC, 66.
96. Irenaeus, *Adversus haeresis* IV.14.2; *SC* 100, 544–45. Cf. CofC, 50, 66.
97. CdlE, 69.
98. Tillard, "Communion and Salvation," *OIC* 28 (1992) 1.

human adventure with respect to the Creator."[99] The Church, he writes, is "coextensive with salvation."[100]

On the other hand, Tillard notes the "kingdom [of God] is broader than the ecclesial community." Salvation and the Church are not coterminous because salvation, like Christ, subsumes the Church and transcends it.[101] The Church is a *communion* in the salvation offered by God through Christ in the Spirit. In the eucharistic liturgy, this is why the Church may claim to represent and effect the agapic love of the reign of God. To be a *sacrament* of salvation, the Church does not have to exhaust the meaning of salvation. To be a *sacrament* of salvation, the Church need only receive and offer the *whole* of salvation *in the part that it can.*

The fourth-century bishop Cyprian is attributed with the now classic formula: *extra ecclesiam nulla salus,* "Outside of the church there is no salvation."[102] For Cyprian, it is fair to say "church" was the controlling factor in this equation. For Tillard, however, the controlling factor is "salvation." This difference is not slight. The principle attributed to Cyprian presumes that membership in the visible Church through baptism is prerequisite to paradise. Cyprian could not imagine charity outside of the Church; and the actions of heretics, he thought, are a poor caricature of love. As a rule, modern Christian theologians emphasize the priority of love and mercy in God's saving design. Membership in the Church through baptism is a sign of salvation. The "Church of all whom God will ever save," the "Church triumphant," may in reality be composed of a much larger number of people than all who were ever baptized into our earthly churches. Baptismal certificates, adherence to a bishop or to the pope, these alone do not constitute a church. God's desire to save the entire human race, the mystery of God's election does.

In a 1984 essay, "What is the Church of God?," Tillard states an important ecclesiological principle. The communion of eucharistic gatherings, the local church, he said, establishes a criterion against which church structures must be measured. Church structures which do not serve our dependence on God in love have no justification. Stated negatively, to fail to serve the communion in Christ is to be "ecclesial" in no meaningful sense.[103] This principle is related to Tillard's preference for, what he calls, a "doxological" ecclesiology.

Tillard compared a "doxological" ecclesiology to a "pragmatic" model in a 1983 article, "An Ecclesiology of Councils of Churches."

---

99. *Ibid.*, 2–3.

100. Tillard, "One Church of God," *Mid-Stream* 20 (1981) 286.

101. CofC, 62.

102. Cf. Cyprian, *De ecclesiae catholicae unitate* 8, 19; *Ancient Christian Writers* 25 (New York: Newman Press, 1956) 50f., 61.

103. Tillard, "What is the Church of God?" *Mid-Stream* 23 (1984) 374.

"Pragmatic" ecclesiology supposes that Christian communities are to provide their members what is sufficient for their salvation. Anything more than the "necessary" is secondary. "Doxological" ecclesiology, Tillard's preference, supposes that Christian communities are to give their members what they need in order to become what God wants them to be, "to his praise and glory."[104] The pragmatic ecclesiology assumes that the doctrine of salvation refers primarily to the salvation of individuals. The salvation of each member is the minimum standard to which the Church and its pastoral action is directed. The doxological ecclesiology assumes that salvation refers not only to the final, heavenly (or infernal) destiny of individuals, to their redemption. Salvation includes the continuing movement during this earthly life through which men and women fulfill (or fail to fulfill) their destiny as members of Christ's body, to their sanctification. Salvation refers not only to the forgiveness of sins, but also to their participation in the love of Christ. The result of salvation is not only a "lack of the bad," it is also a "surplus of the good." The only fitting and adequate response to this "surplus" is praise.[105]

In effect the pragmatic ecclesiology encompasses only half of a thorough ecclesiology. It implies a one-sided emphasis upon the forgiveness of sins, but overlooks the reason why God should choose to forgive us in the first place. God forgives us *so that* we may respond in love and choose to dwell in God's love. The doxological ecclesiology restores this dynamic to a more balanced perspective. The communion we experience in the Church today is a foretaste, a "token" (in Greek: *arrhes*) of the full and final communion of the reign of God.[106] Moreover, the Church's existence as a communion, Tillard writes, "constitutes its essence. And the relationship of *communion* with the Father, Son and Spirit shows its deep rootedness even in the eternal reality of the mystery of God."[107]

Communion is a *soteriological* term. It represents, Tillard says, the destruction of barriers made possible "by the blood of Christ."[108] In this life ecclesial communion represents the restoration of the fundamental relationship between life as an individual and life in community. Communion is a remedy for alienation, holding the person in one hand and society in the other. Communion affirms the authentic destiny of each individual, while giving it meaning and perspective as part of the "collective destiny of humanity."[109]

---

104. Tillard, "An Ecclesiology of Councils of Churches," *Mid-Stream* 22 (1983) 196.
105. See LaCugna, 319–68.
106. Eph 1:14.
107. CofC, 29.
108. Eph 2:12-17. CofC, 147.
109. CofC, 18.

Communion is the best starting place for any discussion of salvation. The existence of the human person receives its best affirmation only in communion with others, for the individual is never discounted or jettisoned. Just as the "universal" Church cannot exist without the fullness of communion in each local church, so the communion of the local church cannot exist except as it is lived in the life of each and every person called by Christ to be a part of it. In other words, communion depends upon the *authentic* individuality of human persons. Authentically human people have been transformed by grace so as to live in harmony with God and one another.[110]

Communion, Tillard concludes, is an antidote to the dissolution of humankind brought about by sin and antagonism. "Salvation," he says, "can be found nowhere except in *koinonia*."[111] The redemption of individuals is the precondition of their sanctification. Their sanctification is the precondition of their salvation. Their salvation is the precondition of the recreation of the world. Put simply, the salvation of the many depends on the salvation of the one.

110. CofC, 17.
111. Tillard, "The Church of God is a Communion," *OIC* 17 (1981) 120.

Questions for meditation and dialogue on "Church of God—A Communion of Local Churches"

1. *Offer and acceptance.* The "two Amens" of the Eucharist are at the heart of Tillard's conception of the Church. How do you understand the Church as a gift of God? How does your church talk about or enact its innermost nature as an offer of God's forgiveness for others? In your life or in the history of your church, can you identify special moments of grace when you seemed to move into a deeper and more profound moment of reception or acceptance?

2. *Sacramentality.* Tillard says that sacraments adjust their recipients by inserting them into new relationships with God and others. How do you understand the sacramentality of the Mass or Lord's Supper? Do you agree the Church is a sacrament of Christ's presence? How can churches in your community more effectively convey their character as a sacrament of Christ's sacrifice?

3. *Communion of communions.* With what words, ideas, or actions does your church symbolize and establish its communion with other churches of the same denomination? Could your church ever use any of the same words, ideas, or actions to symbolize or establish communion with churches of other denominations? What is said or done at the Eucharist in your church that shows it to be opened or closed to the influence of other churches?

4. *Doxological versus pragmatic.* Tillard contrasts a pragmatic understanding of the Church to a doxological understanding. Following Tillard's definitions, does your congregation seem to function more pragmatically or more doxologically? Supposing that most churches function both pragmatically and doxologically, at what times does your church seem most "pragmatic"? At what times does it seem most "doxological"? Do you see "doxology" as a fitting remedy to society's problems?

FOR FURTHER READING

Evans, Gillian R. and Michel Gourgues, eds. *Communion et réunion: Mélanges Jean-Marie Roger Tillard*. Leuven: University Press, 1995.

Tillard, Jean-Marie Roger. *Chair de l'Église, chair du Christ: Aux sources de l'ecclésiologie de communion*. Paris: Cerf, 1992.

_____. *Church of Churches: The Ecclesiology of Communion*. R. C. DePeaux, tr. Collegeville: The Liturgical Press, 1992.

_____. "The Church of God is a Communion," *OIC* 17 (1981) 117–31.

_____. "'Communion' and Salvation," *OIC* 28 (1992) 1–12.

_____. *L'Église locale: Ecclésiologie de communion et catholicité*. Paris: Cerf, 1995.

_____. *The Eucharist: Pasch of God's People*. Dennis L. Wienk, tr. Staten Island, N.Y.: Alba House, 1967.

_____. "Roman Catholics and Anglicans: The Eucharist," *OIC* 9 (1973) 131–93.

_____. "Sacrificial Terminology and the Eucharist," *OIC* 17 (1981) 306–23.

CHAPTER SIX

The Eucharistic Succession
of the Church

Jean-Marie Tillard describes a church that is radically open in relationships to other churches. The Church of God, he says, is a communion of local churches. It is the "communion of all the baptized."[1] In this chapter, I would like to explore the idea of a Church that is radically open in relationship to other churches through time. The Church of God exists as a communion of churches through time with all who have ever been baptized.

Transmission of doctrine is one of the chief ways the churches symbolize and maintain continuity through time. Central terms and phrases, like the creed or the baptismal formula, assume a rich life of meaning. Doctrines are transmitted not only in words. Central rituals assume a rich life of meaning across history. Christian worship practices connote relationships between Christians today and yesterday. Furthermore, the transmission of doctrine is one of the chief ways the churches symbolize and maintain their divisions. Churches closed to one another today look to their past and identify decisive events that symbolize the rupture of their former communion. If the members of the "closed churches" are going to move toward one another in full communion, they must do so in ways that do not destroy the communion they already possess with Christians of their heritage. Anglicans, Lutherans, and other Christians possess lively histories and heritage. When they enter upon new levels of communion with one another, they must bring their heritage and traditions into the new communion as well.

Historians have identified a broad range of teachings about Jesus of Nazareth from the beginning of Christian doctrine during the apostolic and sub-apostolic ages. They see diverse and contradictory beliefs even in the earliest layers of sayings about Jesus. Why should we suppose that Jesus himself was thoroughly consistent? The Gospels depict him tailoring messages for his audience. The Bible contains the Synoptic Gospels along with John, the letters of Paul and the letter of James. Christian

---

1. LL, 148.

diversity is "canonized" in the Scriptures. A legitimate diversity of belief and opinion about Jesus and his saving mission lies at the roots of the Church in its apostolic heritage.

In the apostolic churches and later, the range of acceptable beliefs narrowed gradually. Some beliefs and practices were rejected as "heretical." Beliefs and practices were rejected because they seemed to threaten the authority of church leaders, the Church, or the possibility of salvation in Christ. For example, consider the fourth-century Quartodeciman controversy. A large group of Christians in Palestine and Asia Minor were convinced that Easter should always coincide with the Jewish feast of Passover. Called "Quartodecimans"—the "*Fourteeners*"—by their opponents, they observed Easter on the fourteenth day of the Jewish month of Nisan, the day Passover begins. The practice of celebrating Easter in conjunction with Passover is very ancient, possibly apostolic in origin. However, the majority of bishops at the fourth-century Council of Nicea were convinced that Easter should always fall on the first day of the week, always on Sunday. For them it was more important to maintain the connection between Sunday and Easter than the connection between Easter and Passover. When the Quartodecimans were officially condemned as heretics by the council in 325 C.E., the range of acceptable diversity for the Church had again narrowed. Quartodecimans were severely persecuted in the years to follow.

Modern Christians are not usually faced with the question of reconciliation with Christians who do not observe Easter on Sunday. Jehovah's Witnesses and Seventh-day Adventists may be the only contemporary Christians ideologically close to the Quartodecimans. Nonetheless, one is hard-pressed to defend the oppressive actions of the Nicene, Sunday-observing Christians. Whether to observe Easter on Sunday or on the fourteenth of Nisan may strike modern ears as a trivial question, one that hardly touches on the "essentials of faith." Yet, because of the action of the council and the active suppression of the Quartodecimans in intervening years, nearly all modern Christians are faith-descendants of the Sunday-observers. Few would wish to revive this fourth-century controversy.[2]

In the modern ecumenical context, many suggest that the division of the churches obstructs their mission and witness. While no single church can claim to be the Church of God as God intends it to be, each church possesses a certain fullness of communion. Even those churches that claim to possess the apostolic faith in its fullness are diminished by their inability to comprehend the legitimate diversity of faith and its expressions. The Roman Catholic Church, for instance, is arguably dimin-

---

2. For more examples see Elaine Pagels, *The Gnostic Gospels* (New York: Vintage Books, 1981).

ished by the division of the churches. The reconciliation of churches would enhance and augment the quality of communion and unity which the Catholic Church already claims as its own.

Communion ecclesiology supposes that doctrine is both "one" and "diverse." The monolithic church is moribund; the church of limitless options is fruitless. Thus, full agreement to the substance of faith is required before a fruitful eucharistic communion can exist. Likewise, a variety of beliefs and practices are required for the Church's vitality. The Church's communion must manifest unity in essentials and diversity in non-essentials. It is far easier to assert this principle than to apply it. Ecumenical dialogue groups have worked faithfully to define the essentials and non-essentials for faith. It is time to receive their work and to incorporate their wisdom into the lives of the churches.

A *soteriological norm* may assist the churches and church authorities in determining the relative worth of doctrines and practices. Doctrinal items fulfill the soteriological norm if they pass a simple two-question test. If salvation is impossible when certain beliefs or practices are suppressed, then they are essential for faith. If salvation is impossible when certain beliefs or practices are expressed, then their suppression is essential for faith. All the rest are matters of indifference or *adiaphora*. In actual practice, however, church authorities are more easily persuaded to increase the number of essential doctrines than to decrease them. The extension of "essential" status to marginal doctrines and practices is an easy and effective way for church leaders to manage and increase their authority. Whether this represents an authentic exercise of ministry, I respectfully register doubt.

Strongly confessional churches and church leaders sometimes exert their wills powerfully in order to preserve their institutions and offices. Their actions reveal a desire to remain *who they are*. They esteem *status quo* more than communion. Doctrines and practices become disengaged from real soteriological questions and concerns. They proliferate because they are so effectively used as tools for social control. The confessional churches and their leaders have difficulty hearing the voices of criticism from within and from without.

In cases of extreme confessionalism, doctrines are drafted to serve the distinction of social states. Power is used to create powerlessness among the people. Knowledge is limited and made inaccessible to the powerless, who are now also made ignorant. Powerless and ignorant people are easily manipulated by propaganda, which impersonates the expression of faith. By contrast, communion ecclesiology would end this dynamic. Doctrine and the transmission of doctrine are limited to the minimum essentials, those items necessary for a thoroughly Christian apprehension of salvation. The powerless are freed to share in Christ's power. The ignorant are allowed to apprehend the mystery of Christ's word directly.

Can one act simultaneously in the interest of self-preservation and for communion in Christ? Communion ecclesiology asserts the Eucharist as the central focus of the Church. The Church is sustained in communion through time and place in the Eucharist. The paschal mystery of Jesus is the central focus of the Eucharist, hence also of communion ecclesiology. A church which proclaims itself indebted to communion ecclesiology must therefore be willing to abandon self-defensive rhetoric, dismantle institutional boundaries, and modify structures of authority according to the pattern of Christ's self-offering. A self-abandoning, kenotic Church is the practical outcome of a communion ecclesiology. One cannot both claim to support communion ecclesiology and act in ways which undermine the real possibilities for communion among the now divided churches.

When the Church receives the Eucharist, faith is both personal and immediate. There is no way for communicants to insert a codicil into the "Amen" when one receives the bread and drinks from the cup. The open table fellowship of the Eucharist was not just for Jesus and the people of his day. The Eucharist must conform to the table fellowship of Jesus. It must be open with respect to every social distinction. When we say "Amen" we are also saying "Amen" to everyone whom Christ has called to live with him *without exception.*

The sacrifice of the Cross is radically egalitarian in its impact on humankind. It was performed once, and for all. The Church that desires to be eucharistic must also be conformed to the radical egalitarianism of the Cross. When the Church is drawn up into the sacrifice of Christ, it may not believe that its sacrifice is offered only for a few people or only for that Church's own people. The openness of the Church is an outcome of the openness of Christ's sacrifice. The Church's desire to be conformed to the *ephapax* character of Christ's sacrifice, therefore, is identical to the sacrifice of the Mass.

In communion ecclesiology, the Eucharist is the main sign of the reception of Christ's paschal sacrifice in each time and place. If the Church's doctrine is coordinated to a soteriological norm, then it must also be coordinated to the signs through which we receive our knowledge of salvation. Doctrine must be coordinated to the Eucharist. The Eucharist must be a central location for the reception and transmission of doctrine. The Eucharist makes the Church. It also *makes* the Church's doctrine. This is the eucharistic *paradosis.*

1. Paradosis *and communion*

Paradosis is the noun form of the Greek verb *paradidomi*, which means, "to transmit" or "to hand along." It also means "to betray."[3] The term occurs twice in the biblical texts we have been considering. In 1 Corinthians 11:23 and 15:1-3, Paul spoke of the contents of the Christian *paradosis*. He had received something from Christ directly and has passed that along to others within the Christian community.

In 1 Corinthians 11:23, Paul said he had received the knowledge of the Eucharist "from the Lord" and had "handed it on to you." The implication is that the Corinthians knew two origins for the tradition of the Eucharist. It was taught to them by Paul, and so has an *apostolic* origin. It was taught to the apostles by Christ on the night in which he was "handed over *(paredideto)*," and so has a *dominical* origin. Insofar as the Corinthians received the Eucharist at all, they received it *apostolically*, "from the apostles." Insofar as anyone ever received a share in the Eucharist, they received it *dominically*, "from the Lord."

Lietzmann, remember, thought that Paul's claim to have received the Eucharist "from the Lord" meant that Paul had received an instruction on the Eucharist directly from Christ in a vision. There is no evidence to prove or disprove such a belief. Considering the accounts of his conversion, Paul may have been disposed to receiving visions, yet nowhere else did Paul appeal to visions for his exposition of the faith. What did he mean when he said he had received the Eucharist from the Lord? [4] If he meant "immediately," that would only affirm Lietzmann's "mystical vision" idea. If he meant "indirectly," then one may only interpret Paul's statement as a claim in support of the mediation of the apostles. Paul would in effect be saying, "I received the Eucharist 'from the apostles' *as if* I had received it 'from the Lord.'" Jerome Murphy-O'Connor takes the argument far beyond these interpretations. He claims Paul equated the Church and Christ. Paul, he says, received the Eucharist "from the Lord" *because* he had received it from the Church, which is the Lord's body.[5]

Oscar Cullmann's discussion of this passage, however, is more nuanced than either Lietzmann's or Murphy-O'Connor's. Cullmann suggested that the word "Lord," *(kyrios)* in this text does not refer only to the earthly Jesus, but to the Risen Christ "at the right hand of God" and now present in his Spirit.[6] The tradition of the words and works of Jesus

---

3. *TDNT* II, 173, s. v. παραδοσις, *Paradosis* by Friedrich Büchsel.

4. Acts 22:6-11, 26:12-19.

5. Murphy-O'Connor, *1 Corinthians*, 196.

6. Oscar Cullmann, "*Paradosis* et *Kyrios*," *Revue d'histoire et de philosophie religieuses* 30 (1950) 15.

belongs now to the entire community.[7] Cullmann continued, however, to wonder why Paul singled out this one tradition, from all the traditions of the community, to say, it "came from the Lord."[8]

Theologically, there is a qualitative difference between apostolic, ecclesial, and dominical traditions. The entire effect of such qualitative differences implies a real hierarchy of truth among the doctrines and practices the Church has received. Dominical traditions, traditions that bring us into a direct apprehension of the earthly and now risen Savior, are far more important than the day-to-day activities of the local church whose "traditions" might include preferred hymns, where to store the communion linens, or who is particularly good at decorating the church for Christmas. On the other hand, we meet the Lord only in the present, in the everyday life of the Church.

Cullmann concluded that the proper subject of the Church's *paradosis* is Christ himself, in his person, the "incarnation of the New Law."[9] Apostolic tradition safeguards the Church's ongoing encounter, by the Spirit, with Christ. The little "traditions," the ones that often cause the most fuss for pastors and church leaders, are tertiary. All three streams exist within the wide and living stream of the Church's *paradosis*. Salvation history, as such, is the place where the Church will live out and transmit life in communion with God, the living *paradosis*.[10]

In 1 Corinthians 15:1-3, Paul reminded the Corinthians of the fundamental message of the Gospel. The good news of Jesus' death and resurrection is handed on through the Church. In New Testament Greek, the word "gospel" is a verb. Literally translated, Paul refers to the "good news with which I have 'good-newsed' *(evangelisámen)* you."[11] The good news is active and comes by way of the apostles. Faith is the outcome of the apostolic ministry.[12] Still, Paul did not say that the good news originated with him. He is only the mouthpiece, a vehicle for the message, which possesses him. The message and its power come from the Spirit, from the "grace of God that is in me."[13]

To hand on and to receive the Gospel are linked. One cannot receive what has not been given. The Church's ministry, if it is truly apostolic, is consumed in handing on the message, but it is consummated in the reception of the message by others. The Church's ministry has no other

7. Cullman, 16.

8. Cullman, 17.

9. Cullman, 24.

10. Cf. Oscar Cullmann, *Unity through Diversity*, tr. M. Eugene Boring (Philadelphia: Fortress Press, 1988) 28.

11. 1 Cor 15:1.

12. 1 Cor 15:11.

13. 1 Cor 15:10.

reason except to give voice to the living traditions of the Church. Tillard reminds us the office of the Church is to proclaim the Word. But the Church, he continues, "has no power over the act of faith," over the moment of reception.[14] The Church does not require belief in the one who is doing the proclaiming. We are not required to believe in John, or in Paul, in Peter or James. We are called to believe in the God that saves us—whom they proclaimed. In other words the apostolic *paradosis* does not serve itself or its own ends. The Church continuously and generously pours out (*kenotically*, i.e., to the point of emptiness) the contents of faith before the world. The apostolic *paradosis* exists only so that the *paradosis* of Christ may continue to be received. The apostolic ministry is consummated in the faith of those who receive Christ, whose faith, in turn, becomes *apostolic*.

Ministry to the transmission of faith is the apostolic vocation of the Church. In a particularly important analysis of the apostolic vocation, Tillard concludes that "apostolicity" is both transmissable and non-transmissable. The transmission of apostolicity was already described in the last few sentences. The proclamation of the word of God continues to this day. However, apostolicity is also non-transmissable in the sense that the apostolic age is definitively closed.[15] The vocation of the apostles, as first-hand witnesses to the resurrection, has ended. The pastoral office of the Church, therefore is "apostolic" in a secondary sense. It is not apostolic because church leaders and authorities today are not apostles. They are no more first-hand witnesses to the resurrection than any other contemporary Christians. The pastoral office *is* apostolic, however, insofar as its members continue to protect and guard our accessibility to the non-transmissible witness of the apostles. Pastors continue in apostolic ministry whenever they uphold the soteriological norm in the development of doctrine and tradition.

Paradosis therefore is part of the ongoing event of God's self-disclosure. It includes the revelation of God's word, and is part of the events which establish the Church and give the Church its characteristics and qualities. Some complain or fear that the Church has fallen from apostolic purity. From time to time, the contents of the tradition, they say, have been tainted by human elements. This fear is relevant to our discussion. The reception and transmission of doctrine is a process that develops through time and place.[16]

Edward Kilmartin, for instance, drew a useful distinction between "vertical" and "horizontal" consensus. He writes that doctrinal consensus through time ("the vertical consensus") has priority over the doctri-

---

14. CofC, 250.

15. Tillard, "The Eucharist in Apostolic Continuity," *OIC* 24 (1988) 17.

16. Cf. E. J. Kilmartin, "Reception in History," *JES* 21/1 (1984) 34–54. George Tavard, "Tradition as Koinonia in Historical Perspective," *OIC* 24 (1988) 97–111.

nal consensus at any one time ("the horizontal consensus").[17] Similarly, George Tavard focuses on the sacramentality of tradition in general. The communion of the churches, Tavard says, manifests the tradition at each moment in time. The "horizontal" consensus is expressed in the communion of churches today. The "horizontal" consensus and the "vertical" are not the exclusive domain of bishops or clergy, but there is truly an apostolic succession among the entire people of God. All the people take part in the movement of the Church in consensus of faith from each moment to the next.[18]

Historical study shows that the witness of the apostles was not as clear and self-evident as some may prefer. Knowledge of the apostolic witness is further clouded by sparse documentation. Layers and layers of historical and cultural changes, set down over the past two centuries, must be unearthed before the "apostolic" perspective could look up at us out of the rubble. The developments of history and culture, then, must not have removed the apostolic faith so far from us that we cannot be saved. Even in our humble knowledge of the apostolic witness, there is something in the central core of today's consensus of faith which touches us where we need in order to be redeemed.

In my family we own several copies of old Dutch psalters and Bibles. For my ancestors, singing the psalms from those books was an essential part of their faith. To sing those words with those tunes was part of what it meant for them to be Christian. The books themselves have been handed on, but sadly, in my family, there is no real *paradosis* on the psalter. My late grandmother recognized none of the tunes I once played for her. What was once a living tradition among my ancestors, texts and tunes committed to heart, is now only a few pages and texts, archaic tunes with nearly incomprehensible words. Though I must express the substance of faith in distinction from my Dutch Calvinist forebears—I am an American, late-twentieth-century Roman Catholic—there is still a real and substantial handing on of faith from them, through my parents, to me. If they had not been Christian, could I still be today? If they had not had faith, would they have successfully immigrated to northwest Iowa and western Michigan? I am convinced the faith I can express today would have been immeasurably impoverished if they had not passed their faith along to their children and their children's children. The books of psalms and Bibles remain, for our family, a *symbol* of the precious *paradosis* that did take place. It is also a powerful reminder of the traditions we lost. Faithfulness and loss walk side-by-side in *paradosis*.

---

17. Kilmartin, "Reception," 50.
18. Tavard, 111.

Some might have thought that "doctrine" means catechism texts, or snippets of solemn pronouncements from the pope or the great church councils. *Paradosis* of faith, however, refers first to the transmission of the substance of faith. Words in doctrine, catechisms, and so forth, are the symbols by which the transmission occurs. *Paradosis* depends on far more than the words alone. It implies the transmission of a world-view, of a common ethos. It implies the transmission of "rules for living," the way one should live with God and with others. *Paradosis* implies the transmission of a way of being human along with a way of speaking about what being human means.[19]

The conveyance of such an enlarged sense of *paradosis* was one of the chief aims of Paul's letter to the Corinthians. Recall that Paul's rhetorical strategy sought to encourage the Corinthian church to live together more peacefully. The concord of Christians, Paul seems to have been saying, is one of the chief benefits of the reception, in faith, of the apostolic *paradosis*. Concord, therefore, could not have been the result of merely assenting to verbal declarations. It involved also living together in an agreeable fashion, with no other "lord" among us, except the Savior. "Ecclesial life," Tillard writes, "does not rest on an abstract acceptance of doctrine. Doctrine must be embodied in a concrete *communion*."[20] Doctrinal statements must be interpreted in light of the ecclesial context in which they are made. Unity in practice occasionally conceals diversity in faith and vice versa. We should not be surprised by this.[21]

Our understanding of *paradosis* is impoverished to the extent that we believe it is constituted by the transmission of information. Instead, it is chiefly constituted by the transmission of communion through time and place. *Christian paradosis* involves the transmission of the love and Spirit of Christ. In this sense, again, the Church is not so much the agent for the transmission of faith, but the recipient, grasped in faith by the Spirit of Christ. Tradition, Tillard states, is not a body of texts. "It is the Church *en marche*."[22]

2. A succession of eucharistic assemblies

The meaning of *paradosis* is not very far removed from that of *kenosis*. In the communion of trinitarian life, the Father gives over the Father's entire being to beget and enter into relationship with the Son. The *paradosis* of the Father is *kenotic*, because the Father does not withhold any part of the Father's being to beget the Son. The Son is coequal to the

19. CofC, 145.
20. CofC, 130.
21. Tillard, "How Do We Express Unity of Faith?" *OIC* 14 (1978) 319.
22. CofC, 140. Cf. Michael O'Connor, "The Holy Spirit and the Church in Catholic Theology: A Study in the Ecclesiology of J.-M. R. Tillard," *OIC* 28 (1992) 334.

Father only because the *entire* being of the Father has been given to the Son. When *paradosis* is complete and thorough, *it is kenotic.*[23]

The Church experiences the *paradosis* of God as the revelation of the fullness of God's love for the world. The incarnation is a transmission *(paradosis)* of the Word into the world, for the sake of God's love for the world.[24] The gift of the Spirit is likewise a *paradosis*. The Spirit is poured out over the world. Those who respond, in faith, to this Spirit are drawn up into the Church. Tradition is therefore both charismatic—referring to the gift of the Spirit—and personal—for God constitutes persons in this loving self-offering. The Eucharist is at the heart of the *paradosis* of the Church because it is the primary location where communion is given and received. Moreover, the eucharistic *paradosis* of the Church establishes the Church in an unbroken succession of Christian assemblies.

The eucharistic communion of the Church is mediated through the apostles, yet it is immediate by the gift of the Spirit. The eucharistic communion is mediated through the apostles because it is part of the legacy of the apostolic Church. The apostles recognized the risen Lord in the breaking of the bread. They remembered their meals with the earthly Jesus in a new way following their experience of his resurrection.

Paul, too, is part of the tradition of the Eucharist. We have a Eucharist because of Paul's ministry. His testimony in the letter to the Corinthians is the first witness to the Lord's Supper. Paul's tradition of the Lord's Supper strongly influenced the story's retelling by the authors of the Synoptic Gospels. The sayings gospel, Q, did not include an institution narrative. The *Didache*, an early Christian liturgical document, is similar to Q in that it too has no institution narrative. In both Q and the *Didache*, the Eucharist is presented as an extension of Jewish table practices, with the inclusion of strong eschatological references. In John, there is again no institution narrative. In John, Jesus blesses and praises God, breaks the bread and shares it. The stories of the multiplication of loaves, I suggest, belong to the earliest strata of eucharistic traditions. In these stories, Jesus is the "eucharistizer." In the Pauline and synoptic institution narratives, a later development is represented. There, we see the beginnings of a later trend in the eucharistic tradition. In Paul's letters, Jesus becomes the message; he is "eucharistized." Von Harnack once wrote that, in the Christian traditions of the first century, we see Jesus, the "proclaimer" of God's kingdom, become "proclaimed." So in the eucharistic traditions of the first century, we see Jesus, the "eucharistizer" of God, become "eucharis-

---

23. Constantine Scouteris, "*Paradosis:* The Orthodox Understanding of Tradition," *Sobornost* 4 (1982) 30ff.

24. John 3:16.

tized." The agapic and agrarian meal traditions of the *haburah* become the cultic and sacrificial meal traditions of Eucharist.

The eucharistic communion is also received, immediately, as a gift of the Spirit. Like the entire *paradosis* of the Church, the Spirit creates eucharistic communion among us each time it is offered and received. Communion depends upon the Spirit for its efficacy and while each Eucharist depends on the transmission of ritual knowledge from one generation to the next, the saving effect of the rite depends upon the Spirit's power every time the ritual is enacted.

We depend on the Spirit to bring the work of salvation near us. The Spirit is the being of God insofar as we are given and receive any communion with God at all. We must therefore admit that God *can* bring about a new thing among us. God *does* bring about an entirely new communion among us when we gather around the table for the Eucharist. Each Eucharist is performed in a new time and by a new assembly. If we could not depend on the Spirit to bring about the work of God in us each time, then we would have to imagine that our rituals and words are the sole means for establishing the continuity of the Church. The continuity of the Church depends on the continuity and permanence of God. It does not depend to the same degree on the continuity or permanence of the assembly, its people, its doctrines, or its leaders.

Misunderstanding the Spirit's work in the liturgy is the origin of false rubricism. Rubricism consists of the idea that the reality of Jesus' presence among us can be entirely encoded within a set of words and actions, handed down in minute detail from the time of Christ. The rubricist fears that changes in the Church's ritual imperil their sacramentality. The attempts by some to restore an imaginary, "perfect liturgy" stems from these fears and concerns. There are no recipes for salvation. There are no recipes for good liturgy. Rubricism obscures the graciousness of God and implies that God cannot or does not choose to save us unless we say and do the right things.

The historical study of Christian liturgy during this century has helped to address the problem of false rubricism. The liturgy, we know, has responded to historical, cultural, and social demands. The Eucharist has changed over time and is observed in many different ways. How, then, do we recognize authentic forms of the rites and distinguish them from false or unfruitful developments? Such questions cannot be answered in the abstract and our answers rely on the common sense of faith. That is, the Church *as a whole* must discern the Word and works of the Spirit. All that we can be assured is that God is faithful and does not secretly plot our undoing.

Hope for salvation is not founded on words. It is not founded on rites. The communion we accept and receive in the Eucharist is a revelation of the saving love of God. Human beings have it in their power to say words and perform deeds that threaten or injure their own or other people's ability to respond in love to the love of God. Those words and deeds cannot threaten or injure God's love. They can, however, destroy the possibility of communion, because they can literally impair, injure or kill the person whom God had hoped to receive in love.

Apostolicity is not merely a succession in ministry. It is not even a chain of unbroken doctrines or practices. Merely holding onto forms of words, like the creeds, is no guarantee that any person or church still lives in communion with God. The apostolic succession of the Church is certainly symbolized in the laying on of hands and in the succession of bishops and priests.[25] The office of the bishop *is* a sacrament of the apostolic succession of his church. But the succession itself neither exists only among clergy nor is it guaranteed by the clergy alone. The apostolic succession, in its first meaning, must apply to the succession of eucharistic assemblies, constituted in the Eucharist as the body of Christ. The constitution of the ministry of the Church in apostolic succession derives from the apostolicity of the Church and not the reverse.

Communion ecclesiology describes the Church as a succession of local churches, faithful in doctrine and practice to the soteriological norm, immersed in the sacrificial love of Christ by the power of the Spirit. Through the Spirit, communion is manifested anew in myriad times and places. There is a relationship between these manifestations. The succession of one assembly into another, its openness toward others in communion, their common *paradosis*, forms the core and purpose of apostolic succession.

Consider the humble example of a mother preparing her daughter for First Communion. For this family, First Communion means white gowns and gifts, a large family meal—huge bowls of pasta. Going to Mass, walking down the aisle, gathering around the altar, receiving the bread and cup, are totally ensconced within the family's other observances. In passing along the entire complex of familial and ecclesial "rites," the mother has a vital role to play in the apostolic ministry of the Church. The child's living *paradosis*—including the gown and veil, the gifts and dinner—is no less a part of her reception of Christ than are the liturgical rites. The entire, rich context of the day is the "first communion" for this child and her family.

No less true in other contexts, baptism, confirmation, or marriage, liturgical rites are richly contexted events within the lives of individuals and local churches. To focus exclusively on the supposedly "essential" or

---

25. "Apostolic Continuity," 16.

"immutable" elements of the sacraments risks ignoring the places where the "grace of the sacrament" is truly recognized and experienced.

From the perspective of the local church, First Communion represents another level in the consummation of its *paradosis* with respect to this child. The introduction of another person into the local communion culminates the apostolic ministry of the Church. Simply put, the Church that has taken bread, blessed it, broken it, and given it has fulfilled its apostolic mandate. The Gospel is fulfilled in its simplest form during the interchange between child and eucharistic minister. Her response, "Amen," to the minister's "The body and blood of Christ," is embedded within a dense constellation of significant actions. There is the displaying, the praying, the holding, grasping, extending of the hand, eating, drinking, chewing, swallowing. Where is the minimal essence of the rite in this? Christ is sacramentally offered and sacramentally received in the entirety of the rite. In giving away its bread and its cup, the Church is sacramentally offered and received. One communicant at a time, the Church is made not to forget the sacrifice of Christ, his *kenosis* in love. One communicant at a time, the Church comes into being.

Receiving the Eucharist makes the Church since the Church that is generated by the Eucharist is a "receiving church." The Church that offers the Eucharist is always a "dying church," a "self-giving church." To borrow a phrase from Paul, the Church is so wed to the "forms of this world," it is, along with the world, "always passing away."[26] This Church is always being poured out into the being of another, into the next generation, into the poor and lowly of the world. Inasmuch as the Church lives, it lives because its entire being is always being given away.

There is no guarantee that the Church will survive another generation—or even from one moment to the next. By some catastrophe, it would be possible for the Christians of the world to simultaneously "forget" or fail to pass along the faith they had received. Only consider the history of northern Africa to witness the demise of the eucharistic *paradosis* and of the Church. The Church in North Africa once thrived. Home to hundreds of saints, Augustine, Monica, Perpetua, Felicity, the churches of Hippo and Carthage, Alexandria and others are now withered giants. The vigor of Islam was certainly a factor in their demise. In the end though, the African churches failed during the seventh century because faith was no longer being received. The people had died, were refugees, or converted to the new religion. The Church can only control and measure its own self-surrender. It is powerless to control how others receive Christ's message.

26. 1 Cor 7:31.

3. Communion through time

The *paradosis* of the Eucharist describes communion through time. The churches of the year 998 and the year 1998 are not usually thought to exist outside of communion from one another. Temporal discontinuity is not, in itself, a threat to Christian communion. The Church of 1998 would have had to explicitly disavow its communion with the Church of 998. Even then, it is difficult to imagine what could possibly amount to a full, complete, and thorough rejection of the Christians of an earlier age.

Recent official apologies for past abuses by the Church and by church authorities are not signs of rejection. Apologies for the pogroms against the Jewish people, for the treatment of Galileo, or for the abuses of the Inquisition, are a witness to our communion with earlier Christians. We apologize and repent for the actions of earlier Christians because their abuses were real and because those abuses were conducted by members of our own family of faith. Admitting the fault in beliefs that were once considered unquestionably "Christian" witnesses to our ability to receive the faith of earlier Christians. Receiving their false beliefs as departures from Christian faith, we also challenge and critique faulty and inadequate opinions at large today. Communion is not destroyed when the Church moves beyond the beliefs and practices of yesterday's Christians. The Church of each age must receive the faith anew.

The Church of 1998 similarly needs to remain open with respect to the judgements the Church of 2998 will make. The Christians of the future may look on our age as we look upon the "early church." They may wonder why the status of women for ordination was such a problem for us—they may have finally resolved this issue. They may wonder why our churches were closed to one another—they may have formed new unions or new divisions. Today, we must look for the salvation to come and respond in obedience to the Spirit's promptings. We must be content to suppose that Christians of the future, similarly obedient, may reverse or surpass everything we tried to accomplish. Can we still live in communion with the churches of unborn generations? We must be open to their contribution and should not seek to bind them too tightly. "Openness," as an essential character of the Church, does not pertain only to communion in the present.

Receiving and rejecting the doctrines and practices of the churches of the past, the contemporary Church is not normally thought to have defected from communion with the past. To eschew its apostolic character, the Church would have to do far more damage than rejecting one or more categorical expressions of the faith of an earlier epoch. Faith is far more malleable than doctrine, because faith is the result of the loving communion of persons. For the Church to damage its apostolic character, it would have had to make salvation in Christ an impossibility for itself or for others. Thus *paradosis* does not require uniformity, but still permits us to speak about a Church as united in communion with Christ across the years.

3.1. *Paradosis* as sacrament

In the actions of the Eucharist, taking bread, blessing, and breaking it, the Church finds itself entangled in a new and independent subjectivity. The Church finds itself drawn into relationship with a person greater than itself. The ritual actions of the Church, in effect, *hypostasize* the Church's communion. The Church is confronted, in its own words and deeds, with a vision of its own true personality. Such claims rest on the idea that the meaning of "the body of Christ" or "the blood of Christ" are discovered whenever we break bread or drink from the cup. The meaning of the terms will always be affected by our daily experience of the liturgy.

The Eucharist, Tillard writes, is the source of the "network of mutual relationships and exchanges that . . . the community weaves together in order to be the church which God wills."[27] To receive Christ in the Eucharist is to participate, sacramentally, in a huge network of relationships with all who have this relationship in Christ. One rediscovers one's identity in the context of a nearly infinite number of new, loving relationships. This is no "metaphorical" claim. Men and women who come to the Church discover this every day. These new relationships are rich or poor, better or worse, fair or injured, healing or injurious. In the Church, however, the sick, the poor, the weak, the infirm, and the wounded are brought together beneath the infinitely large tent of God's mercy. To live in communion with them, we are saying, is essential to life in communion with Christ.

3.2. Sacraments of our salvation

Sacramental theology easily accounts for the presence of Christ in any one Eucharist. He is present in the proclamation of his Word, in the person of his minister, in the sacraments, especially in the bread and cup of his body and blood.[28] The eucharistic *paradosis* assists sacramental theology for it helps account for the presence of Christ in the *succession* of eucharistic assemblies. Communion is not one event in isolation. It is received in a series of events. Communicants come to the table in every situation of their lives. Through ongoing encounter with Christ and one

27. CofC, 155.
28. SC, 7.

another, they acquire a far more detailed understanding and knowledge of who Christ is for them. A naive eucharistic realism might claim that "now Christ is present" after the consecration and "now Christ is not" after the communion. A more robust eucharistic realism, however, must maintain that Christ is present as savior also in the relationships which link one eucharistic assembly to the next.

Christ's promise of enduring presence, "until the end of the age," makes possible a discussion of the Church's continuity in being.[29] If Christ were not present in Eucharist after Eucharist, if there were no eucharistic *paradosis*, or if Christ's promise to be present had gone somehow, tragically, unfulfilled, then the Church, too, would have remained an isolated, one-time event. Perhaps there would have been a single day of "Pentecost" in the first century, a brief fizzling of fervor, then extinguished. But the Pentecost continues and the Spirit is given with such lavishness it "spills over" from one gathering into the next and from each gathering into the world.

The Church is not simply an event. It is a series of events. The Church is not simply an institution, though it takes the complexion of an institution because of the faithfulness of God through time. The Church is built up in an entire history of events where God's grace has injected itself into human lives and cultures. The Church's institutional complexion may not be divorced from its saving mission. The institutional characteristics of the Church entirely depend on God's will to save us. The Church recognizes a continuity of being in its history of eucharistic assemblies. No single, living Christian may claim to have been present at the Last Supper. The Church, however, may claim to have been there, performing and receiving the meal with its founder.

The eucharistic *paradosis* is given for the purpose of salvation. I suggest the eucharistic *paradosis* is another mode of Christ's presence for us. If so, then the *paradosis* of the Church, the succession from the apostles, is given for the purpose of our communion with Christ and one another. The *paradosis* of the Church is a sign of the steadfast continuity of God's grace for the human creature. The institutional and historical characteristics of the Church are less the indications of human faithfulness to God. They are more indicative of the absolute faithfulness of God toward women and men.

The saving mission of the Church depends on its being part of a richly ambiguous, ongoing history of communion. By itself, the "first communion" does not have an intrinsic value for the person. It must include and imply the hope and commitment to further, future events of communion. To speak of the "Church" as though it meant a single, eas-

29. Matt 28:20.

ily identifiable group or class of people is always a problem. We do not always know who will join us in our next communion, and how they will affect and change us. Christ suffers these changes along with us. Pluralism, ambiguity, doubt—these are signs of a Church that, though it knows the outcome of the "last day," does not know the outcome of "tomorrow." *Paradosis* leads us to the "last day" only by way of "tomorrow." The Church's eucharistic *paradosis* therefore includes pluralism, ambiguity, and doubt.

Pluralism, ambiguity, and doubt in our explanations and understanding of the Church and the Eucharist are not only the signs of human finitude and ignorance. They have an interesting and unexpected value for our understanding of salvation. The Church's *paradosis* on the Eucharist shows, even more clearly, the borderlessness of salvation and the love of God. God can love us and save us even though we are ignorant and can be surprised. Understanding the Eucharist and the Church precludes knowing "once-and-for-all" what they are and what they mean. As men and women join the Church, the accretion of their lives and love infinitesimally alters the meaning and nature of the Church and the Church's communion. *Paradosis*, if it is to continue, requires that the Church *move* to meet the Other, the ones who will come to the table tomorrow, and the day after that.

The borderless character of the Eucharist is not necessarily limited to the meals that Jesus shared with the socially marginal men and women of his day. If the Church is to succeed into the future, the Eucharist must be opened at least with respect to the next generations, the poor, and the marginalized. Ambiguity, finitude, and uncertainty in the doctrine of the Eucharist are also part of the borderless character of the Church. Though the Church may be infallible and certain on essentials, it must also be open with respect to the manner in which its doctrines will be received. The Church is free to develop its eucharistic *paradosis* and to extend it, in accord with the fundamental, soteriological character of the Eucharist. If the Eucharist must be a "borderless board" with respect to the number and kind of people who may dine there, then it must be also somewhat "borderless" with respect to the number and kind of explanations these people will give to their experience of communion with God.

The eucharistic *paradosis* is sacramental. The eucharistic *paradosis* does not denote an absolute presence of Christ, but a "presence in absence." The sacramentality of the eucharistic *paradosis*, moreover, does not describe a limit with respect to God, but with respect to humankind.

The eucharistic *paradosis* gives the Church a rhythmic quality. The Church, as a sacrament of the presence of Christ, finds itself gloriously exalted by this experience. However, the Church is simultaneously minimized, because its ability to signify Christ and the kingdom does not persist. The Church does not abide, but from time to time, the Church draws its life and love from Christ, from the Spirit, for the future kingdom. The rhythmic character of the Eucharist gives the Church its sense of time and allows it to seem to abide. At the Eucharist, John Zizioulas states, "the church becomes what she is delayed in being," the body of Christ, the kingdom of heaven.[30] To describe the eucharistic *paradosis* as a sacrament denotes its limitations. The Church can never be so certain of its communion with God than when it actually subsists in the communion God is offering us in the reception of the Eucharist.

Whatever the Church "hands on" in *paradosis* is a finite and partial knowledge of Christ. Nonetheless, however partial, whatever the Church receives and transmits *signifies* the entire Christ for us. Christ is known as much in his absence as in his presence. He is the object of the apostolic witness to his resurrection and heavenly exaltation. He is the object of historical study, which barely knows him as the leader of a peasant revolt, executed by the Romans. Finally, Christ is known today in the eucharistic actions of his body. While the entire Christ is represented and received in *paradosis*, he is represented and received in partial, finite words and signs. While the whole Christ is known and loved in the communion of the Eucharist, no one Church can know and love him entirely or impartially. No one Church can know and love Christ so thoroughly that the knowledge and love of the other Churches is rendered superfluous.

Consequently, the *paradosis* of any Christian church, of any Christian community, is a partial *paradosis*.[31] The Church's affirmation of faith is always historically conditioned. The way in which each church confesses and lives its communion in Christ is limited and this limitation cannot destroy the possibility of their being redeemed and saved. This is another reason why individuals and churches must be joined to one another in communion. As parts of the whole, they must be drawn into communion, and so be opened to the whole. The churches that are closed to the whole, that are not "catholic," cannot know, live, and confess the entirety of the Christian *paradosis*. While each Church represents, in its teachings and in its sacraments, the fullness of God's salvation, each church may not claim to signify salvation in so perfect a fashion that it can "go it alone" and pretend not to need the strength, the wisdom, or the correction of the others.

---

30. John Zizioulas, "L'Eucharistie: quelques aspects bibliques," in *L'eucharistie*, ed. John Zizioulas, J.-M. R. Tillard, J. J. von Allmen, Églises en dialogue 12 (Paris: Mame, 1970) 31. McPartlan, 287f.

31. Cf. Richard McBrien, "The Church: Sign and Instrument of Unity," in *Structures of the Church*, ed. Jimenez Urresti, Concilium 58 (New York: Herder and Herder, 1970) 50.

Finally, the eucharistic *paradosis*, like all sacraments, describes a limit with respect to creatures but not with respect to God. Both communion and *paradosis* originate in Christ through the Spirit and are signified and transmitted through signs that human beings are capable of enacting and receiving. Whatever is required for salvation must be communicated mediately—through signs—or immediately—by grace—to human beings and communities. Whatever is defective in the communication of signs—in the eucharistic actions, in the words which constitute a living *paradosis*—is supplied by God's grace. Human signs and human communication acts are always limited vehicles. The *paradosis* of the Church is thus not a merely human act. Like all sacraments, it consists of words and deeds. The *paradosis* is made through songs and prayers, hymns and catechisms, taking, gathering, blessing and breaking. However, God remains free yet faithful with respect to these actions. God is free to use other actions and signs to proclaim the message of salvation, and so is not limited to our use of official rites, official books, special formulas of words, prescribed patterns of ritual. God can use our actions, and because God is faithful, God does.

4. Conclusion

Perhaps the best way the Church hands on the Eucharist, its best *paradosis*, is the mere doing of the actions which comprise the Eucharist. Does one acquire a better knowledge of Christian communion except by being drawn into the love of others? Does one acquire a better understanding of the Eucharist except by taking bread, blessing, and breaking it with others? Christians *remember* the Eucharist with their bodies. They bear this memory into their lives away from the table. They *remember* the Eucharist when they write, when they eat, when they fail or sin. The Eucharist, some have said, exercises or "rehearses" us in relationships and behaviors that, though alien to our self-interest, exhibit the kenotic love *(agape)* of Christ. Having rehearsed this love around the table, it begins to permeate, one hopes, the rest of life. The Eucharist acts as a leaven for our common life. A church's ability to behave "eucharistically" outside the context of the liturgy is one measure of the quality of its communion in Christ within the liturgy.

Eucharistic doctrines and their transmission through time constitute, within and among the churches, unique cultural and sociological constituencies. Particularities and peculiarities, if left unchecked and unsupplemented by communion with the whole Church, set in and reproduce across generations. Thus we find the development of "communions" within the communion of the Church. This is not necessarily a negative development, for the genius of the various communions—East and West,

North and South—contributes to the rich complexion of Christianity. Would Christians want to sing Russian chants or Lutheran chorales exclusively? There is more than a single succession of doctrines and practices within the limits of the "essentials" suggested by the soteriological norm.

The existence today of separated ecclesial communions is linked directly to the divergence of *paradosis* on the Eucharist. Even within the imposingly monolithic Roman Catholic Church there is a valid and cherished plurality of *paradosis* on the Eucharist. This is no indication of "corruption" or "error." It is, I suggest, an utterly benign indication of the truly rich comprehensiveness of the salvation which Christ is offering the Church.

Future ecumenical dialogue, then, will want to focus on the convergence of diverse *paradoses*. The churches will recognize that they, alone and uncorrected, do not possess the entire *paradosis* of the Eucharist. *Paradosis*, like communion, is not generated through human effort alone. The churches are possessed in *paradosis*, they do not possess it. Fidelity to tradition is not just another form of "ancestor worship" or "filial piety." On the contrary, fidelity to tradition must walk within the limits described by a soteriological norm. There must be a discernment of the quality of traditions. Is this practice dominical? Is it apostolic? Is it ecclesial? Is it an aberration?

God saves us by giving us over to one another in love. The Church's *paradosis* must be consistent with the communication of signs of love. Handing on doctrine, teaching the catechism, preaching from the heart, hearing the Gospels again and again, these ministries are not to become the means for exerting power, for managing and controlling. They, too, must be performed in an ethically consistent manner. Even the truth has been used, by the corrupt, to debilitate and enslave the powerless.

If the churches receive faith and the contents of faith as a gift of God, will they be less likely to impose that gift on others? Will they be more likely to recognize the diversity of gifts among one another? Will they be more eager to listen and allow the *paradosis* of other churches to permeate their own? Because the *paradosis* of the Church culminates in the Eucharist these "ecumenical dreams" will not happen as long as the churches maintain and sustain divided tables.

Questions for meditation and dialogue on "The Eucharistic Succession of the Church"

1. *Paradosis.* What are some ways your church and churches in your community use to perpetuate themselves from one generation to the next? From the history of your family, your church, or denomination can you describe any examples of doctrines or practices which have fallen by the wayside and are now no longer enforced or considered essential for faith and communion? The Greek verb *paradidomi* can refer to "tradition" and to "betrayal." Is there ever a sense in which the "traditions" of your church are both faithful and less than faithful? How would you distinguish between "dominical," "apostolic" and "local" traditions? In what traditions do you more fully experience Christ or the Church than others?

2. *Succession of assemblies.* The Church is constituted as a communion through time. Can you see a way to renewed communion among the churches of your local community through this concept? Can the churches ever "turn back the clock" on their differences? Or, can you identify a way forward to a reconciled *paradosis* in the churches of your community? What are some simple ways this task could begin?

3. *Institution or event.* Those who say that the Church is an "event" tend to emphasize the charismatic role of the Spirit in the Church or they tend to emphasize the occasional nature of the Eucharist. Those who say the Church is an "institution" tend to emphasize the Church's continuity from each moment of time to the next. Is your church more an "event" or an "institution"? What elements of your church's life make it seem more like an "event"? More like an "institution"? If the Church is only an "event," what ensures it will continue into the next day or into the next millennium? If the Church is only an "institution," what ensures it can change to meet new circumstances in society and culture?

FOR FURTHER READING

Congar, Yves M.-J. *Tradition and Traditions: An Historical and Theological Essay.* Michael Naseby and Thomas Rainborough, tr. New York: MacMillan, 1967.

Kilmartin, E. J. "Reception in History," *JES* 21/1 (1984) 34–54.

Scouteris, Constantine. "*Paradosis:* The Orthodox Understanding of Tradition," *Sobornost* 4 (1982) 30–37.

Tavard, George. "Tradition as Koinonia in Historical Perspective," *OIC* 24 (1988) 97–111.

Tillard, Jean-Marie Roger. "The Eucharist in Apostolic Continuity," *OIC* 24 (1998) 14–24.

_____. "How Do We Express Unity of Faith?" *OIC* 14 (1978) 318–27.

CHAPTER SEVEN

Borderless Church

The salvation of the soul is the supreme law.[1]

Robert Jenson's book *The Unbaptized God* disposed many arguments which have been used to stall ecumenical dialogue. He concluded that Christians, particularly Western Christians, share in a tragic unanimity. They share in an incompletely christianized or, as he put it, "unbaptized" conception of God. Impasse in ecumenism, Jenson argues, represents our failure to appreciate the reality of God *in history*. God *among us* is an essential part of the Christian message of salvation. The intellectual problem for the West has been to understand "God *among us*" while still allowing God to be God. Over time, we have "distanced" God. God is not so much "among us" as God is "over us," "around us," but certainly not "with us." Jenson observes that nearly every issue on which ecumenical dialogue has failed, shares the presupposition that the Church and individual believers inhabit ". . . a temporality to which the risen Christ is intrinsically alien."[2]

The divided table at the Christian Eucharist is one tragic example of this "tragically flawed consensus." The divided table indicates how far the churches have failed to confess God together, how little they have recognized Christ *in their midst* and *in their neighbor*. We do not agree on a common doctrine of the Eucharist. Yet nearly all Christians say they can (usually) discern the body of Christ in the Eucharist of their own Church. The Ecumenical problem of the Eucharist is that many Christians fail to recognize Christ in the breaking of the bread on the tables of other churches. They do not recognize Christ in the Other.

1. God for us in communion with others

John Zizioulas asks, "Are there no limits to otherness in the euchar-

1. "Salus animarum suprema lex." Cf. Rahner, *Shape of the Church to Come*, 111.
2. Jenson, 146. See also Maurice Villain, "Ecumenical Understanding and the Theologian," in *The Future of Ecumenism*, ed. Hans Küng, Concilium 44 (New York: Paulist Press, 1969) 89–97.

istic communion?"[3] Answering his own question, he says, the only "exclusion" in the Eucharist is the "exclusion of exclusion." Schism, apostasy, and heresy are properly "exclusionary" acts. They destroy the dynamics of communion, for they already represent a rejection of the other. Zizioulas is not so clear, though, on the exclusionary practices of the supposedly "non-heretical" churches. Leaders of "non-heretical" churches sometimes exclude men and women in the name of protecting communion within their Church. Sometimes the Church unwittingly excludes only because it is too peculiar in its ways or seems antiquated or strange to modern men and women.

Is there a difference between making communion impossible and protecting the communion that exists? To destroy, deface, or obscure the sacraments of salvation, this kind of obfuscation *does* make communion impossible. On the other hand, the Church easily lives in communion with the proponents of hundreds of controversial and contradictory, sometimes odd, opinions. We live in communion because we *love* one another, not because we *agree* with one another.

Diversity enhances the prospects of communion. Möhler, Schleiermacher, Vatican II, Zizioulas, Congar, Tillard, and many others, all have registered their opinion on this side of the discussion. The hierarchy of truths, they have said, poses the best prospect for communion within diversity. We must learn to distinguish between the "fundamentals" and the "non-fundamentals" in faith, even if Pius XI had enjoined Christians not to do so.

Diversity is the sign of God's having entered a world full of *free* creatures. God is not rapacious, but enters human life *according to the abilities* of those who receive God. God in Christ Jesus represents the absolute fullness of truth. The truth among us, however, is known only partially—according to our ability to know and recognize it. Likewise, God in Christ Jesus represents the absolute fullness of love. Yet, love among us is expressed only partially—according to our ability to know it and share it with others. This dynamic is no less true for individual men and women than it is for individual churches. I would add, it is no less true for the Church as a whole. It is part of the universal condition of humankind.

Our approach to God varies by time and place. We meet God in greater and lesser depths throughout the course of life's history. God can touch us deeply or lightly, recognizing when we can and when we cannot adjust to the experience. Looking back at life's history, we see deeply profound moments of faith and love and we see equally profound moments of rejection or fear.

---

3. Zizioulas, "Communion and Otherness," *Sobornost* 16 (1994) 15.

The communion of the Church is much like this. God is always close to the Church. God does not "defect" or "withdraw" from any of the covenants God has made. But the churches are not always so close or faithful or free. They are not always so near to one another in love. They are not always able to draw close to one another in the communion of the Spirit. Wounded, they withdraw into isolation. Isolated, they turn inward and will not listen to the other churches. While God is still close to that church, and finds a way to love and to save it, that church, the confessional church, remains a much less effective sign of God's love than the other churches.

The quality of communion in any given church is diminished to the extent that its altar is closed to any other baptized Christians. For the churches, to be "open" is first to receive God's constant, abiding, nurturing love freely and without reservation. For the churches, to be "open" is to give the entirety of the love it has received to others in kenotic self-giving. Eucharistic communion, and therefore also the communion of the churches, we have shown, consists in these two dynamics. Accessibility to Christ and his sacrifice epitomizes the divine plan for salvation and establishes the Church as a radically "open" and borderless society. Ecumenism consists in our openness to this dynamic since ecumenism is the result of the churches' faithful striving to live in ever deeper communion.

For the Church, to exist is to exist in communion. For the Church, to exist in communion is to exist ecumenically. Therefore, the ecumenical problem of the Eucharist is no marginal issue. It cannot be treated after other matters of faith or church order. It is the nexus where all other doctrinal issues and concerns come home to rest. The Eucharist is where we learn what it means to know and love God in the knowledge and love of one another.

2. Necessity of structures versus the structures of necessity

Paul used his description of the Lord's Supper to endorse a certain style of Christian community. The Church, he said, must not be divided. It must not have factions. Christians must live as one body, always discerning the body of Christ in the others with whom they share the Supper.

In intervening centuries, the primordial structures of the Church have solidified into several standard juridical, organizational models or systems. So intricate are some of these systems, "hierarchology" has come to impersonate "ecclesiology." "Hierarchology" is a poor substitute for "ecclesiology," for it focuses too exclusively on the structures of earthly power. Its analysis ignores the soteriological dynamics at the heart of Christian communion. I suppose that Soviet Russia is an apt demonstration of "hierarchology" gone amok. Marx's utopian values were sacrificed at the altar of conformity. To make the "structure" of the state work more efficiently, the ideal of freedom for workers was abandoned and the realities of oppression were conveniently ignored. The good of the Soviet state—secrecy, unquestioned authority, conformity—was substituted for the good of society—freedom, the cultivation of human talents, nurturing collective action for the common good. It is one thing to suggest that certain social and cultural structures *are able to* serve the common good. It is another thing to suggest that certain social and cultural structures *are necessary* for the common good.

Much the same holds true in the Church. After all, God allows the churches to exist, in freedom, as totally human, social and cultural institutions. It is one thing to suggest that certain church structures can serve the common good. It is another thing to suggest that certain church structures *are necessary* for our communion in the kingdom of God. Here lies one of the most potentially church-dividing issues revealed by this study. The Church *necessarily* exists in and through social and cultural structures. Some of these structures, all agree, are *essential* to the nature of the Church as a communion of human beings with God. However, none agree that *all* of the structures of the Church are necessary. Neither would all agree on any one kind of structural system for the Church.

There is a difference between affirming the value of a given church polity and insisting that the Church, always and everywhere, in order to be the Church, must exhibit that polity. The "polity" described by the Eucharist, I have argued, *is* one of those essentials. In the Eucharist we have access to Christ and are able to give ourselves to him and to one another in kenotic love. However, the essential place of the episcopacy or the primacy of the bishop of Rome in the structure of the Church is far less obvious from this perspective. For example, one could easily admit that a "primacy" is part of the Church. A certain kind of primacy is evident on every level of the Church—in the presidency of the parish Eucharist, in the ministry of the bishop, in the synodal service of metropolitan archbishops and the patriarchs of East and West. However, many Christians in good conscience have difficulty affirming the absolute essentiality of the Roman pontiff exercising sole, infallible primacy over the entire Church, East and West. The "structure" of primacy may be essential to the Church; but the way the primacy is now exercised is not. One easily imagines primacy exercised quite differently than today. Any number of historical contingencies could have led to a different sort of papacy: had Rome been destroyed in a nuclear holocaust, had St. Peter died in Antioch, had Gregory the Great never been elected bishop of Rome. Christians validly differ on the extent to which the modern Church is bound by the historical developments of earlier periods. The past is a "closed book" and not one of the deeds of the Church and its leaders can be undone.

Roman Catholic ecclesiologies—and Tillard's is no exception—have developed ways to speak about historical developments in the life of the Church which make them sound as though they are ontologically binding on the Church. "There must be only one bishop," we say. "The pope is first among equals," and some more folks will pipe in, adding "but more 'first' than 'equal.'" Reading arguments that amount to sloganeering, it is easy to become impatient with authors who beg the historical questions. "So what if Ignatius could not imagine a Church with more than one bishop?" "What matter if the early councils determined that the Church of Rome should be first among equals, '*primus inter pares*?'" Why should particular and peculiar, historically contingent developments have been drawn—without question and without argument—into orbit about the substance of faith? Showing how historical developments are not inconsistent with the divine plan is not the same as having made arguments for their necessity within salvation's design.

3. The memes that divide—applying the soteriological norm

Social psychologist Mihalyi Csikzentmihalyi's discussion of the competition of ideas sheds light on the (sometimes irrational) persistence of ephemeral ideas long past their usefulness. Most ideas, he says, evolve like objects do. Bicycles and trains, for instance, once they are invented are never "uninvented." Bicycles, trains, and now automobiles, must all now learn to "share the road." In American cities, we still find horse-drawn carriages, now used almost exclusively for "traditional" occasions like wedding processions and moonlight romance. Cultural artifacts—like bicycles, carriages, or cars—and ideas—like freedom, justice, or monarchy—seem to take on lives of their own.[4] Such things are called "memes." The term "meme" Csikzentmihalyi reports, was introduced by English biologist Richard Dawkins about twenty years ago to describe "a unit of cultural information." In its effects on society, a "meme" is comparable to the effects of a gene on an organism.[5] Bricks are memes, symphonies are memes. Gregorian chant and Renaissance polyphony are memes just as much as punk rock and the blues.

In the Church, because it is a human, social and cultural institution, there are many thousands of memes at work. I attempted to distinguish some of them in my discussion of the eucharistic *paradosis*. For American Catholics First Communion memes usually include white dresses and gifts of rosaries and missals. Then there are memes like Gregory Dix's

---

4. Mihalyi Csikzentmihalyi, *The Evolving Self: A Psychology for the Third Millennium* (New York: HarperCollins, 1993) 124f.

5. Csikzentmihalyi, 120.

"four-fold shape" of the liturgy. Until Dix, no one had ever considered the "shape" of the liturgy as such, let alone the number of "-folds" that shape might comprise. Yet, the "four" or "seven" actions at the heart of the Eucharist, Dix admirably showed, have been there from the beginning of the tradition. All agree that breaking the bread and blessing the cup, as Jesus once did, are essential memes in the eucharistic *paradosis*.

Since the Great Schism of 1054 and the Reformation of the sixteenth century, the "memes" that comprise Christian faith have been shunted along several paths. So there are now memes that unite and memes that divide. The polemical memes are still a problem for us. "Outside of the Church there is no salvation," *Sola scriptura*, "The Lord's Supper is *only* a memorial," transubstantiation, the eucharistic sacrifice, polemical interpretations of the *ephapax* character of Christ's sacrifice: all of these are memes. Together they suggest the mimetics of a divided *paradosis* on the Eucharist. Such phrases and practices take on lives of their own. And, as was seen following Vatican II, the reform of the liturgy could not take place without division because adherents to the "old memes" were not going to stand by and idly watch the cultural monument, in their judgment, disfigured. From one perspective, the traditionalist followers of the French archbishop LeFebvre were only "following their memes." They were not radical, but like the Quartodecimans of the fourth century, were defending the *paradosis* they had received in the best way they knew. They could barely imagine a Church that included the Tridentine Mass and Communion under both kinds.

The "memes that divide" are not only doctrinal. Envy, suspicion, class distinctions, and racial strife divide the churches because they divide Christians from each other. Should the day ever come when all Christians are united in a single, world-wide communion, it will have meant that these memes had been overcome as much as any doctrinal disparities. It is not enough that we should agree on the temporal extent of Christ's presence. Christians should agree not to offend each other. They should work together to end attitudes that consider the disposal of the consecrated elements an "irrelevancy" or their worship a matter of dogma. But these things, alone, will not guarantee full communion.

In living memory Catholic children were not allowed to join the YMCA. In living memory Protestant children were not allowed to dance or play cards. In living memory Catholics and Orthodox have come to blows in the Ukraine over which Church owned the buildings. If anything, the Eucharist should have been a place for conflicts to be eased, for the communion of the Church to be renewed, for prejudice and enmity to dissolve in the communion and peace of the Holy Spirit. Ironically and tragically, the sicknesses that need most to be healed by communion so easily thwart communion at every stage.

4. *Accessibility,* kenosis, *openness—primordial qualities of the Church*

Tillard says the communion of the Church is a reconciled communion. It is the place where hatred is buried and distinction has no place. It is the place where the paschal mystery of Christ is drawn near to us, and we are invited to enter. This is the eucharistic heart of the Church. Christ is accessible by the Spirit. We are given a communion in his sacrificial and saving love. We may experience entry into communion as a loss, as a sacrifice of the self, as the "similitude of a holocaust." But we choose to enter, not for our own sakes, but for the sake of the world that must be healed of strife.

Accessibility is a primordial quality of the Church. The Spirit and Christ are *always* accessible to the Church. The accessibility of God culminates in communion. Accessibility is just another word for God's steadfast faithfulness to everyone. Accessibility to God and one another in the Church is the result of God's faithful promises.

Kenosis is a primordial quality of the Church. The eucharistic Church must be a sacrificial Church. The Church enters into communion as an act of self-giving. This is not an act of the Church by itself, but it is an act of the Spirit in the Church. The Church that gives itself away, wholly, is an effective witness to the Spirit's presence within it. *Kenosis* is fundamental to the success of ecumenism, for the voluntary abandonment of cherished, non-essential, yet divisive, practices is not a "sell-out." In Tillard's estimation, they are acts of homage to God.[6]

Finally, the Church that lives in communion with God has such a surplus of being. Ecstatically the Church pours itself out in absolute openness before God and others. Openness is a primordial quality of the Church. The Church that exists in communion is radically open. It is a sign of the kingdom of God for all people. Its only exclusion is the "exclusion of exclusion."

Accessibility, sacrificial self-giving, and openness are part of the fundamental dynamics at the heart of the Eucharist. They operate on the level of the individual, in the offer and reception of communion at the Eucharist. They operate on the level of the local churches, in their relationships to other local churches and the societies of each place and time. They operate on the level of the entire, universal Church of every place and time, as a sign of God's having chosen to dwell among us.

Accessibility, self-giving, and openness lie beneath many traditional qualities of the Church: unity, apostolicity, holiness, etc. The "primordial" qualities are eucharistic qualities since the Eucharist creates the possibility of the higher order characteristics. Each Church will be "one," "apostolic," and "holy" in a unique way because it exists and responds to

---

6. "Preparing for Unity," *OIC* 16 (1980) 18.

God's calling, uniquely and freely, in response to unique circumstances. The ministry of unity among the churches exists to call each church to respond faithfully and freely. It does not exist to call each church to respond uniformly and identically.

5. Leaning together into unity

To date, perhaps the most objective yet optimistic "program" for church unity was proposed by Karl Rahner and Heinrich Fries in their 1983 essay, *Unity of the Churches: An Actual Possibility.*[7] Rahner and Fries did not propose that the churches simply open their tables wide, all at once in indiscriminate table-fellowship. Christian attitudes and beliefs remain too fractious. The attitudes and practices that keep us from joining together in a common table have very little to do with the Eucharist or with communion. Far more do they reveal our failure to be the kind of people God intends us to become.

Rahner and Fries proposed eight "theses" which, they believe, can lead to the reconciliation of churches. These are objective strategies which, if ever followed by church authorities and other leaders, could possibly ameliorate many of the attitudes and practices which continue to divide us. Churches should agree, they said, on the "fundamentals of faith," the priority of Scripture and the historical creeds. They should recognize the faith of others and should not condemn the dogmatically held beliefs of other churches. Neither should any church attempt to impose its dogmatic formulation of faith upon Christians from other churches.

In the reunited Church, they said, local churches might continue in partnership with regional sub-bodies which represented the old denominations. For instance, formerly Anglican churches would be joined officially and unofficially, on the local level with the united leadership of the churches and, on a regional level, with an interjurisdictional leadership. The charism and gifts of partner churches would be united, but not absorbed by a reunited church.

There are several more theses, but underlying all of them is Rahner's and Fries's insistence that the unity of the Church does not yet exist. There are several conditions, they said, which must exist before Christian unity can become a reality. These conditions, they maintained, are neither utopian nor idealistic. The churches are not acting in faithfulness to Christ so long as they postpone the steps necessary to establish unity in the Church. The work for unity and its fulfillment will most certainly be

---

7. Karl Rahner and Heinrich Fries, *Unity of the Churches: An Actual Possibility,* tr. Ruth C. L. Gritsch and Eric W. Gritsch (Philadelphia and New York: Fortress Press and Paulist Press, 1985). See also Nilson, "Chapter Four: What the Roman Catholic Church Can and Must Do Now for Church Unity," *Nothing Beyond the Necessary,* 65–92.

a gift of the Spirit. But that is no excuse, they said, to act as though unity will appear like a "bolt out of the blue." Grace and cooperation with grace are not antithetical but complementary.[8]

The theses of Rahner and Fries work well for universal communions, like the Roman Catholic Church, the Anglican communion, churches in communion with Constantinople or the Lutheran World Federation. They do not describe as thoroughly the ecumenism that must take place now in the local churches. The "memes that divide" must be allowed to wither on the vine if the "memes" that unite us will ever be able to flourish. Disunity and division can only disappear one relationship at a time, one church at a time, one parish at a time. If anything, communion ecclesiology shows that the Eucharist should be the place where disunity and divisive behaviors are put to an end. Therefore, communion is always local and is always built from the "ground upward." Confrontation, Tillard writes, must be converted into unity on the local level.[9] Ecumenism must be unleashed on the local level or else our regional and worldwide efforts will amount to little.

The Eucharist of Jesus is a meal without borders. The Church is born in that meal and shares in the borderless character of Christ's love. This "Church without borders" does *not yet* exist. However, every time we are possessed by the Spirit in a communion of sacrificial love, the fullness of communion *already* exists among us. "Already," though "not yet;" this is neither an excuse for ecumenical "quietism," nor is it an argument for a "triumphal" and "god-like" Church. They are the grounds only for a simple argument in favor of renewed vigor in ecumenism among the local and regional churches of the world. The law of salvation is the limitless, merciful, and faithful love of God known and expressed in communion with others through Christ and the Spirit. The law of salvation is the only norm for the Church. Again and again, it is time to begin living like the Eucharist we have received. What better place to begin than where we are? At home, together around the table, with a simple meal of bread and wine in Jesus' name.

8. Rahner and Fries, 139f.
9. CofC, 228.

Questions for meditation and dialogue on "Borderless Church"

1. *Human communion, divine salvation.* Do you experience human communion as a sign or sacrament of God's plan for salvation? If human communion is a sign or sacrament of God's plan for salvation, how does that challenge or affirm your fundamental convictions about salvation or about God? Do your ideas of salvation or about God challenge your church, or other churches in your community, to act and respond differently?

2. *Necessary structures.* Imagine the possibility of a truly ecumenical communion among the local churches and congregations of your community. What structures would be necessary to create and maintain a fruitful local communion? If members of your dialogue group provide different answers to this question, how would they resolve them? How would they distinguish between "necessary" structures, "helpful" structures, and "harmful" structures? Could your group devise a model for church governance which enhances the values and traditions of all the churches in your community?

3. *Leaning into unity.* What steps can members of local churches take together to enhance prospects for unity in your community? What avenues or methods have been followed in the past? What offers the best hope for ecumenism in your community? Among churches that already celebrate at an open table, what can be done to welcome Christians from "closed" communions? Among churches that celebrate "closed" communions, what steps can be taken now, within existing guidelines, to enhance prospects for full communion? Could the members of your congregation enter into communion with members of other churches? Can you or your group identify some simple, yet effective, ways to proceed?

4. *The Eucharist and ecumenism.* As an experiment in hope, describe a fully united Church for the members of your dialogue group. Describe its patterns of worship. How will it be governed? What will be its central message and values? Then, consider your current parish or congregation. Describe the path your parish or congregation would need to follow to walk toward the fully united Church you imagined earlier. Ask the members of your dialogue group to describe the ways their church could support your church along the road toward unity. What role will the Eucharist play in establishing your churches in Christian unity?

FOR FURTHER READING

Csikzentmihalyi, Mihalyi. *The Evolving Self: A Psychology for the Third Millennium*. New York: HarperCollins, 1993.

Rahner, Karl and Heinrich Fries. *Unity of the Churches: An Actual Possibility*. R. C. L. Gritsch and E. W. Gritsch, tr. Philadelphia: Fortress, 1985.

Zizioulas, John. "Communion and Otherness," *Sobornost* 16 (1994) 7–19.

Index of Citations to Scripture

General Index

A

absence, 134

accessibility, 16–17, 22, 95, 177; catholic character, 102–03; soteriological considerations, 22; of Christ, 78; pneumatological character, 18

adiaphora (matters of indifference), 131, 151

agape (love), 66, 157

aggiornamento (openness), 62
See also openness.

anamnesis (having not forgotten), 22, 83, 86, 127, 134, 136; sacrificial character, 86

Anathema Study, 87

Anglican-Roman Catholic International Commission (ARCIC), 75–76

apostolic ministry, 154

apostolic succession, 160

apostolicity, 156, 160

arrhes (pledge), 144

ascesis (assent in practice), 110

assent, 129; the "two Amen's," 126–27, 129

atonement, 88

autocephaly, 142

B

Babel, 131

baptism, 77

Baptism, Eucharist, and Ministry (BEM), 80; responses to, 109

Beauduin, Lambert, 47

Bellarmine, Robert, 40

belonging, rituals and symbols of, 13

body and blood of Christ, 25

body of Christ, 63, 138; in Pauline theology, 21, 94

body, 60; physical, social, and mystical, 51; theological considerations, 94

borderless board, 5, 26, 104

Bradshaw, Paul, 12

C

Canberra assembly, WCC, 1

catholicity, 75, 100; of Christ's presence, 102; of churches, 142; of sacrificial love, 101; of the local church, 140–41; through time, 102

Chair de l'Église, Chair du Christ (CdlE), 122

christology, prophetic, 18; pneumatological, 18; sacramental considerations, 79

Church of Churches (CofC), 122, 140

Church of God, 143

Church, borderless, 179; of churches, 140–41; as communion, 56, 128; continuity of, 159; definition of, 173, 179; as divine society, 52; ecumenical character, 179; as event, 164; eucharistic character, 173; as incarnation, 21; as institution, 164; as mystical body, 53; as sacrament of salvation, 55, 64; as sacrament, 54, 56–57, 60; as social body, 55; eschatological considera-